The Embodied Psychotl

The therapist's body is a vital part of the therapeutic encounter, yet there is an inherent inadequacy in current psychotherapeutic discourse to describe bodily phenomena. Until recently, for instance, the whole area of touch in psychotherapy has been given very little attention.

The Embodied Psychotherapist uses accounts of therapists' own experiences to address this inadequacy in discourse, and provides strategies for incorporating these feelings into therapeutic work with clients. Drawing on these personal accounts, it also discusses the experiences that can be communicated to the therapist during the encounter.

The description and exploration of the ways practitioners use their bodily feelings within the therapeutic encounter will be valuable for all psychotherapists and counsellors.

Robert Shaw first trained as an osteopath, later as a counsellor and psychotherapist. He now works in private practice as an integrative psychotherapist, supervisor and osteopath in Derbyshire. He is also a freelance lecturer specialising in the body in psychotherapy, and qualitative research methods for psychotherapists, and currently teaches on masters and doctoral courses in the UK and in Europe.

The Embodied Psychotherapist

The Therapist's Body Story

Robert Shaw, Ph.D.

Brunner-Routledge
Taylor & Francis Group
HOVE AND NEW YORK

First published 2003
by Brunner-Routledge
27 Church Road, Hove, East Sussex BN3 2FA

Simultaneously published in the USA and Canada
by Brunner-Routledge
29 West 35th Street, New York NY 10001

Brunner-Routledge is an imprint of the Taylor & Francis Group

© 2003 Robert Shaw

Typeset in Times by Regent Typesetting, London
Printed and bound in Great Britain by T J International Ltd,
Padstow, Cornwall
Paperback cover design by Jim Wilkie

British Library Cataloguing in Publication Data
A catalogue record for this book is available from the British Library

Library of Congress Cataloging in Publication Data

Shaw, Robert, 1961-
   The embodied psychotherapist : the therapist's body story /
Robert Shaw.
        p. cm.
Includes bibliographical references and index.
   ISBN 1-58391-268-1 — ISBN 1-58391-269-X
   1. Shaw, Robert, 1961- 2. Mind and body therapies. 3.
Psychotherapist and patient. I. Title.

RC480.8.S52 2003
616.89'14—dc21

2003008052

ISBN 1-58391-268-1 (hbk)
ISBN 1-58391-269-X (pbk)

For Elizabeth

Contents

Acknowledgements

This book has required the support and goodwill of many people. First, I would like to thank all those who participated in this study, which included therapists from several countries, all of whom were very generous in giving their time and in sharing intimate aspects of their practice lives.

Throughout the course of the research for this book I have received some excellent support. I would in particular like to thank my director of studies for my Ph.D., Ursula Sharma, who was a constant source of encouragement and support; her constructive comments throughout have been a source of stimulation and inspiration. She also gave me invaluable help at the proposal stage of this book. Diana Shmukler, my second supervisor, also provided helpful guidance through-out the research phase.

I am very grateful to the University of Derby School of Education and Social Sciences for providing me with a bursary to help me take time away from my practice and teaching commitments, enabling me to complete the research for this book.

Thanks also go to my friends and colleagues who have supported me in many ways during the course of this research. Particular thanks go to Geoff Heath, who has given generously of his time to read, comment on and discuss in depth earlier drafts of this book. His honest and constructive feedback has helped to shape this book.

Introduction

It is through my body that I understand other people.

(Merleau-Ponty 1962: 186)

In this statement Merleau-Ponty neatly encapsulates the essence of this book, namely that we can only perceive other people through our own bodies. This perspective on embodiment that I am going to discuss relates to how we as psychotherapists come to be aware of, and then use, our bodily reactions to clients during our therapeutic work. Merleau-Ponty's statement appears at first glance simplistic and self-evident. To view it this way is to ignore its importance for our work as therapists. It is my contention throughout this book that psychotherapy has ignored for too long the importance of therapists' bodies in the consulting room. As a profession, we have certainly tried to incorporate the bodily feelings by using notions such as countertransference, but I feel we end up locating the therapist's bodily reactions back into the client. As Merleau-Ponty suggests, I can only ever come to understand another person by how my body responds and reacts to them. The importance of taking our own bodies and our own sense of embodiment seriously is a crucial aspect of this book. I strongly suggest that, as a profession, it behoves us all to become more bodily literate, and this book offers an opportunity to do this.

Every book tells a story and this book is no different. Several of the stories that are told here are those of therapists and how they come to use their own physical sensations while working therapeutically with clients and, in this process, form a 'body story' which relates to the therapy with their particular client. In addition, there is also the story of how this book came to be written. During this introduction I will also provide some background information on the therapists who kindly agreed to take part and share their body stories.

Since this book focuses on the embodied experience of therapists, it seems only right that I state my own interest in the topic: this book is based on the research I undertook to complete my Ph.D., but I am also a practitioner. Prior to any training in counselling or psychotherapy, I trained and then practised for several years as a registered osteopath. I am, therefore, well versed in a body-orientated discipline. I then decided to study counselling to gain more of an understanding of the emotional life of the patients presenting in osteopathic practice. I became aware of the ambiguous nature of the body in the therapy world and the fear relating to touch; the body seemed to be viewed with considerable unease. After completing my master's degree in counselling, I underwent psychotherapy training.

At the beginning of this research project I had a clear agenda, which was to bring the body back into psychotherapy. I made the assumption that, due to the contentious nature of the body within psychotherapy, it was ignored or somehow marginalised. Initially I intended to achieve my aim by exploring somatisation in clients[1], and, by so doing, I intended to reclaim the body for psychotherapy. I appreciate that this sounds rather grandiose, but I thought I might as well aim high!

Thus I bring to this book a background as both osteopath and psychotherapist. I have professional training in both disciplines and am registered with the General Osteopathic Council (GOsC), the United Kingdom Council for Psychotherapy (UKCP) and the British Association of Counselling and Psychotherapy (BACP). The GOsC is now regulated by an Act of Parliament. This is an important fact to bear in mind, as there is no such formal regulation (as yet) within the counselling or psychotherapy world. I graduated as an osteopath in 1989 and worked part-time as a tutor in a London teaching clinic and in private practice. I became aware that my education as an osteopath was lacking a major perspective: the psychological aspects of patient care had, to all intents and purposes, been ignored. I decided to rectify this by training first as a counsellor, then progressing to psychotherapy training. During this time my intention was to treat my patients in private practice using a combination of osteopathic and psychotherapeutic skills. However, as a part of my counselling course I undertook a research project for a master's degree and became intrigued by the concept of somatisation and the language used by osteopathic patients to describe their pain (Shaw 1997c). I discuss this concept in some detail in Chapter 1.

At that stage I found myself in a practice dilemma: I was now trained as both an osteopath and a counsellor, yet the two disciplines somehow seemed incompatible. I found myself confronting the age-old dualism of 'mind' and 'body'. It was as if in osteopathy the mind was not considered important, and in the realm of counselling the body was a taboo subject. I was a practitioner in both, so I thought a good way to understand my dilemma would be to deepen my research. I then decided to explore the concept of somatisation in more depth and, with guidance from my research supervisor, the idea of studying somatisation within general medical practice arose. I was about to embark on a participant observation study in general practice when I had to take a break for a year away from this research to take up a post as a 'new blood lecturer' in counselling, during which time I completed my psychotherapy training. On returning to my research my interests had moved on. I was now qualified as a psychotherapist and had begun to look in some depth at how the body was viewed in the therapy world. This move in interest corresponded to my career changing. Originally, working primarily as an osteopath, exploring the concept of somatisation seemed to be a good way of combining a professional practical issue with a research project. However, as my career began to be more influenced by psychotherapy, I became more intrigued by the body within therapy and, having written some articles on the subject, I was invited to talk on the issue of the body in therapy. During a series of three talks I held some discussion groups on the role of the body in therapy and it was at that point that the focus for this study became clear. What was the experience of the therapist's body within the therapeutic encounter? This seemed to fit within my interest and provide a project which could contribute something to the mind-body debate. I was making the clear assumption that, as in osteopathy, where the mind appears largely absent within the treatment regime (Randell 1989, 1992), so too within psychotherapy the body remains absent or removed from the therapeutic consulting room. My hope was that, by investigating the therapist's body, I could somehow reclaim the body for psychotherapy, just as I have tentatively tried to reclaim the mind for osteopathy (Shaw 1994a, 1994b, 1995). I began this research hoping to reconcile my two professional lives, and that my work as both psychotherapist and osteopath would become more integrated. This book is, therefore, the culmination of several years' study, and is also an example of how research can be relevant to practice.

The research sample[2]

As I have used the verbatim accounts of therapists in this book, I would like to spend a little time discussing how they became involved in the research, which focuses on 14 in-depth interviews I conducted with them. In addition, I conducted five discussion groups, three before the interviews and two afterwards. In all some 90 psychotherapists took part in the discussion groups, and my thanks go to all those who did so. The post-interview discussion groups were conducted following a presentation which included a preliminary analysis of the data collected in the interviews and in the three initial discussion groups.

The initial discussion groups were set up to explore the issue of the body in therapy. My intention was to explore in a very general way the main issues that interested therapists relating to the body in therapy. These discussion groups took place at conference and training workshops where I had been asked to present my work on the body in therapy (Shaw 1997a, 1997b). Before these workshops began I asked those present if it would be possible to talk and record their responses about aspects of the body in therapy. It was after this phase of my research that I decided to focus on the therapist's body, and at this stage I conducted in-depth interviews with 14 psychotherapists. A summary of each therapist who was part of the interview group is provided in the Appendix.

Throughout this book I refer to each therapist by their number in the Appendix. For inclusion in the interview group, certain criteria were required to be satisfied. First, therapists had to have been in practice for at least five years – this was considered an adequate amount of time to have experienced working with a variety of clients, and to be aware of issues relating to the body in therapy. The years of practice experience ranged from 6 to 35 years (average 13 years). Second, participants were required to hold membership of at least one professional organisation, and to have completed a recognised training programme. The majority of the sample had studied in training programmes recognised by the BACP or the UKCP.[3] These are the two main organisations in the UK currently responsible for professional accreditation in counselling and psychotherapy respectively. Other training programmes were also considered suitable – for example, T5 was a fully trained and experienced dramatherapist and a member of the British Association of Dramatherapists, and T13 had trained to a high standard in New Zealand. Very few of the sample claimed to work in one single model of therapy, most describing their practice in terms of two or more therapeutic modalities (e.g. integrative, Gestalt and person-centred models). Other models which were used included clinical theology, cognitive-behavioural and psychodynamic. I also decided to interview therapists mainly from the humanistic school as I made the assumption that they were more likely to be body conscious. However, I now realise that this assumption was incorrect as all therapists, whatever their theoretical orientation, are likely to be aware of their bodily reactions to clients. Therefore, this book will be of interest to therapists from all theoretical models.

At this stage of recruitment there was no attempt made to form a sample representative of the psychotherapy profession in terms of gender. However, it was apparent during all the discussion groups that most of the therapists present were female. The interview group mirrored this with 11 women and three men. Thus, the overwhelming number of responses for this research have come from women. It is interesting to note that the membership of the BACP, which totals 19,000, is made up of a ratio of 3:1 women to men (BACP 2000), so those taking part in the interview and discussion groups would seem to be representative of the therapy profession in general if only in terms of the female to male ratio.

The therapists in the interview sample were people I came to meet via my contacts in the profession. Many I knew through my own training as an integrative psychotherapist, and through my training to become a clinical supervisor. Some I met through my teaching commitments at a psychotherapy institute, while others heard about my work and volunteered to be interviewed because they were particularly interested in the subject of the body in therapy. The end result was a group of highly qualified, experienced psychotherapists who were highly motivated to meet with me to discuss my research topic.

During the post-interview discussions in 1999 my preliminary findings were presented to two groups of psychotherapists, one in Vienna, Austria (Shaw 1999) and one a group of Gestalt psychotherapists in Stockholm, Sweden. I was interested to discover if my findings meant anything to other groups of therapists, and to provide an opportunity for my findings to be scrutinised by professionals in the field.

In summary then, this research included therapists who used different models of therapy, and the pre-interview discussion groups and in-depth interviews included therapists from all parts of the UK. The post-interview discussion groups included therapists from the UK, Estonia, Germany, Italy, New Zealand and Scandinavia.

Ethical considerations

Attention has been paid to ethical considerations throughout this research. At the beginning of each interview or discussion group, the issue of informed consent was addressed. As the participants in this study all worked as therapists or counsellors, the concept of informed consent was well-known to them. I provided information as to the purpose and nature of the study by way of an introductory talk. Confidentiality was assured in that names and place names would be changed. I also informed them that I would be the only person to have access to the audio tapes of the discussion or interview, and that I would be transcribing these. I suggested that they make anonymous all client details and that, if they wished to remove their responses from the research they could contact me after the session; otherwise it was assumed that consent had been given for their responses to be included for the purposes of the research.

All the therapists who took part in the in-depth interview stage received a transcript of their interview, later returning the transcript with amendments; they were all happy for their responses to be included in my research and any future published work.[4]

Layout and organisation of this book

I have divided the contents into three parts: Part 1 looks at theory, Part 2 at practice, and Part 3 at implications and recommendations for practice.

Part 1 focuses primarily on the body in psychotherapy. In this section I concentrate on the theoretical aspects which I bring to my work on embodiment. I have therefore included sections which address particular issues which are pertinent when talking about the body in psychotherapy. For example in Chapter 1, I discuss issues around mind-body dualism and how this has had an impact on how the body has become theorised in psychotherapy. I also offer some perspectives taken from other disciplines such as sociology. In Chapter 2, I have gone on to examine how the body is currently addressed in psychotherapy training, highlighting the issue of touch and how problematic this has become for our profession. Chapters 3 and 4 build up a theoretical framework which can incorporate a way of bringing our bodies into the therapeutic encounter without relying on theories such as transference and countertransference. Instead, I suggest that we can build up a 'body story' or narrative of the therapy which can be shared with our clients and help to construct a therapeutic narrative. In this way I demonstrate that our embodied experiences as therapists can become a central, crucial and valuable part of a co-constructed therapeutic story.

Part 2 focuses on how therapists actually describe their bodies and the wide range of physical reactions they experience during their everyday working lives. Chapter 5 focuses entirely on the physical reactions that therapists experience and, in Chapter 6, we discover that it is possible for the therapist's body to become a 'receiving device'. I contend that we use this ability in our practice and incorporate these sensations within a narrative framework in order to be able to share these experiences with our clients. Chapter 7 looks at some of the strategies therapists have adopted to help them understand their physical responses. Some therapists also discuss the potential health implications for their work, and we review some of their coping strategies. Part 2, therefore, very much focuses on practice and how therapists bring their bodies into their work.

Building on Parts 1 and 2, Part 3 looks at recommendations for practice. In Chapter 8 I suggest the term 'body empathy' as a means of incorporating an embodied narrative perspective into the therapeutic encounter. I also suggest that body empathy could be used as an alternative to the notion of countertransference. The implications of taking my discussion on embodiment and narrative seriously are discussed in Chapter 9, one of these being a need to seek a more egalitarian way of viewing therapy, moving away from the psychoanalytic model of interpreting our bodily feelings as aspects of countertransference, always originating from the client. Instead I argue it is imperative that, as therapists and as people, we own our physical reactions. Rather than viewing them through traditional psychoanalytic theory, we can allow our sense of embodiment to be explored through a more liberal narrative perspective.

Part I

The body in psychotherapy

Part 1 is devoted to an exploration of how the body has been incorporated into psychotherapy. I begin with a historical overview and address issues such as *mind-body dualism*, discussing how this has had a profound impact on how we as therapists approach the body, and the types of language we currently employ to describe bodily phenomena. This leads us to an exploration of how psychotherapeutic techniques of the body are acquired by therapists and opens up a debate on the importance of incorporating a knowledge of the body within psychotherapy training. In the final two chapters of Part 1 I suggest that there are alternative ways of looking at bodily phenomena; that the bodily feelings we experience as therapists can be framed within an embodiment perspective. I therefore spend some time discussing embodiment in Chapter 3 and suggest a novel means of interpreting our bodily feelings in the therapeutic encounter. Chapter 4 builds on these ideas and adds a further layer to the embodiment framework. I discuss the narrative movement and how therapy can be perceived as a joint storytelling venture, by both therapist and client. My suggestion is that our embodied experience as therapists can be incorporated into the therapeutic encounter, and we can use an embodied narrative approach to therapy.

Chapter 1

The psychotherapeutic body

I have been intrigued for some time by how the body has been perceived within psychotherapeutic culture. A question I have posed and attempted to answer in this chapter is: how has the body come to occupy such a peculiar space within psychotherapy? It is as if, as psychotherapists, we are not sure where to put the body, or even whose body to concentrate on: the client's or the therapist's. Bodies can be seen as fearful objects where certain taboos come into play – for example, the whole area of touching in psychotherapy is fraught with ambivalence, or even anxiety. In some sense the body becomes silent and is almost written out of psychotherapy as a dangerous 'thing'. When it is written about, it is predominantly the client's body that becomes the focus of attention; the therapist's body is marginalised or seen as merely a receptacle for transferential phenomena. This chapter looks at these issues and the key debates around the body in psychotherapy. These are crucial areas to debate due to the centrality of psychotherapist embodiment within this book. I will begin with a *historical overview* of the body in psychotherapy which provides a context for the importance of addressing the body within the therapeutic encounter. There will be a critical discussion of the impact of *mind-body dualism* on psychotherapeutic culture, and the difficulties of integrating bodily phenomena into psychotherapy. An example of this is provided by exploring the concept of *somatisation*. This is also a key concept, and its use within psychotherapy discourse is ambivalent. Indeed, it was the concept of somatisation that started my interest in the research presented in this book.

Other disciplines within the social sciences are also beginning to acknowledge the importance of the body, so at the end of this chapter I have included a brief overview of how sociology is addressing the bodily perspective.

Historical overview: the origins of mind-body dualism[1]

> The body is the tomb of the soul.
> (Plato)

Before embarking on an overview of the body in psychotherapy it is important to provide a brief sketch of the meanings of the body within western culture, and the impact this has had on viewing the body as a separation of mind and body. I start with Plato (d. 347 BC), not as a means of privileging Greek knowledge but as a reasonable place to begin. I am not intending to marginalise other ways of looking at the body, such as eastern traditions which perceive the body as a physical manifestation of the mind (Capra 1975). Different cultures inscribe the body with different meanings. At this point I am deliberately looking at the western perspective of the body, since psychotherapy is a western cultural practice.

The ancient Greeks celebrated the human body, this being demonstrated by their art and literature, and by their organisation of the Olympic Games. However, as the founders of western philosophy they also began the intellectualisation of the mind-body split. Plato, in the quotation at the beginning of this section, sees the body as a captivating force, an armoured carapace locking in the soul. Also, in one of his dialogues, the *Phaedo*, (Hutchins 1952) he describes body and mind as fighting against each other in a constant struggle.

This image of the body is echoed in Roman times when Stoicism was a dominant philosophy of Seneca the younger (d. AD 65) who said: 'Nature has summoned our soul with the body as its cloak' (Synnott 1993: 10). Again, we see the body acting as some kind of concealer, an object to prevent seeing, a definite entity in its own right. Indeed, Seneca goes on: 'a high minded and sensible man divorces soul from body' (Synnott 1993: 10). Although 'soul' here does not necessarily mean 'mind', these quotations do emphasise that the body *per se* is somehow separate, somehow distanced, and are a clear demonstration of mind-body dualism.

The early Christians seemed to have difficulty in reconciling their bodies as part of themselves. St Paul, for example, said 'Your body is the temple of the Holy Spirit' (Synnott 1993: 7), while Francis of Assisi believed that 'We must hate our bodies with [their] vices and sins' (Synnott, 1993: 16). There is thus a confusing message that the body is something to be worshipped as it contains the Holy Spirit, but at the same time it is full of evil as demonstrated by desire. Bayer and Malone (1998) describe how early Christianity viewed the body as a site of sin and of weakness, and how St Augustine of Hippo (AD 354–430) insisted that pleasures of the body be denied. Badaracco (1997: 108) also makes a link between illness and punishment, and links this to Christianity, which 'considered the body as the origin of the sin of the flesh, and illness as a consequence of guilt'.

The body as a beautiful object was rediscovered in the Renaissance of the fourteenth century. Artists such as Botticelli, da Vinci and Michelangelo produced images glorifying the body. The body was something to be admired, adorned and enjoyed. However, as civility and refinement increased, so basic bodily instinctual behaviour was frowned upon. The body became distant and, as Synnott (1993: 19) puts it, 'New notions of civility began to privatize the body'. Throughout this period, the mind is considered as higher, of greater worth, and the body as a vehicle for the mind. This was given credence by the work of René Descartes (1596–1650), 'the patriarch of Western philosophy' (Boyne 1990: 1) and by his famous statement, '*Cogito ergo sum*' ('I think therefore I am'). The view of the body as machine was given a philosophical meaning and, combined with the monumental work of Isaac Newton, the prevailing Cartesian attitude was that 'the rules of mechanisms are the rules of nature' (Synnott 1993: 23). It was believed that everything could be reduced to its constituent parts, analysed and therefore understood, and the mind was that which was capable of this understanding. Modernity was born with the fundamental belief that mankind could at last, via scientific tools and reductionist philosophy, understand the universe. Mankind, of course, included the mind and that irritating encumbrance, the body.

Scientific knowledge increased during the eighteenth and nineteenth centuries, and scientific discourse was founded. It is still a powerful discourse today, with the entrenched belief that the mind is separate from the body. Sanitary science in the 1870s put the body in its place. An acknowledgement of the scientific dangers of human waste led to phobias of diseases from without affecting the body. Although advances in sanitary disposal undoubtedly helped to improve people's health in general, they also established 'a new anatomical space' (Armstrong 1993). In the eyes of public health administration the body became political. However, during the nineteenth century certain cracks started to appear in this dualistic paradigm. Charles Darwin demonstrated that our bodies were still evolving, thus implying that 'mind was dependent on body' (Synnott 1993). Karl Marx suggested that, if a body can be viewed as a machine, it can become a disposable asset (Fox 1993; Synnott 1993), therefore pointing out that 'body as machine' can be used as a manipulative tool, and that power is knowledge. If that knowledge comes from a philosophical base of reductionism, then workers are units, units are machines and machines are expendable. He therefore exposed a cruel extrapolation of Cartesian thought. Later, in 1895, Freud's studies on hysteria led him to see that psychological phenomena converted into physical symptoms (Freud 1905); in effect, he founded psychosomatic medicine. However, far from introducing the idea of an integrated system of medicine, Freud's ideas became subsumed into general medical discourse. Medicine thus promoted the mind-body dualism by providing specialisms in mind and body. Medicine has taken control of our bodies and our minds: 'The magic bullets work better and quicker than prayer' (Synnott 1993: 28).

Mind-body dualism and psychotherapy

The problem of mind-body dualism is not only located within psychotherapeutic culture, but appears to be endemic within western culture (Bayer and Malone 1998). However, within psychotherapy it is worthwhile to trace the sources of this dualistic attitude. As McLeod (1997: 15) notes: 'All the pioneers of psychotherapy were scientifically trained doctors, and they brought with them into the new discipline of psychoanalysis a battery of medical procedures and principles'.

We see that the founders of psychoanalytic psychotherapy had a medical training (e.g. Freud, Jung, Reich, Adler, etc.). This is echoed in many other models of therapy. The founders also had a strong medical background – for example, Joseph

Wolpe, who influenced the behaviour therapies, was a medical doctor and Albert Ellis, who founded cognitive behaviour therapy, had initially trained as a clinical psychologist (Prochaska and Norcross 1994). It is interesting to consider the absence of the body in much current psychotherapeutic theory. Perhaps, as the founders had such a grounding in medicine, the body was taken as a given; it was simply not worth mentioning. Clearly, their view of the body would be that as seen through a medical lens, and this therefore may be one of the reasons for the embedded nature of the mind-body split within psychotherapy culture. Medicine clearly focuses on the patient's body; we can see that a history of the body within psychotherapy could also be considered to be a history of the client's body. The therapist's body is written out and almost absent in most of the literature, except in cases of issues like erotic countertransference or touch. Even then, somehow the therapist's body is reacting to the client's body. This in effect is another form of dualism: there is a client body separated from a client mind, and a therapist body separated from a therapist mind.

Clearly the body has been given much significance in psychotherapy – as Freud stated, 'The ego is first and foremost a bodily ego' (Freud 1923: 364). Freud's perspective on the body has been critiqued from a feminist standpoint and Bayer and Malone (1998: 95) point out that for Freud 'women's bodies posed not only an impasse to full psychosexual development, at least insofar as development of the super-ego went, but also a mystery about femininity'. Yet, for psychotherapy there remains the issue of how to work with bodily phenomena, and how to make sense of such bodily information. One way of dealing with client's bodies is via the use of touch, which has its own particular set of problems (see Chapter 2). However, Freud's assertion about bodily ego led to a very important developmental implication – that 'the lack of certain body sensations will limit ego development' (Smith et al. 1998: 5). I agree with Smith et al. that the importance of the idea of the body ego actually provides for a rationale for the use of touch in psychotherapy. However, when looking at the history of psychotherapy, it was not Freud who developed this idea but one on his students, Wilhelm Reich, who took the idea of the body seriously and developed a method of treating the body within a psychotherapeutic framework. He further developed Freud's notion of libido and applied it to his observations of his clients' bodies. Reich extended Freud's theory of libido to the realm of body armour. Reich (1983, 1990) observed in his patients areas of rigidification within the soma; he termed this 'body armour' and suggested a mechanism for this process in that the ego assumes a definite form in the conflict between instinct (essentially libidinal need) and fear of punishment. He suggested that the ego becomes rigid. It is this rigidity that can be felt within the body, but this required touching his patients. Therefore, according to Reich, rigidified areas within the soma represent unconscious conflict. These areas of armouring can also be considered as an adaptive response to past or present events.

Reich provided a further rationale for his theory by suggesting that armouring reduces the capacity of the body to feel pleasure by blocking out libidinous urges. Reich's observations led him to believe that areas of the body become numb by encapsulating the libidinal feeling into a site of muscular tension. Such areas of high muscular tone symbolise denied preconscious and unconscious feelings. It requires energy, physical and psychic, to maintain such tightness; in a sense these areas can be regarded as psychic defence mechanisms aimed at preventing the conflict becoming conscious (Reich 1983, 1990). Thus, armouring reduces the capacity to achieve libidinal pleasure by decreasing the body's ability to feel, and that character armour 'fulfils its function by absorbing and consuming vegetative energy' (Reich 1990: 339). Reich therefore advocated a system of therapy which involved touching patients and encouraging an awareness of body tensions.

There have been many developments of Reichian therapy (for a good review see West 1994). However, one of the criticisms of this way of working is that without the associated verbalisation of these somatic phenomena it is unlikely that a meaningful understanding of bodily phenomena will be achieved. Therefore, authors such as Frankl (1990, 1994) and McDougall (1989, 1993) advocate the use of some form of insightful talking therapy as an adjunct to body work.

The net effect of these techniques for addressing bodily phenomena is not the solving of mind-body dualism but a perpetuation of this dichotomy. In some way this apes the medical model from which the founders of psychotherapy came and in which physicians treat physical phenomena and psychiatrists treat mental phenomena. Also in the world of psychotherapy there are now particular models of *body* psychotherapy which are identified as using *body* techniques. However, the use of 'body' in their title emphasises the split from 'mind'. Perhaps Reich was closer to addressing the mind-body split in psychotherapy when he advocated that all psychotherapy practitioners should undergo training in physiology and anatomy (Prochaska and Norcross 1994).

A good example of mind-body dualism within psychotherapy culture is the use of the term 'somatisation'. This also highlights some of the difficulties of integrating bodily phenomena into psychotherapy. It is to this concept that I shall now turn.

Somatisation

> . . . communicating personal problems through complaints about the body is the universal language of mankind.
>
> (Szasz 1987: 37)

The discussion of the concept of somatisation is important because of its use within the therapy world and because it is a notion frequently referred to by therapists. Somatisation is a medical term that is used to describe bodily pain which does not appear to have a medically clear physical cause. A simple definition of somatisation is provided by Kellner (see Rodin 1991: 367): 'the presence of somatic symptoms in the absence of organic disease'. An example of how the term is currently in operation in the medical world is given by Servanschreiber *et al.* (2000: 1423): 'Somatisation is the experiencing of physical symptoms in response to emotional distress. It is a common and costly disorder that is frustrating to patients and physicians'.

Somatisation is included in the generic term 'somatoform disorders' which appear in the *Diagnostic and Statistical Manual of Mental Disorders* (DSM IV) published by the American Psychiatric Association (1995). This is a comprehensive classification of mental disorders which has become an invaluable tool in assessing patients for mental health problems. It is, therefore, a manual in widespread use, not only in the USA but also in the UK, and has become accepted currency within the health care professions dealing with mental disorders. However, it is of interest to note that classifications change; for example the passive aggressive personality disorder is present in DSM III (American Psychiatric Association 1987) but absent from DSM IV (1995). Drew Westen (2002) has also noted this absence from DSM IV, and wryly observed that a possible reason for this omission is that patients with this personality orientation did not fill out the relevant questionnaire, which could be construed as passive aggressive behaviour! The classification of mental disorders is therefore not immutable but subject to change, and it is interesting to speculate on who decides on this change and for what reason. However, for the purposes of this discussion, somatoform disorders are classified in the DSM IV. There are seven classifications, namely: somatisation disorder; undifferentiated somatoform disorder; conversion disorder; pain disorder; hypochondriasis; body dysmorphic disorder; and somatoform disorder not otherwise specified. A definition provided by the American Psychiatric Association (1995: 457) is as follows:

> The common feature of the Somatoform Disorders is the presence of physical symptoms that suggest a general medical condition (hence, the term somatoform) and are not fully explained by a general medical condition, by the direct effects of a substance, or by another mental disorder (eg Panic Disorder).

The term within medicine tends to be used in a pejorative manner as patients who have this 'condition' are viewed as not having an organic disease, and thereby in some sense not suffering from a 'proper' pathological condition. A demonstrable pathology can be classified, and then presumably treated by medical means; however, somatisation poses a problem for medicine as, if it cannot be classified within pathological parameters, the manner of treatment becomes problematic. Patients who regularly present with symptoms which can be described as somatisation are termed by the medical profession as 'crocks, turkeys, hypochondriacs, the worried well, and the problem patients' (Lipowski 1988: 1361). Somatisation has thus come to be an accepted medical label for this group of patients. It is an apparently ubiquitous phenomenon within western primary health care settings (Ford 1986; Fisch 1987; Lipowski 1988; Coen and Sarno 1989; Barsky 1992; Craig *et al.* 1993). It is almost as if patients attending their general practitioner (GP) use their symptoms as a calling card to gain access to medical services (Mechanic 1972; Hannay 1980). It may well be that the patient is referred on for expensive and time-consuming further medical opinion, when the underlying reason for consultation is psychosocial distress, which remains untreated. Since this group of patients tends to use up large amounts of time and to be investigated using expensive medical techniques and equipment (Shaw and Creed 1991) the medical profession is now looking at this group as a resource issue.

It would seem that the issue of classification proves problematic since, once the label 'somatisation' has been applied, the assumption is then made that the pain is 'all in the mind' (Evans 1993). It almost seems that the ethic of 'all in the mind' somehow diminishes the experience of the pain for the patient, as though if it is in the mind then it is not as worthwhile as if it is 'really' in the body. Thus a hierarchy of symptoms is implied based on an explicit mind-body dualism, with organic pathologies which can be viewed with a medical lens perceived as real and important, and those which somehow seem beyond the range of this lens perceived as less important.

There is an acceptance that somatisation and psychosomatic disorders are related. This implies that there is some linkage between the mind and the body, but within the entrenched Cartesian world of medicine this leaves the patient in a quandary. Since the patient with physical symptoms has consulted a doctor, usually their GP, for physical treatment, they are not expecting to be told their symptoms are all in the mind with the concomitant assumption that they need to seek psychological help. Indeed, I have noted this phenomenon within my own psychotherapy practice (Shaw 1996a, 1996b), and a related phenomenon when working as an osteopath. In the latter case, patients would not be interested in a holistic approach, but instead wished their bodies to be treated as machines, having the broken bit fixed or put back in place (Shaw 1997c). It is not surprising that within a culture dominated by the body as machine (Featherstone *et al.* 1991; Seltzer 1992) patients seek out a practitioner to alleviate what they perceive to be a straightforward physical pain. Therefore, to be told that they have a problem that is 'all in the mind' presumably does not fit in with their construction of the symptoms based partly on the 'body as machine' myth.[2] Capra (1982) gives a comprehensive account of the major impact exerted by the mechanistic world view on western thinking, and how this has promoted a culture of the body as a machine. He explores in some depth the notion of 'Newtonian psychology', which is based on how Newton's world view has been extrapolated to the body and has promoted the idea that the mind can be viewed as a glorified machine.

Somatisation as a concept is far from new – for centuries physicians have recognised the phenomenon (Lipowski 1988). It has been suggested that the first person to coin the term was Stekel, early in the twentieth century, who suggested that 'a deep-seated neurosis could cause a bodily disorder and was thus related to, if not identical with, the concept of conversion' (Lipowski 1988: 1359). The term 'conversion' originates from psychoanalytic discourse. Fenichel (1990: 216) describes conversion in the following way:

> Any neurotic symptom is a substitute for an instinctual satisfaction; since excitement and satisfaction are phenomena that express themselves in a

physical way, the leap into the physical sphere, characteristic for conversion is perhaps not so strange. However, conversion symptoms are not simply somatic expressions of affects but very specific representations of thoughts which can be retranslated from their 'somatic language' into the original word language.

Conversion is thus assumed to represent an unconscious conflict erupting in the soma as a physical pain. In the nineteenth century words which were used to describe a similar process – that is, emotional distress with somatic involvement – were 'hysteria' for women and 'hypochondriasis' for men. It is interesting to note that hysteria was viewed in a pejorative and negative manner, whereas hypochondriasis did not carry the same stigma (Turner 1995).

It is interesting to note that the term 'hypochondriasis' has now found its way into the DSM IV (American Psychiatric Association 1995: 462), where it is not gender specific but defined as 'the preoccupation with the fear of having, or the idea that one has, a serious disease based on the person's misinterpretation of bodily symptoms or bodily functions'. The term 'misinterpretation' implies that the patient is somehow wrong and that the physician is somehow right. It is almost as if in medicine physical illness is somehow privileged over mental illness. The perennial problem of the mind-body split is evoked along with an imposition of will or, as Leder (1984: 35) puts it: 'there is an ironical fulfilment of Cartesian dualism – a mind (namely that of the doctor) runs a passive extrinsic body (that of the patient)'.

Thus there remains the problem of trying to understand such physical pain in medical terms. Our western culture more or less expects doctors to be able to take pain away. Medicine encourages this belief by purporting a reductive discourse; as Foucault (1973: xix) puts it: 'The restraint of clinical discourse (its rejection of theory, its abandonment of systems, its lack of a philosophy; all so proudly proclaimed by doctors) reflects the non-verbal conditions on the basis of which it can speak'. However it is the body which is able to communicate, and eloquently at that. The postures and gestures we make are all taken for granted. One aspect of this communication is pain, a personal experience, but one full of meaning. There is a tendency in western culture to 'focus on the body only when ill' (Leder 1984: 35). The body therefore becomes an area where medical discourse can exert control. As suggested by Fox (1993: 12): 'the body is a site for the exercise of power'. Medicine thus provides a means for exercising this power. Its discourse is not objective and purely scientific, but full of prejudice, disempowerment, and related to society's mores (Armstrong 1989; Fox 1993).

Thus within our culture the body as a separate entity cannot be avoided. The reductionist medical discourse firmly separates mind from body. An integrated view of mind and body is harder to draw into focus, especially when viewed through the mechanistic lens. Indeed, within the realms of psychotherapy the body occupies a peculiar space (Shaw 1996b). There is the fear of the touch taboo, and appropriateness of touching bodies (Wilson 1982) among other bodily aspects; in a way the body is placed off limits or seen as a site of danger.

The idea of somatisation is not a purely western one; other cultures have acknowledged the phenomenon. Shamanism, which dates back at least 20,000 years, recognises the psychosomatic aspects of illness and disease (Achterberg 1985). As Lipowski (1988: 1359) has suggested: 'the tendency to experience and communicate distress in a somatic rather than a psychological mode is widespread in our own and other societies'. There was a belief in ancient Buddhism that the ability to convert psychological pain into somatic pain was an adaptive achievement (Goldberg and Bridges 1988). This begins to hint at the process being seen in a positive light, almost to suggest that if the psychological pain can be converted into a physical pain then something can then be done to alleviate suffering. Other ways in which the psychosomatic component of disease is acknowledged can be seen in Afghanistan, where sadness or depression is referred to as a 'squeezing of the heart', which is also reminiscent of our western term 'broken heart'. This terminology may in part be due to the culturally unacceptable notion of depression (Craig and Boardman 1990). Traditional Chinese medicine also makes the link between emotions and bodily organs by using diagnostic categories like 'the angry liver' and 'the melancholy spleen' (Ots 1990). These methods of description may indicate a way of looking at disease which moves away from the mind-body dichotomy to a sense of mind-body unification.

As a concept, somatisation seems to mean different things to different professions. Since in this book I am discussing the world of psychotherapy, it is appropriate to explore how somatisation is viewed by the psychotherapy profession. The First Congress of the World Council for Psychotherapy (1996) obviously considered somatisation a serious phenomenon in that:

VIENNA DECLARATION (First Congress of the World Council for Psychotherapy, 4 July 1996)

That the governments of all countries from all continents of our earth

1. integrate psychotherapy better in their preventative health-care programs because it reduces somatisation resulting from emotional conflict and thereby:
a) cuts the cost of expensive medical measures
b) reduces social follow-up expenses.

Apart from the rather grandiose style of this statement, there is an assumption of causality between somatisation and emotional conflict. Although this is often mentioned in the literature it is far from proven. The bold statement that psychotherapy reduces somatisation is, therefore, debatable. It does, however, bring into focus the use of the term within the psychotherapy world, whereby the body is brought into the realm of psychotherapy. Also, somatisation is seen as a result of emotional conflict, thus making a direct causal connection. This would imply an agreement with the medical use of the term somatisation, as mind-body dichotomy is suggested by this statement. Also, this would seem to be aligning politically with the ideas of somatisation as a resource issue, and making a claim that psychotherapy can make an impact on reducing the numbers of potentially expensive somatising patients.

However, as we shall see, somatisation as a concept employed by the therapists in this book is used differently to its mode of reference in the literature. The term as discussed so far has a distinct and clear meaning, and is generally viewed by the medical profession as a problem. Many of the therapists who took part in the research for this book use the term to describe a bodily phenomenon occurring in their own bodies. There is a very different quality to the use of the term somatisation in this context and this may provide an example of how psychotherapy tends to incorporate terms from medical and biological discourse and use them with a different meaning. Initially in my research project, I was excited to hear that therapists used the term somatisation to describe themselves; this was most unusual as it is used in such a negative sense within the medical literature. However, it became clear that psychotherapists used the term to describe a process wherein their body reflected something from their client, and that they somehow 'picked up' this information. It was an example of how psychotherapists borrow from other discourses (in this case medical) to try to make the phenomenon seem real. In effect, it was a way to reify or make concrete subjective phenomena, a tendency to describe subjective experiences as though they are somehow tangible, and can be 'really' captured in language. One of the consequences of my research for this book was the growing realisation that reification was an endemic practice within psychotherapy. I shall discuss this in more detail later, once I have presented some of the verbal accounts of the therapists. But for the moment I wish to describe just one further example to illustrate my point: the use of the word 'osmosis'. This has a particular biological meaning and is an essential part of the regulation of cellular metabolism (Stryer 1981); if osmosis did not occur, we would not be able to survive. The term is clearly defined within the biological sciences to refer to the passive process of movement across cell membranes of essential molecules for cell functioning. It is not used in any pejorative manner, but is a term that describes a particular biological process. I have come across this term in psychotherapy training, but unfortunately it does not tend to be written about so I cannot provide a literary source; my evidence is anecdotal. Within the humanistic psychotherapy movement I have heard that osmosis is used to describe how infants assimilate 'introjects' or messages from their primary caregivers. In a psychotherapy context this tends to have a rather negatively loaded meaning due to the abuse that many therapists' clients have suffered in childhood. It can also be viewed in a positive light in that good messages can be taken in or modelled by caregivers. In either case an emotional element is added, which is patently not there in the original biological term, and the use of scientific discourse implies that this process is a real event, and is thereby an attempt to reify a subjective phenomenon.

I would suggest that the term somatisation is problematic when used in a psychotherapy setting. Not only is it steeped in medical discourse and therefore heavily imbued with reductionistic and mechanistic thinking, but it perpetuates the mind-body dualistic world view. As a term it has become pejorative, and patients labelled as 'somatisers' are akin to latter-day lepers, with the contemporary argument now viewing them as a resource issue. A new term is required which acknowledges this subjective experience in a way that is not pejorative. One suggestion is provided by Ots (1990), who rejects the notion of somatisation on the grounds that it is embedded in mind-body dichotomy. In arguing against the use of the term, he makes the link with the lived-body paradigm (which we will look at in Chapter 3) and suggests that the German word *leib* could be employed. This is a 'pre-dichotomatic term that denotes the 'body-mind entity' and is used to describe how mind, body and person are considered to be all part of lived experience. Obviously we are a long way from a language which can move away from the dualistic frame of reference. The purpose of our discussion to date is to highlight the problems of western dualistic thinking and suggest that this does not help us in our quest to come to understand bodily phenomena within the therapeutic encounter.

Before moving on to discuss how the body is brought into psychotherapy, which is the subject of the next chapter, it is important to acknowledge that the subject of the body is attracting much interest in disciplines such as sociology. This in part is a reaction to how science has attempted to monopolise body technologies – the social sciences are now waking up to the importance of the body.

The body in sociology

Shilling (1993: 204), writing from the perspective of a sociologist, boldly states: 'The body is centrally implicated in questions of self-identity, the construction and maintenance of social inequalities, and the constitution and development of societies. It is far too important a subject for sociologists to leave to the natural sciences'. I would echo this and argue that psychotherapy needs to address the body seriously. There appears to be much interest within sociology on the subject of the body (see e.g. Featherstone *et al.* 1991; Shilling 1993; Synnott 1993; Yoshida 1993; Turner 1996). Shilling (1993) points out how we are becoming body conscious. This, he suggests, is an aspect of our postmodern society, in that the body becomes more relevant in assessing our self-identity. This is certainly an aspect of modern living where images of the body within consumer culture abound. However, far from integrating the idea that mind and body are one, this perpetuates the notion of mind-body dichotomy. For example, the idea of 'body maintenance' within our culture enhances the machine metaphor, yet it is a commonly-held belief that 'like cars and other consumer goods, bodies require servicing, regular care and attention to preserve maximum efficiency' (Featherstone *et al.* 1991: 182). This is an ethic also found within branches of complementary medicine such as osteopathy which purport to be holistic therapies. Osteopathy leans heavily on the serviceable body paradigm, looking for causes of back pain in the design of beds (Norfolk 1993) or car seats (McIlwraith 1993).

The sociologists of postmodernism are beginning to acknowledge the existence of the body (Featherstone *et al.* 1991; Fox 1993; Shilling 1993; Synnott 1993) but still treat it as separate, as a discrete entity worthy of separate research and enquiry. This must surely be a reiteration of the mind-body dualism, since there is little mention of the mind. It is, however, strange that a society needs to turn its gaze towards the body. We already live our bodies, so why is there a need to turn a sociological microscope on the body? I would suggest that a prime reason is that we do not *know* our bodies; we feel them and live them. Within western society there appears to be an overwhelming need to know, to understand. It is as if cognitive understanding is privileged over other forms of knowing. This perpetuates another dualism: that of objectivity and subjectivity, the objective being associated with a more significant and therefore important sense of knowing. However, the body, imbued with all manner of organs geared to sensing and to feeling, poses a problem, if not a threat, to objective understanding, since how can one understand subjective feelings? The body is therefore a reservoir of subjective phenomena. Since the work of psychotherapy is to deal with subjectivity, the argument to acknowledge the body within the therapy world is a compelling one.

The importance of introducing sociological ideas at this stage is that sociologists are taking the body seriously and much of my research for this book has relied on sociological theories in order to create a conceptual framework to discuss psychotherapeutic embodiment. The arguments within sociology have had an important impact on our bodily understanding and this is linked to how we perceive our bodies, and to our sense of embodiment. Gender must therefore play a significant role in this, and is an area which has been debated by social scientists. As we have seen, not only were many of the founders of psychotherapy theory steeped in the traditions of medical discourse, but the vast majority of these people were male. The scientific world view which came to be known as the modernist project can also be viewed as a means of privileging objective knowledge over subjective knowledge. This form of knowledge production has become strongly identified with masculinity. As Emily Martin (1987: 21) observes when describing how women have been seen by the medical profession, 'women are not only fragmented into body parts by the practices of scientific medicine, as men are; they are also profoundly alienated from science itself'. One of the reasons for this, according to Martin, is that science operates a belief system which links objectivity to masculinity and thereby regards objective knowledge as superior and downgrades subjective knowledge, which is associated with femininity. Scientific methodology has also been sexualised by Carl Linneaus' classification of plants. Bayer and Malone (1998: 100) point out that this was a gendered project:

> classifications of plants were drawn along the lines of (hetero)sexual differences and relations that coincided with transformations in modern European science and in sexuality and gender. Furthermore, Linneaus's designation of a class of animals as 'mammalia' occured at a time when . . . men of medicine and politics heightened attention around the importance of the mother's milk and so to infants' need of a mother's as opposed to a wet nurse's breast.

This suggests a political motive for gendering scientific knowledge, and we can see that throughout the history of science 'gendered embodiment runs deep' (Bayer and Malone 1998: 101). The significance of this argument for psychotherapy is that it has roots in modern medicine and therefore in science. A good example of this was Freud who at the turn of the twentieth century tried to combine his theories of psychoanalysis with the neurological sciences. He attempted this via his Project for a Scientific Psychology (Bloom *et al*. 1985; Cooper 1985). He was forced to abandon this project due to the crude techniques available at that time for studying neuroanatomy. This did not prevent him from theorising, and some of his ideas on neurology have since been substantiated (Bloom *et al*. 1985). It was, though, an attempt to see how psychoanalysis and neurology could be combined via a scientific method. Freud, like the other founders of psychotherapy theories, was a product of his time and had to operate within the cultural mores of his era. However, by incorporating ideas from sociology, and in particular notions of gendered knowledge, the founders of psychotherapy must have been influenced by these ideas. This must also have had an impact on how they viewed their bodies and the bodies of their clients, and on the types of theories that arose relating to the body in therapy. It is to this latter aspect that I wish to turn in Chapter 2, and look at some of the ways that therapists are trained to use the body in their work with clients.

Summary

We have looked briefly at the origins of mind-body dualism and opened up a debate on how this is an endemic way of thinking within western culture. Psychotherapy evolves from western culture, and is therefore not immune from the consequences of viewing the body and mind in a dualistic manner. One of the results of seeing the body within a mind-body framework is the use of language, and we have seen how psychotherapy borrows terms from medicine and science and that there is a potential problem in this process – namely, the reification of subjective phenomena. We have also seen that the body is becoming an area of study in other disciplines and that the problem of viewing the mind and body as separate is not just related to psychotherapy – disciplines such as sociology are also grappling with this issue. Before we explore in more depth how, as psychotherapists, we can employ the ideas from the social sciences it is important to examine how the body is currently brought into the psychotherapeutic encounter.

Chapter 2

Psychotherapeutic techniques of the body

In this chapter I wish to address how the body becomes a part of the therapeutic encounter. In particular, I want to explore how the body is addressed in psychotherapy training. The main therapeutic intervention which therapists employ to bring the body directly into their work is touch; therefore I will address this particular intervention in some depth.

How is the body brought into training?

This question was one that intrigued me at the beginning of my training, both as a counsellor and then as a psychotherapist. I came into this form of training having already qualified as an osteopath and having had several years working as such; therefore, for me, the body was very much part of my practice life and I was aware that, in the world of counselling and psychotherapy, the body was highlighted as problematic. The context of my training was that of an osteopath interested in exploring the emotional side of my patients, and the sometimes bizarre phenomena I experienced which osteopathic methodologies did not seem to address adequately. I therefore entered this training well versed in the osteopathic techniques of handling bodies and made the assumption that psychotherapists as a whole were not literate in the language of the body. In some ways this assumption was borne out by both my counselling and psychotherapy courses: the body was largely absent. Passing reference was made to topics such as somatisation and body work, but there was no real depth of coverage. Touch was considered to be problematic, but with some potentially very beneficial consequences, and the level of physical contact (i.e. hugging and supportive holding) was very high within my particular psychotherapy training group. This training was very much located within the humanistic tradition, although it was integrative in that it drew on theories from the psychodynamic and self-psychology schools. Touch in this context was seen as beneficial if it fulfilled a developmental need, so that if it was clear from a client's history that touch had been withheld, or was somehow abusive, then the judicious use of touch from a benevolent therapist could be seen as reparative of a longed-for need. Indeed, there is much literature around this subject, but it still remains a very contentious area of debate due to the danger of touch being a need of the therapist and not of the client. This also highlights the fact that there are both ethical and clinical implications around the issues of touch.

Clearly there are now types of psychotherapy training which directly address the body, and these can be broadly described as 'post-Reichian therapies' (West 1994). The types of therapy included here would be Lowen's bioenergetics therapy (1976), and more recently the work of Boadella (1988) where he introduces the ideas of biosynthesis. Lowen underwent analysis with Reich, and based his ideas primarily on the notion that 'the freedom to enjoy life can only come from a body that is fully alive' (Prochaska and Norcross 1994: 235). Bioenergetics therefore addresses areas of rigidification within the client's body, and relates this to past patterns of repressive behaviour.

Biosynthesis (Boadella 1988, 1997) emphasises the use of all the bodily senses that are available to listen to the client. Therefore, therapy is considered to consist of much more than talking, and body language as well as listening to the tone and modulation of the client's voice are very important. Boadella terms these modes of listening 'channels of contact'. His later work specifically addresses the issue of embodiment within the therapeutic relationship, although this does focus on the body of the client, not the therapist (Boadella 1997). What these therapies have in common is that they stress the importance of viewing the mind and body as inseparable. Whether this is achieved is debatable but at least there is an attempt to grapple with the problem of mind-body duality.

It is now possible to train as a 'body psychotherapist' in the UK, for example, at the Chiron Centre. Chiron are an organisation registered with the UKCP, and for further information you can visit their website (see Chiron 2002). Body psychotherapy views the mind and body as inextricably connected, but focuses on bodily unease or tension as a means of trying to verbalise emotional discomfort.

The client's body is the body most frequently referred to when therapists tackle the subject of the body in therapy, and of course the way that the body is referred to is representative of the particular model the therapist uses in their work. For example, Susie Orbach (1994: 165) draws upon her psychodynamic background to explore the relationship between women's bodies, eating disorders and body image:

> I have been grappling with theoretical aspects of an endemic clinical problem: the problem of the body. The body for the women with a distorted body image is not only the site of an expressive symptom but it is also the principal medium through which she negotiates her psychosocial existence.

This is a laudable attempt to address a particular aspect of the body in therapy – namely, the experience of body image and how this fits in with the client's psychosocial experience. It is, however, concerned with the *client's body* and it would be interesting to see how therapists viewed their own body image. Also, as we have seen, psychotherapy discourse emanates from a patriarchal system, so it must be questioned whether a psychodynamic model is an appropriate one with which to interpret women's bodies. However, in general it is rare for the body to be directly addressed in therapy training, although I have come across some literature from The Scarborough Psychotherapy Training Institute which provides notes on the supportive therapeutic use of touch in counselling (Wilkinson 1997), and some discussion notes on using touch in psychoanalytic psychotherapy (Wilkinson 1997). At the institute where I trained there is a module on somatisation and defence mechanisms (SPTI 1999/2000) within the Gestalt psychotherapy programme; also on the Gestalt programme, external trainers teach on aspects of body work. Some of my colleagues have received direct training on body work, but the emphasis is always on the client's body and I am not aware of the therapist's body being addressed in the course of such training. One attempt at addressing this is the intro-duction of courses which include modules on psychosomatics, as described by Turp (1999). She describes a method of working with the body using body story-lines. The emphasis again is on the client's body but this does introduce the idea that the body of the client is also a narrative account for that client. The therapist's bodily experience is also brought to awareness in this approach. Turp (1999: 303) suggests that:

> I believe that we often unconsciously echo the posture of another person, par-ticularly where we wish to understand a little more of their experience in the world. Our own physical way of being in the presence of a particular client is therefore a useful source of information.

A major theme to arise from the research presented in this book is that the therapist's body is an actively present agent and highly tuned to receiving sensitive information. However, how is this taught? Within my training and that of my colleagues, and within the psychotherapy world in general, this sophisticated process is not directly addressed. Certainly bodily phenomena, when they arise, are considered seriously, but the range and variety of these phenomena and the significance that therapists place on such information seems so great that it is curious that this is not a significant part of the training.

It may be that such bodily phenomena are so obvious that there is an implicit assumption that they will somehow be subsumed as part of the therapeutic endeavour. This may account in some way for the difficulty mentioned by some of the interviewees in expressing what it was they were experiencing. It is almost too obvious, so taken for granted, that to describe the phenomenon becomes very difficult.

How are boundaries taught?

The major boundary that is addressed is that of touch, although this is an issue that arises not necessarily as a part of the curriculum but as a part of practice. I can recall this issue arising within supervision, where trainees would take their caseload to a supervisor and discuss issues to do with their work with clients. This was a place where the application of theory to practice occurred, and issues to do with the ethics of touch were sometimes addressed, as well as the appropriate use of touch with particular clients. It is in supervision that many of the boundaries concerning bodies are addressed, together with some of the embodied phenomena arising from therapy with particular clients. Although it is an assumption that supervision is a place where *all* issues are addressed, there is some evidence to suggest that issues relating to touch are actually avoided in supervision due to the contentious nature of this area. Tune (2001: 170), in a preliminary study on the use of touch as a therapeutic intervention, observed that 'There were numerous contradictory statements made about touch by the therapists who participated in this study. Touch was generally a hidden topic that was not easy to talk about comfortably'.

Touch is an important area for psychotherapy training to consider, if only to allow free exploration of its use within the therapeutic encounter. There is a potential danger of therapists burying their heads in the sand over this issue and assuming that, as it doesn't arise in supervision, then there is not a problem to address. In fact, the notion of bringing the body into mainstream psychotherapy training is not a new one. Reich advocated such an idea by suggesting that mental health professionals be trained in anatomy and physiology, as well as undergo some form of body-orientated therapy (Edward Mann and Hoffman 1980; Prochaska and Norcross 1994). However, this is clearly not the case in contemporary psychotherapy training. It would therefore seem appropriate to examine just what therapists *are* expected to know about bodies.

What are therapists expected to know about bodies?

At the end of a training programme it could be assumed that some issues of bodies in therapy would have been addressed in some form, either in the training itself or via external speakers or supervised practice. The body as a topic may even come into the personal therapy which each trainee is required to undertake throughout the course of the training programme. The emphasis in this learning is predominantly on the role of the client's body, and the potential dangers of touching the client's body.

The therapists interviewed for this study were all experienced, each with at least five years of practice behind them. Since the majority were from the humanistic tradition, the idea of incorporating the body in some form into their work was not an alien notion. Some of the therapists had a training in Gestalt psychotherapy which directly addresses the use of the body (Perls *et al.* 1951). The ideas of Perls are directly related to those of Reich (1983, 1990), since Perls was analysed by Reich. However, the phenomena described by the therapists interviewed did not seem to fit in with their initial training, and a variety of mechanisms were employed to try and make sense of what they were saying. Even though these bodily phenomena were unexpected, the therapists did not seem to feel particularly perturbed by them, but were generally interested and regarded them as useful information for the therapeutic encounter. In fact, one of the aspects of training is a realisation that, in therapeutic work, it is important to establish a support network to help deal with the sorts of phenomena that are experienced; thus all the therapists had access to supervisors or colleagues with whom they could discuss these phenomena. Again, this refers back to the fact that these phenomena are not uncommon, and it is almost a part of psychotherapeutic folklore that they do occur; even more surprising then that there is little written or taught on the subject of the therapist's embodied response. Another surprising feature, when put into the context of psychotherapy training, is that the dominant methodology is experiential learning: this would seem a useful method with which to explore embodiment. Talbot (1998) has also observed that such bodily phenomena are frequent occurrences in psychotherapy. She suggests that what she terms 'listening with the body' is much more of a feminine trait, and its absence from psychotherapy theory, and therefore training, is related to male-dominated psychotherapy theories. This has echoes of the objective-subjective dualism discussed in the previous chapter, and perhaps highlights the predominance of male theorists in psychotherapy culture.

Nor is the idea that the therapist's body becomes affected by the client a new one. Badaracco (1997: 107) makes a link with the ancient healing rites of the Babylonians and Brahmins which used embodied phenomena within the priest to cure illness within the patient. He goes on to observe:

> The way in which the Supreme Priest had to embody evil in his body to exorcise the patient of illness may be found today in the transference-countertransference relationship, especially in patients with severe mental illness, for whom Fairburn once said that the analyst should sometimes be a true exorcist.

I would contend that such phenomena are by no means linked to severe mental illness, but are ubiquitous within therapeutic settings. Therefore, these phenomena are not only in the domain of psychotherapy but are likely to be present in all communication between persons. Indeed, there is mention of this within the medical literature. Gothill and Armstrong (1999: 7) point to some of the literature which actually suggests that the doctor's body has been recognised to reflect somatic reactions to the patient's reporting of symptoms:

> In a humorous aside to their [Byrne and Long] discussion of the meaning of patients' verbal behaviours, the authors commented . . . most doctors agree that when they hear these words they start to suffer unpleasant feelings in various parts of their anatomy which have no clear organic cause.

It would seem then that doctors are susceptible to 'picking up feelings' from their patients. This is similar to the way the therapists in this book describe some of their bodily phenomena, although with the introduction of terms like 'heartsink patients' (O'Dowd 1988) and 'crocks, turkeys, hypochondriacs, the worried well, and the problem patients' (Lipowski 1988: 1361), the problem of the patient's bodily symptoms reflecting in the body of the doctor has been successfully, or perhaps safely, relocated into the patient's mind (Gothill and Armstrong 1999: 7). The distinction that I would like to make clear here is that these phenomena are extremely important within the realm of human relationships. We are embodied beings and thus bodily communication is of great import in how we relate to each other. Therefore, instead of relocating the therapist's body reaction back into the client, I would like to suggest that these bodily experiences are brought out into the open and allowed to become part of the therapeutic encounter. There is a danger within the therapeutic community of viewing such phenomena as merely aspects of countertransference. I would suggest that this is a ruse akin to the medical trick of locating doctors' physical responses back into the body of the patient. I hope to demonstrate throughout this book that the somatic phenomena felt by therapists are important features of the therapeutic relationship, but are, and can only ever be, the *therapist's responses*. These responses are dependent on many factors and the therapist's relationship with their client is but one of them.

Touch in psychotherapy

Bodies are seen as fearful things in relation to touch (Smith *et al.* 1998), even though touch is a psychotherapeutic technique employed by some therapists. Another way in which the subject of the body has been introduced into therapists' training is via the subject of the client's health: if a therapist suspected that their client needed medical treatment, then that client should be referred to their GP. I am also aware that trainees with a background in Gestalt psychotherapy tend to use information about a client's body language and bodily demeanour, and make interpretations based on these observations. Kepner's (1993) work on body process has been influential within the Gestalt community.

Bodily techniques tend to be dealt with as they arise as issues in practice, rather than addressed in a more formal way in training. The exceptions to this are somatisation and, in some instances, touch. This may, of course, reflect the western dualistic method of splitting mind from body but, since a discipline like psychotherapy explores subjectivity, it seems strange that the body has become somehow distant and removed from training. As for the therapist's body, this appears to be as absent in the training as in the literature.

Since psychotherapy is predominantly a therapy of talk, there is, understandably, an emphasis on the use of verbalisation as the mediator of subjective phenomena within the therapeutic encounter. However, this indicates the problem of mind-body dualism, since there is an assumption that problems of the mind must be dealt with via a talking therapy and problems of the body require a physical intervention. Despite this, the therapeutic encounter *is* embodied. One way that bodies can communicate is via touch, which is used in many physical therapies. A good example of this is the osteopathic touch. Much of the training to become an osteopath revolves around the differentiation of various muscle and articular states by touch, and learning to palpate different qualities of muscle tone and assess joint mobility. The training becomes a means of learning from the body by means of touch. Thus the osteopathic clinical encounter incorporates high levels of touch in order to reach an osteopathic diagnosis. The nature of touch in a psychotherapeutic setting is, of course, very different to that in an osteopathic setting, where the osteopathic patient *expects* to be touched. The psychotherapy client does not necessarily expect to be touched, and the type of touch employed by psycho-therapists tends towards that of comfort or consolation; it is the type of touch which would be expected from a close friend or relative. The nature of touch is therefore very different, and negotiating this intervention is fraught with problems for the therapist, since the possibilities for misinterpretation are many. Indeed, the whole idea of touch of any sort is treated with great caution in the psychotherapeutic world. A culture of the touch taboo has evolved, which leaves many therapists in a confused state as to how to approach the issue of touch in therapy.

The origins of this touch taboo lie in the historical links to psychoanalytic theory, where any form of touch was forbidden (Kertay and Reviere 1993). Even touch via a handshake is considered an inappropriate contact by some psycho-analysts (Masson 1990; Sayers 1996) and thus an ambivalent culture has developed around the use of touch in therapy. It is perhaps not surprising that this culture has developed when one looks at the occurrence of misuse of touch in therapy (see Masson 1990; Thorn *et al.* 1993; DeLozier 1994; Jehu 1994). Jehu (1994: 34) sums up the research into sexual abuse by therapists: 'A wide range of sexual acts are perpetuated with patients by abusive therapists belonging to all the main psychotherapy professions in the USA, including intercourse in more than half the cases'. Jehu suggests that there are certain risk characteristics prevalent in abusive therapists, the vast majority of which are older men abusing young female clients. One of these risk characteristics relates to those psychotherapists who reach the top of their profession and tend to be isolated and grandiose in their behaviour; they tend to be isolated from their peers and to be charismatic guru figures.

One of the key features identified in assessing whether to use touch or not is a careful consideration of need – that is, whether or not the need to touch comes from the therapist or the client (Holub and Lee 1990; Halbrook and Duplechin 1994). There is also a clear consensus within the profession that sexual contact should never occur between therapist and client. Indeed, much research has been done on this aspect of touch in therapy: 'It is clear from survey research, and from case study reports, that therapist sexual contact has almost universally negative consequences for the client' (Stake and Oliver 1991: 297).

The current climate, in which it is beginning to be acknowledged that not only is abuse happening in therapy, but that some of the originators of therapeutic theory were themselves abusive to their clients (Masson 1990), understandably leaves therapists wary of using touch. Ilana Rubenfeld (2000) recalls how in the 1960s she was subjected to unwanted sexual advances from her mentor Fritz Perls, who died in 1970. She has since developed her own innovative approach to combining body work and psychotherapy.

Some authors suggest that therapists should never touch their clients in any circumstances (e.g. Alyn 1988). Other authors, while very aware of the dangers of touch, cannot bring themselves to be so abstemious – for example, Hoffman and Gazit (1996: 115): 'The use of touch in psychotherapy is a highly sensitive and controversial issue. It goes without saying that physical contact in psychotherapy should be limited to that which is therapeutically supportive and without erotic overtones'. However, there appear to be danger signals with touch, almost as if touch between client and therapist will automatically lead to some form of sexual contact, or as if touch *per se* has sexual or erotic connotations. Perhaps one of the problems is the setting of psychotherapy, usually in a room (often within the therapist's own home) with just the client and therapist present. Both therapist and client are, potentially, in a very vulnerable position, with no one else present to back up any complaint of misbehaviour on either side.

There is, without doubt, a fear among the profession of complaints and litigation brought by clients. This is especially true of complaints about the inappropriate use of touch in therapy (Imes 1998). This fear is a result of an increasingly litigious culture over the past 20 years, as Glickauf-Hughes and Chance (1998: 153) have observed: 'psychotherapy has become increasingly dominated by fear of lawsuits (particularly lawsuits against therapists for sexual misconduct) and concern about managed care'. The authors are referring here to the state of play in the USA, although the climate is not too dissimilar in the UK. Indeed, client pressure groups have already been organised to address abuse in therapy, an example being POPAN (Prevention of Professional Abuse Network) which is a group consisting of ex-clients who have been abused by therapists (Fasal and Edwardes 1993). Abuse is defined as one of four types: sexual, physical, emotional and financial. There is also the Psychology Politics and Resistance Network, set up to expose abusive practices in psychology (Parker 1996). In the light of the increasing number of cases of sexual misconduct between male therapists and female clients, David Pilgrim (1992: 240) has even suggested that 'The sexual exploitation of clients by male therapists raises the question about the wisdom of training men at all'.

The ambivalent nature of touch is perhaps best summarised by Horton *et al.* (1995: 455), who researched into touch in therapy from the patient's perspective. They found touch to be predominantly perceived as a positive experience, but still urged caution: 'Despite the overwhelmingly positive testament to the helpfulness of touch given by patients in their narrative answers, therapists need to proceed with caution when incorporating touch in their repertoire'. Thus, even when research demonstrates the positive aspect of touch, there is a clear message that touch must be treated with caution. It is not surprising, therefore, that therapists remain confused about this subject.

Yet touch is a normal, everyday form of human contact. It is within a psycho-therapeutic setting that it becomes fraught with possibilities of misinterpretation or, possibly, abuse. There are therapists who positively advocate the use of touch (Wilson 1982; Kupfermann and Smaldino 1987; Woodmansey 1988). The type of touch suggested here is the touching of hands or placing a hand on a shoulder. Although used as a form of reassurance, even this can prove problematic as T2 in this study found to her cost when a reassuring touch from her was misconstrued and led to a complaint against her (see p. 116).

There are even some therapists who work in the psychodynamic world, which traditionally has been averse to the very idea of touch, who can see it has benefits. They view touch as developmentally important, enabling a movement towards the verbalisation of feelings (Goodman and Teicher 1988). A study conducted by Fagan and Silverthorn (1998: 72) concluded that: 'On the basis of this series of studies, we can say that the ability to understand emotional communication from others as communicated by touch is an important component of mental health'.

Thus touch can be a powerful technique to employ within the psychotherapeutic setting. Its use is certainly not new, and there are many authors who advocate a deeper engagement with touch in therapy (Reich 1983, 1990; McNeely 1987; Randell 1989; Frankl 1990; Kepner 1993). It may be that one of the problems around touch is that of *expectation*. Clearly, if one visits an osteopath, there is an implicit expectation to be touched, but this type of expectation is not prevalent in psychotherapy. This could be related to the power dynamics of the therapeutic relationship, and it is refreshing to note that there are some psychotherapists who address this issue directly: 'It is our position that a power differential is inherent to the nature of a therapeutic relationship, with the therapist always holding the superior power position' (Hunter and Struve 1998: 78). Hunter and Struve (1998: 95) explore in some detail this power relationship with reference to touch, and produce a framework with which to view the issue of touch in therapy:

> Numerous factors related to the dynamics of power must be considered prior to using touch in psychotherapy. A therapeutic relationship does not exist in a vacuum, so it is important to acknowledge the ways that touch will be processed through the context of prevailing power dynamics.

They have, therefore, moved the argument towards an acknowledgement of cultural and gender dynamics. While not excluding the use of touch they have made a laudable attempt to view psychotherapy as a cultural practice, and the concomitant result of that is the acceptance that there are many ways of viewing touch. It is also important to realise that psychotherapy does not operate within a cultural vacuum, different cultures having very different views on touch. It is also important to recognise that therapy itself is a cultural enterprise and operates within its own cultural norms. I think it is intriguing that touch is apparently a widespread practice within psychotherapy, yet it remains an area where therapists are particularly reticent about discussing its use within supervision (Tune 2001). An acknowledgement of the use of touch is the first step to opening up debate within the profession, and thereby challenging the touch taboo. Perhaps touch that occurs in therapy can be considered as a part of therapeutic cultural practice. I would suggest that the current taboos on touch provoke feelings of embarrassment and shame in therapists who have touched their clients, and it is this that results in therapists being unwilling to disclose their use of touch.

Summary

The predominant technique that therapists use to bring the body into therapy is that of touch. We can see, then, that touch plays an ambivalent role in psychotherapy. There are clear indications that touch can be both beneficial and abusive. The therapists who engaged in this study were trained in a predominantly humanistic therapeutic modality and, therefore, were more likely to use touch as opposed to therapists who may have trained in a psychoanalytic modality, where touch would be considered inappropriate. In general, the psychotherapy profession remains confused on the issue of touch as a therapeutic intervention. One way to bring the body into therapy which does not necessarily involve touch is via an exploration of embodiment. By this I mean actively bringing the somatic phenomena that therapists feel while working into the therapeutic encounter. Clearly we need a framework to do this, and in the next two chapters I will introduce the ideas of embodiment and narrative which I argue will help provide such a framework for working with therapeutic embodiment.

Chapter 3

Embodiment and the lived-body paradigm

The concepts of embodiment and the lived-body paradigm help to provide a theoretical framework which moves away from traditional psychotherapeutic discourse of the body, towards a way of viewing therapists' embodied phenomena as part of the therapeutic narrative. I am suggesting that the embodied experience of the therapist is a significant aspect of the intersubjective nature of therapy. By viewing embodied phenomena through the perspective of the lived-body paradigm, meaning can be created out of the embodied experience of the therapist. This is a significant aspect of the intersubjective nature of the therapeutic relationship, and so we will, at the end of this chapter, be discussing the importance of intersubjectivity. In particular I will highlight the role of empathy during the intersubjective encounter between therapist and client.

Embodiment

Within the psychotherapy world there is some literature relating to embodiment, which I will discuss in this section. However, in order to explore this phenomenon in more depth and obtain a broader perspective, it will be necessary to cast our net further afield and draw on the disciplines of sociology and psychology.

The perspective of embodiment I am exploring here is taken primarily from the phenomenological movement. It is, therefore, influenced by the work of Merleau-Ponty (1962, 1968) who was part of the French phenomenological philosophical movement which rejected the idea of Cartesian dualism.[1] Turner (1996: 78) summarises these debates and provides the basic premise and starting point for the concept of embodiment I am employing here:

> The body is never simply a physical object but always an embodiment of consciousness. Furthermore, we cannot discuss the body without having a central concern for intentions: the object, 'outside' world is always connected to my body in terms of my body's actions, or potential actions on them. To perceive the world is to reflect upon possible actions of my body on the world.

Embodiment in this context is a dynamic concept where the body is not rigid or unmoving, but a fluid entity which is inscribed with individual as well as cultural meaning. It is, therefore, a means of understanding experience within a broad perspective, and with an emphasis on mind-body unity. It is a concept which examines and highlights the subjective nature of being. This way of looking at the body is compatible with the lived-body paradigm, which is discussed in more detail later in this chapter.

The nearest that psychotherapy theorists come to addressing embodiment is by an exploration of bodily subjective experience (Schwartz-Salant and Stein 1986; Kepner 1993; Boadella 1997). Authors such as Kepner and Boadella stress the importance of the client's bodily experience and, while not addressing the concept of embodiment, do acknowledge that there is a somatic element to the therapeutic encounter. This does little to solve the problem of mind-body dualism and, in a sense, underlines this divide by emphasising the client's bodily phenomena as somehow distinct from the client's mind.

Kepner (1993) provides a comprehensive Gestalt psychotherapy perspective on utilising body experience, and uses the term 'embodiment' as a means for the client to reclaim a sense of embodied self through therapy. Other authors look at bodily subjective experience as a highly important aspect of analysis (e.g. McDougall 1974, 1989; Schwartz-Salant and Stein 1986). We see though that the emphasis within this literature is to look at the body of the client, the therapist's body being largely absent. It is as if the therapist's body is somehow written out of the literature, and yet, as we observed in the previous chapter, the therapist's body is inextricably involved in the therapeutic process and therapists use their own bodily feelings to help guide them in the therapeutic encounter. On reviewing the psychotherapeutic literature it is as though there is only one body in the consulting room: that of the client. This may well symbolise some of the problems of dealing with bodies within psychotherapy. Boadella (1997: 31) has remarked that 'The body which became symbolically banned from psychotherapy with the political expulsion of Wilhelm Reich from the psychoanalytic movement . . . has had 60 years in the cold'. Boadella provides a persuasive argument for taking the body seriously and viewing the rich material emanating from clients' bodies as a form of non-verbal communication. However, the argument is again 'client body orientated'. It is also debatable whether Boadella actually addresses the issue of embodiment at all. It is almost as if the term 'non-verbal communication' has been substituted for embodiment and, as a consequence, it is unclear from his argument what he means by embodiment.

Very few authors directly address the therapist's bodily response. Nathan Field (1989) explores some of his somatic phenomena in a very open account of his practice experience. He puts forward a tentative hypothesis for the appearance of such phenomena which he terms 'embodied countertransference'. His explanation is that this represents some form of pre-verbal or archaic kind of communication. His paper directly addresses the issue of therapist bodily reaction and is thus unusual in seeking to explore the therapist's embodied side of the therapeutic encounter. Although his report is based on his own experience and practice via contacts with colleagues, and while it does not claim to be a serious research project, it does open up avenues for investigation.

Andrew Samuels (1993: 33) openly acknowledges that 'the analyst's bodily reactions are an important part of the picture: the body is an organ of information'. In an earlier work he also used the term 'embodied countertransference' (1985). He conducted a study involving 32 psychotherapists, asking them about counter-transference reactions which could be related to unconscious communication from their patients. From the responses there is a suggestion that there are both reflec-tive and embodied countertransference phenomena. A link is made so that 'patients with instinctual (sex, aggression, food) problems are more likely to evoke reflec-tive and embodied countertransference than other patients' (1985: 57).

Thus therapists' bodily phenomena are classed as important within the thera-peutic encounter. The type of phenomena described range from wearing the same clothes as the patient, to pain and sexual arousal. An intriguing connection is made with the *mundus imaginalis*, the imagined world. This has links to Gestalt psycho-therapy notions of the 'in-between' – the space between therapist and client (see Hycner 1993; Hycner and Jacobs 1995). This space could also be referred to as the intersubjective space between client and therapist and is, therefore, important in the examination of intersubjectivity. Samuels (1985: 59) suggests that the *mundus imaginalis* can provide a framework in which to view these embodied counter-transference experiences, since 'the experiences of countertransference in this paper, may be regarded as visions'. There are links also to mysticism and the work of Buber, where Samuels suggests that 'analysis is a mysticism of persons – and hence polyvalent, pluralistic, many-headed, many-bodied' (1985: 62).

Rowan (1998) has noted Samuels' use of embodied countertransference, and introduced his idea of 'linking'. This is a term describing a special type of empathy, and the embodied nature of the connection between therapist and client is provided as an example of this concept. Rowan is unusual in suggesting a new term; he moves away from the confines of old discursive terms like 'transference' and 'countertransference', and suggests that new ways of thinking are needed to try and explain such embodied phenomena. On discussing empathy he suggests that:

> We try to enter into another person's inner world, but know very well that they are over there and we are over here . . . we are talking about something different, which goes much deeper into the world of the other person: it is as if it actually overlaps with ours.
>
> (Rowan 1998: 245)

Thus the idea of linking offers the opportunity to see the therapeutic relationship as an embodied encounter. There are two bodies in the room, the client and the therapist, and the types of embodied phenomena which therapists experience may be viewed in the context of an overlapping of experience. This also suggests (though not explicitly in Rowan's paper) that some form of bodily communication is at work. This view of embodiment is very different to the prevailing attitude in psychotherapy, where it is often perceived as a form of countertransference.

An example of this countertransferential perspective is given by Mathew (1998: 17). She has become aware through her own psychotherapy practice of powerful physical reactions to clients. She provides an account of the many varied responses which she terms as somatic countertransference:

> The body is clearly an instrument of physical processes, an instrument that can hear, see, touch and smell the world around us. This sensitive instrument also has the ability to tune in to the psyche: to listen to its subtle voice, hear its silent music and search into its darkness for meaning.
>
> (Mathew 1998: 17)

Authors such as Mathew, who are steeped in the psychoanalytic tradition, not surprisingly view these processes through a psychoanalytic lens. Thus, when describing a particular patient who evoked strong bodily responses in her, Mathew reported: 'perhaps that had something to do with the very concrete way I experienced him in counter-transference' (1998: 17). A little later she goes on to say that 'This time it was possible for me to collect and process my objective bodily response to my patient's unconscious material fairly quickly so that I could offer it back to her during the session' (1998: 21). I highlight the last two quotes in particular as they link into my later discussion on reification in psychotherapy (see Chapter 9). The use of the terms 'concrete' and 'material' suggests a tangible substance, and the problem with this is that Mathew is describing intangible subjective phenomena. This does, however, begin to open the debate relating to the type of language or discourse used to describe embodied phenomena, and highlights the problem of using terms like 'transference' and 'countertransference' as a means to describe these intersubjective phenomena. We shall return to this debate on psychotherapeutic discourse in Chapter 9.

The author who moves closest to describing embodiment in the context of this book is perhaps Schwartz-Salant (1986: 23), a Jungian analyst who suggests that 'Clinical material can often be approached with reference to either body or psyche'. This 'either body or psyche' description does tend to evoke the Cartesian mind-body split. However, Schwartz-Salant proposes the use of the 'subtle-body' concept in analysis, which he describes as follows: 'The subtle-body experience is often a background, a subliminal field of imagery, against which we form interpretations and other cognitive acts' (1986: 38). His work clearly acknowledges that the therapist's somatic experience is of significance during therapeutic work. Also, his description of the subtle-body concept evokes the concept of embodiment I am exploring in this book, although he does not use the term 'embodiment'. However, in an earlier work, when discussing empathy, he differentiates between two types – namely, psychic and somatic (Schwartz-Salant 1982). This has particular relevance to this book as the types of bodily phenomena described by therapists have been attributed to a form of empathy.

Another angle employed to address the therapist's body has been an investigation by Arthern and Madill (1999) of the use of transitional objects. The outcome of their research suggests that embodiment is a significant part of the use of transitional objects. However, although the therapist's body is present in this research, the embodying phenomenon is still seen as that belonging to the client: 'the model focuses on the TO [transitional object] as embodying the client's sense of the relationship' (1999: 19).

If we examine how the related discipline of psychology views the body, then we see that the body has historically been seen through a physiological lens – i.e. the body as an organism where 'organisms are just organised bodies' (Stam 1998: 1). Psychologists are beginning to incorporate some of the thoughts from the sociological movement which looks at aspects of the body, and are now starting to see the relevance of embodiment to practice (Radley 1998; Sampson 1998). A consequence of this is that the body is viewed in a rather abstract and disembodied way, as an entity existing in a sociological space, remote and removed from subjective experience.

The use of the concept of embodiment may help in understanding some of the subjective phenomena described in the research discussed in this book. Radley (1998: 13) suggests that: 'embodiment, rather than the body, is central to psychological life and to social relationships'. The way that I am employing the term embodiment throughout this book is as follows. Our bodily sense arises from how we perceive the world; this is related to how we have come to know the world, and therefore our embodied sense necessarily incorporates our biographical experience. This includes how we have perceived and have been perceived by other bodies. Thus embodiment is also related to how we relate to others. In a sense this is an attempt to break free from the western cultural mind-body dichotomy and to see embodiment as symbolising a 'being in the world'. This clearly echoes those authors who have written on the phenomenological aspects of the body (e.g. Merleau-Ponty 1962, 1968; Leder 1990).

Phenomenological readings of the body are not without problems. As Sampson (1998) suggests in his critique of phenomenology, it excludes history and culture. He argues that it is the 'uncritical taking of the body as a ground' (1998: 35) which leads to the individualisation of experience outside history and culture. He attempts to resolve this problem by putting forward social constructivist concepts as a means of reading embodied experience. This would seem to be a worthwhile endeavour: 'I am not suggesting that we are in the world through language or through the body separately, but because language is in-itself embodied even as the body is en-worded, we are in the world in a unified manner' (Sampson 1998: 39–40).

Since psychotherapy is a 'talking therapy' I would suggest that we need to take seriously the language we use. This is a crucial argument as we can see that language is itself an embodied experience. Radley's suggestion that we are in the world in 'a unified manner' derives from Merleau-Ponty's work, where he tried to deconstruct the Cartesian view of mind and body as separate (1962, 1968). This concept of unification, which is alluded to frequently within the humanistic psychotherapy world, is often accompanied by that nebulous term 'holistic', which frequently comes across as a catch-all phrase to try and encompass everything at the same time. While it can be a useful term to attempt to describe complex interrelations there are some problems with its generic use.

This sort of terminology is particularly common in Gestalt, where therapists regard themselves as 'holistic practitioners'. They use concepts such as field theory to attempt to explain holistic phenomena. However, much confusion reigns over what these terms actually mean, and some rather lax arguments are proffered to try and describe complex phenomena. An example of this loose thinking is provided by Roberts (1999), whose argument is that field theory helps us to understand subjective experience; he then begins to refer to 'the field' as though it were a real thing, and thus implies a reification of subjective experience. This is clearly problematic as it implies that therapeutic phenomena can be experienced as real and substantial. Clearly, subjective phenomena are not substantial and, therefore, not tangible. The problem for psychotherapists who believe that, for example, countertransferential phenomena are real things in themselves, as suggested by Roberts (1999) and Mathew (1998), is that this implies such phenomena may be malleable, that they may be manipulated as if they were real. Such assumptions about subjective experience imply a dogmatic attitude and, I would suggest, require challenging.[2] The issue here is that many psychotherapeutic terms remain unchallenged and are frequently taken as givens or truths within psychotherapy culture. As a consequence there is a tendency to assume knowledge and not to employ critical thinking when addressing unsubstantiated theoretical constructs. This is exemplified by the cavalier way that discursive terms from other disciplines (e.g. medicine) are incorporated into psychotherapeutic discourse. This also highlights the necessity of examining the type of language that we employ as therapists to describe embodied phenomena.

Radley (1998: 27) asserts that 'embodiment is vital to expression', and it is certainly a crucial concept within the context of this book. Radley makes a strong argument for investigating this concept in a way that looks at 'how people deal focally with their bodies' and suggests that this may reveal important information for psychological theory. Crossley (1995) provides a useful account of Merleau-Ponty's work and suggests that phenomenological descriptions of intersubjective experience are a starting point from which to investigate embodiment. The range of bodily phenomena that I am presenting in this book would seem to fit somewhere within this framework; I am attempting to investigate therapists' phenomenological experience of their bodies and thus gain a deeper insight into the embodied experience of the therapeutic encounter.

Gender is an important concept to consider as an aspect of embodiment. As Parlee (1998: 122) points out: 'human bodies differ in many ways, which are always, necessarily an admixture of biological processes and social history'. Gender is related to both biological processes and social history. It is therefore an important aspect of our sense of embodiment. There are many authors who have looked at gender and the sociology of the body (e.g. Martin 1987; Featherstone *et al.* 1991; Synnott 1993; Turner 1995). Turner (1995: 321) provides a summary of the key debate: 'while we are born either male or female, masculinity and femininity are social and cultural divisions'. Gendered identities are therefore not merely biological characteristics but are also learned through social practices. As Shilling (1993: 107) notes:

> Gendered categories and practices operate as material forces which help to shape and form women's and men's bodies in ways that reinforce particular images of femininity and masculinity. The mind's conceptualization of bodies is closely related to people's experiences of bodies.

Clearly any research which looks at bodies needs to consider the issue of gender. However, in the study discussed in this book gender was noticeable by its absence. By this I mean that therapists did not tend to talk about their bodies in a gendered manner. In some cases there was an obvious link to a gendered body (e.g. in the case of the therapist who experienced a feeling of pregnancy). But in general the types of response that therapists reported were not related to a particular gender. This strikes me as rather curious since, as I suggested earlier, gender is socially constructed and thereby linked to a sense of embodiment; it would have been expected that these issues would have surfaced at some stage when interviewing therapists but, in this research, no mention was made of issues relating to sexuality or gender identity, nor was there any mention of erotic countertransference. This may have been because these issues are too sensitive, or because, as most of the sample were women, they did not feel such an exploration was appropriate with a male researcher. However, the male respondents did not refer to these issues either. Alternatively, it may be that psychotherapy discourse does not as yet have the language to debate these issues, which may indicate a lack of critical reflexivity within the profession. With hindsight, it would have been beneficial to have addressed the issue of gender in the interviews. I would suggest that, for this group of therapists, gender is not an issue worth raising, because it is as yet not a conscious aspect of their psychotherapeutic discourse.

In summary, embodiment as seen through a psychotherapeutic lens appears to be a rather narrow concept, although authors such as Rowan (1998) are engaging in a debate which might develop it beyond the therapy room. The sociological constructs of embodiment potentially provide a broader perspective, and it is this perspective that will be discussed in the next section where we will examine the lived-body paradigm.

The lived-body paradigm

> Everyday life provides compelling evidence of the importance the body plays in our search for understanding.
>
> (Halling and Goldfarb 1991: 313)

The lived-body paradigm derives from the phenomenological school of philosophy which has been influenced by the work of Edmund Husserl (1859–1938), Maurice Merleau-Ponty (1908–61), Jean-Paul Sartre (1905–80) and Martin Heidegger (1889–1976), among others (Schwandt 1997). Phenomenology is concerned with an understanding of a person's life world, and a fundamental tenet of this approach is that 'knowledge is an act of consciousness' (Hughes 1990: 140). The authors who have contributed to the lived-body paradigm are Merleau-Ponty (1962), Straus (1966) and, latterly, Leder (1990).

The lived-body paradigm is a means of acknowledging that our perception of the world, and how we interpret the world via our bodies, is the starting point in acquiring knowledge. The argument here is that we can only understand our lived world with the apparatus with which we are provided to sense it, namely our bodies. As Liedloff (1986) points out, we are born with eyes expecting to see, with ears expecting to hear, with bodies expecting to feel and to be touched. Therefore, any knowledge of our world has to be a body-orientated knowledge:

> an examination of experience reveals that it is the body which first 'understands' the world, grasping its surroundings and moving to fulfil its goals. In phenomenological terms, the body is not just a caused mechanism, but an 'intentional entity' always directed toward an object pole, a world.
>
> (Leder 1984: 31)

The ideas put forward here are essentially phenomenological in nature and vehemently against the Cartesian dualistic method of reducing the body and mind to discrete entities.

Merleau-Ponty (1962) was influenced by Gestalt psychology, which had its heyday in the 1930s and suggested that perception of the world occurred by making relationships between objects. Thus, perception was mediated by seeing groups, perceiving in wholes rather than in discrete entities (Clarkson 1989; Rock and Palmer 1990; Ramachandran 1998). Gestalt psychology (not to be mistaken for Gestalt psychotherapy) was against the reductionistic world view, and in hindsight 'its legacy to the studies of perception, cognition and Social Psychology should not be underestimated even though it often remains unacknowledged' (Richards 1996: 64). I make this point here to put a historical perspective on the psychological theories that were present when Merleau-Ponty was writing. Since he died in 1961, the theories of Gestalt psychology would have been prevalent during his time. Gestalt psychology provided a new framework for understanding perception, one where there was an interaction, a relationship between subject and object. This has echoes of the debate within subatomic physics begun during the 1930s between quantum physics and relativity theory (Capra 1975; Briggs and Peat 1984), and it is interesting to note that two of the founders of Gestalt psychology, Wertheimer and Köhler, had close associations with Albert Einstein and Max Planck respectively (Richards 1996: 64). Thus the paradigm of the lived-body had some roots in the debates raging at that time around the nature of matter and the means by which we perceive the world. Merleau-Ponty's position is clearly against the Cartesian view which perceives the world as physical manifestations, as either *res extensa* (extended substance) or *res cogitans* (thinking substance), thus paving the way for the perennial mind-body problem which has dogged philosophy (Cottingham 1997). It is also interesting to note that Merleau-Ponty held the Chair of Child Psychology and Pedagogy at the Institute de Psychologie, Sorbonne from 1949 to 1952, and was presumably well versed in contemporary psychological theories; indeed he makes more than passing reference to psycho-analytic thought in his works.

The lived-body paradigm allows for an interaction with the environment; it lends a perspective of dynamism to the body. The body is not merely an imbiber of external stimuli to which it responds in an automatic manner, but becomes involved at the very centre of being. Our bodies are the means by which we engage with the world; they are how we come to understand our environment and make sense of our place in the world. As Merleau-Ponty (1962: xi) so eloquently puts it: 'The world is not an object such that I have in my possession the law of its making; it is the natural setting of, and field for, all my thoughts and all my explicit percep-tions'. The question to ask then is: how is the notion of the lived-body relevant to the issue of embodiment within psychotherapy? One way of employing the lived-body paradigm usefully is in exploring the means by which a phenomenological reading of the body can help with a description of pain. This would link with the concept of somatisation, a term frequently used by therapists. I hope that a discus-sion of lived-body phenomenology and pain will help to develop my ideas on embodiment within the therapeutic encounter.

Drew Leder (1984/5: 255) has explored the notion of pain within medical discourse and, influenced by the work of Straus and Merleau-Ponty, has suggested that 'pain cuts across the boundaries of the mental and the physical, belongs both to the self and its enworldment'. In a later work (1990: 69) he brings to our atten-tion the idea of body absence and poses the question: 'why, if human experience is rooted in the bodily, is the body so often absent from experience?' In answering this question he suggests that some 'modes of disappearance' are vital to body functioning, and that it is this very ability of the body to recede into the background that gives us a cultural sense of embodiment in the west. This embodied sense is largely one of absence; hence the body has become neglected.

The argument I am putting forward here is the centrality of the body in any encounter; far from receding into the background, it is essential to bring the body centre stage. An understanding of the lived-body paradigm allows for a phenomenological reading of the body and therefore takes us away from the constraints of Cartesian dualism. As a result the body now becomes 'the very basis of human subjectivity' (Crossley 1995: 44–5).

I have written elsewhere about the body in medicine (Shaw 1997c), in relation to the manner in which osteopathic patients describe their pain in a rather disembodied way, and use the medicalised reductionistic model with which to describe their painful symptoms. Osteopathic patients will frequently be described as somatisers by the medical fraternity, as their pain will often remain undiagnosed from a medical perspective. This view of the body is perhaps not surprising in the western cultural context in which we are taught to view our bodies. Medicine is a powerful discourse which has considerable powers over our bodies from cradle to grave, from immunisation programmes to disposal of bodies at death (Fox 1993). Psychotherapists are therefore likely to be heavily influenced by medical perceptions of the body within western culture. One aspect of this is likely to originate in the clinical encounter, as Leder (1984: 32) suggests: 'the patient presents the lived-body for treatment while the doctor treats the Cartesian or object body'. The encounter, therefore, tends towards an objectification of symptoms and the lived-body is missed. Perhaps this is not surprising when one thinks of medical training. As Leder observes: 'the doctor examines a *physical body*. Much of her/his medical training has de-emphasized lived embodiment from the first "patient" encounter – that with a cadaver' (1984: 33). Within the medical gaze, medical patients are equated with dead bodies. The emphasis on how the living body resembles a dead one is an intriguing idea. This methodology for looking at bodies would seem to have no room or space for the lived-body. This may in part explain some of the difficulties that are experienced by medical practitioners and patients alike when it comes to the medical encounter.

As I wish to examine the form of embodiment that arises from the psychotherapeutic encounter, it is worth discussing the lived-body aspect of this encounter in general terms. Since the majority of the work written on this has focused on the medical encounter, this would seem a good place to start. However, there is an overlap between the doctor-patient and psychotherapist-client relationships in that both involve a therapeutic encounter. Indeed, it is interesting that psychotherapy contains the word 'therapy'. This evokes a medical encounter and the application of some kind of medicalised therapeutic technique.

The disembodied encounter

> As he/she thoughtfully adjusts the patient's laboratory values with medication and intravenous fluids there is an ironical fulfilment of Cartesian dualism – a mind (namely, that of the doctor) runs a passive and extrinsic body (that of the patient).
>
> (Leder 1984: 35)

The type of therapeutic encounter described in the above quote is one that anyone can identify with who has sought out medical treatment in the western world. The relationship between doctor and patient is almost a disembodied interaction from the doctor's point of view, an acting out of objective science onto an unsuspecting subject, that of the patient. There has been much written on the subject of the doctor-patient relationship (e.g. Balint 1955; Gordon 1983; Waitzkin and Britt 1989; Mathers and Rowland 1997; Gothill and Armstrong 1999). As discussed in Chapter 2, doctors' bodies also become involved in the doctor-patient relationship, and apparently react to patients in a not too dissimilar way to that with which psychotherapists' bodies react to their clients. It may well be that the psychotherapeutic encounter apes the doctor-patient consultation. Medical physicians who concentrate on physical disorders are likely to ignore the mind of the patient, just as therapists concentrating on the mind of the client are likely to ignore the body of the client. In both instances there is a disembodiment.

The work of Merleau-Ponty brings us to the realisation that we are neither just mind or body – it is a fundamental part of being human that we are physical beings. Our perception of our world can only come about via our physical abilities to receive information in a bodily form. The significance of this is that psychotherapy is essentially an embodied encounter.[3] There are two lived bodies in the therapy room: that of the client and that of the therapist.

If we can apply the notions from the lived-body paradigm we can highlight the lived experience of therapists' embodied experience within the therapeutic encounter. This in turn becomes a form of body narrative which enables the therapist to make sense of and use their bodily feelings. Those researchers who work with lived experience emphasise the subjective nature of life and therefore focus on: 'human lived experience and the physical, political, and historical context of that experience. It is our intention to return to the goals formulated by pioneers such as Weber, who saw sociology as centrally concerned with human subjectivity' (Ellis and Flaherty 1992: 1). An examination of lived experience has much in common with the lived-body paradigm; perhaps the main difference is that an examination of lived experience allows for the incorporation of political and historical experiences, whereas the lived-body paradigm tends to focus more on the physical body. Both have much to offer when viewing therapists' physical reactions to their clients.

In the context of this book, psychotherapists' lived experiences will include aspects of psychotherapy culture. Therefore, it is important to contextualise the way that therapists talk about their bodies in relation to training, techniques and discourse. It is also important to note that researchers who investigate lived experience are concerned with emotional aspects of life, and this is therefore very applicable to psychotherapy.

An integration of embodiment and lived experience is provided by Csordas (1990: 5), when describing his perspective on embodiment:

> This approach to embodiment begins from the methodological postulate that the body is not an *object* to be studied in relation to culture, but it is to be considered as the *subject* of culture, or in other words as the existential ground of culture.

He is clearly stating a phenomenological perspective, and Busby (1996: 143), drawing on the Csordas' methodology, suggests: 'In the embodiment paradigm, knowledge is seen as being synthesised within the body, rather than being an external or mental explanation'. The significance of this to our argument is that the embodied phenomena that we experience as psychotherapists are a means of acquiring knowledge about the therapeutic encounter. There is therefore the potential for generating new knowledge. In a way this is local knowledge and may only be applicable to that particular instant of therapy. This knowledge is of a subjective nature but highly valuable nonetheless, and may be used to develop a therapeutic body narrative. As Csordas (1990: 39) suggests: 'the body is a productive starting point for analysing culture and self'. The culture under investigation in this book is that of psychotherapy, and the selves are those of the therapists in the study, including myself.

The inclusion of myself is another way that lived experience makes an impact in this book, via an autobiographical narrative. This is an important factor as I am a practising psychotherapist as well as a researcher. I will describe some of my own embodied experiences as a therapist later, in Chapter 9.

Intersubjectivity and empathy

These two concepts are very important in my discussion of the therapist's body experience during therapy. One of the main issues to arise from an exploration of body experience is that our subjective experience is primarily a somatic event – 'subjectivity is truly embodied' (Depraz 2001: 172). It is through the experience of our bodies and interaction with other bodies that we develop a sense of our lived body. This sense is closely related to intersubjective experience – i.e. an important aspect of how we build knowledge about our lived body is by relating to other people. The experience of intersubjectivity is a crucial aspect of this process. In the research presented in this book many of the phenomena that therapists experience could be said to be a form of body empathy (I will discuss this particular aspect in Chapter 8) – i.e. the therapist is in some way resonating in their own body with something significant in the therapeutic relationship. This I would suggest must also say something about the therapeutic encounter and the intersubjective experience occurring between therapist and client. Thus embodied experiences are a means of exploring the intersubjective world between therapist and client. In this way we can see that 'intersubjectivity appears to be this mutual discovery, through the other's own embodiment' (Depraz 2001: 174).

Both client and therapist bring their respective lived-bodies to the therapeutic encounter. Depraz (2001: 172) introduces the idea of lived empathy and provides four stages of empathy:

1   A passive association of my lived body with your lived body
2   An imaginative self-transposal in your psychic states
3   An interpretative understanding of yourself as being an alien to me
4   An ethical responsibility toward yourself as a person (enjoying and suffering).

She goes on to explore the concept of *paarung*, first put forward by Husserl. Here, empathy is considered as a form of passive and primal experience which is inextricably related to our lived-body. *Paarung* refers to a coupling process by which two lived-bodies associate with each other through a similar experience of being able to perceive the world by touch, smell, seeing and hearing (Depraz 2001). This seems to be a similar process to that described by Rowan (1998) with his concept of 'linking', discussed earlier in this chapter (see p. 34). *Paarung* is the ability to understand what it might feel like to be someone else, and it is this that enables empathy to be possible. But we can only really know what it is like to be in our own body. Empathic understanding is therefore always an interpretative understanding based on our own lived experience.

This does not mean that empathy is not a valuable means of communication. Indeed, some authors suggest that there is an evolutionary reason for the development of empathy. Jonathan Cole (2001) has explored this with particular reference to the face. He has suggested that:

> the face evolved as a result of several evolutionary pressures but . . . it is well placed to assume the role of an embodied representation of the increasingly refined inner states of mind that developed as primates became more social, and required more complex social intelligence.
>
> (2001: 51)

The face is obviously a means whereby we can communicate emotional states and from the psychotherapeutic point of view, as well as in other human interactions, the face has 'an important role in interpersonal relatedness'. The face can also be seen to have an important role in revealing 'the embodiment of some emotions'. The evolutionary argument is that the face was a means of conveying inner mind states, and this ability to communicate led to: 'an emotional contagion whereby the observer entered into the states of another, and hence to sympathy and empathy'(Cole 2001: 65, 67, 66).

The idea of emotional contagion would fit well with how therapists describe being affected by their clients. It is almost as if something is 'picked up' in the therapeutic encounter, and this is what I think therapists are grappling with when they use words like 'material' and try to make subjective phenomena concrete and tangible. A different way to view such phenomena is to see them as the embodiment of internal states. To quote Cole (2001: 66) again:

> I may not be able to feel your pain, that most private of feelings, but I can share your suffering. It is through behaviour that this is possible, through the embodiment of inner states in a way which leads us to them being available for others to see and then more, for by taking them into themselves they can then be felt and are used to motivate another.

I would suggest that this is more akin to the process that therapists describe when they feel strong bodily feelings in response to their clients. If this is a normal process and one with evolutionary importance then it is not surprising that therapists report these sensations; what is surprising is the dearth of literature within the psychotherapy world on phenomena which are apparently ubiquitous.

The arguments I am putting forward here are that empathy is a bodily phenomenon and that the experience of empathy occurs via an intersubjective relationship, such as the psychotherapeutic encounter. If we use concepts like the 'lived-body' and begin to view therapy as a meeting of two lived-bodies, then this frees us from searching for psychotherapeutic discourse in an attempt to interpret such phenomena. The aim of such an encounter is, rather, to acknowledge the phenomena arising from the lived-bodies of those involved and use this as the basis for a therapeutic narrative, not as a means of interpreting another body's behaviour. It is therefore essential to acknowledge the client as a living body, not just a physical body (Toombs 2001). This has its problems, as the lived-body tends to recede into the background, but the phenomena that therapists experience in their own bodies is a way of bringing the lived-body into the foreground. The importance of viewing empathy as a part of lived experience is that it gives us the opportunity to see empathy as a means of viewing another individual as an embodied being. Empathy can therefore be a way of experiencing direct awareness of another individual. The lived-body is how we react to another's emotional world so we can see that 'the lived body is also expressive of affective experience' (Toombs 2001: 252) and is the medium for the *construction* of that experience; or to put it another way, our emotions are embodied. If affective experience is embodied it is not surprising that another person can elicit emotions within our own body. These are, however, our emotions as they arise from our body. But as this mechanism is learned via relationships with other bodies it is possible that 'affective experience discloses the intimate relations between self and other' (Toombs 2001: 253).

This has been described as 'reiterated empathy', as Toombs (2001: 253) explains: 'In reiterated empathy, I see myself from the viewpoint of another and thus grasp myself as an individual in an intersubjective world'. This has much relevance for the psychotherapeutic encounter as our bodies can be a vehicle for receiving affective experience, which is likely to be invoked during an encounter with a client. Indeed, there does not seem to be a choice about this: it just happens. There is something passive about this process, almost as if as therapists we are tuned in to 'picking up' these signals. I am not suggesting that these phenomena do not exist outside the therapy room – in fact, I am convinced they are very common and part and parcel of everyday life. It is just that in the therapeutic encounter (and this can include any therapeutic interaction) the chances are that such bodily affective responses will be present. These feelings are, I contend, a vital part of the therapeutic process. It is important to remember that empathy is based on the ability to move into another's experience, to walk in someone else's shoes, as if I were that person (Toombs 2001). Clearly one way of doing this is via experiencing bodily feelings, and these very experiences are a means of building a therapeutic narrative. This narrative will be peculiar to each individual therapeutic encounter as 'the meaning of the patient's experience is determined by her unique biographical situation and the values inherent in that situation' (Toombs 2001: 256). I would add to this that therapists bring their own biographical lived-body to the situation and it is by sharing these experiences that an embodied therapeutic narrative can be developed.

So I am suggesting that embodied phenomena are a normal part of the therapeutic process, and as we will see in Part 2 can sometimes be dramatic in nature. The therapists in this study often make the assumption that these experiences are directly related to the client. There is a danger in this and an implication that therapist's body feeling is somehow transmitted to the therapist by the client, or that there is a direct cause and effect link between the somatic sensation and the client. I take issue with these assumptions. That is not to say that these bodily feelings may not have something important to contribute to the therapeutic encounter, and if disclosed they are a crucial aspect of constructing a therapeutic narrative. But the causal links that are sometimes claimed by therapists about their bodies require challenging. Therapists have a habit of employing naive interpretations for their bodily phenomena. It must be remembered, as Zahavi (2001: 153) so eloquently puts it: 'That I have an actual experience of the other . . . does not imply, however, that I can experience the other in the same way as she herself does, nor that the other's consciousness is accessible to me in the same way as my own is'.

As psychotherapists we must remember that the bodily reactions we experience emanate from our own bodies. The danger of using therapeutic discourse such as countertransference, projection, introjection, etc. is that it actually takes us away from our bodily experience. This type of language, heavily imbued with medical (and by implication Cartesian) discourse, tends to treat the body and the mind as objects. The net effect is that a feeling experienced in the body of the therapist becomes a feeling that is somehow transmitted by the client. The result is an interpretation that the therapist is feeling the client's feelings. This is clearly nonsensical, and a problem of therapeutic interpretation. We need a method of viewing these phenomena and talking about them which is free from the old discursive terms, one which will enable us to take into account the lived experience of the therapeutic encounter. This is crucial when considering embodiment within psychotherapy, and when looking at the important association between intersubjectivity and empathy, which are embodied phenomena: 'one's consciousness of oneself as an embodied individual in the world is founded on empathy – on one's empathic cognition of others, and others' empathic cognition of oneself' (Thompson 2001: 2). Then it becomes clear that the traditional psychotherapeutic way of viewing this type of phenomena via countertransference or some form of projection results in the embodied experience being located back into the body of the client. It is clearly not possible, when taking a lived-body perspective, to justify such interpretations. All the phenomena which therapists experience in their bodies emanate from their own embodied experience. The significant factor here is that the therapeutic encounter results in the therapist feeling emotions and bodily phenomena. As Thompson (2001: 4) has noted:

Affect has numerous dimensions that bind together virtually every aspect of the organism – the psychosomatic network of the nervous system, immune system, and endocrine system; physiological changes in the autonomic nervous system, the limbic system, and the superior cortex; facial-motor changes and global differential motor readiness for approach or withdrawal; subjective experience along a pleasure-displeasure valence axis; social signalling and coupling; and conscious evaluation and assessment.

Affect is a whole body event, not merely in the mind. Thompson goes on to suggest that much of affect is related to the intersubjective experience of self and other and therefore, from the perspective of the psychotherapeutic encounter, this is an important issue to consider, especially when exploring the bodily effects that therapists report when conducting psychotherapy.

An interesting concept that Thompson (2001: 11) introduces in relation to empathy is simulation theory (ST), an idea resulting from work seeking explanations for mind-reading. In ST the theory is that someone has: 'the ability to mentally "simulate" another person, that is . . . on being able to use the resources of one's own mind to create a model of another person and thereby identify with him or her, projecting oneself imaginatively into his or her situation'. This could be an explanation for how we as therapists empathise with our clients and somehow manage to have a sense of what it is like to be in their world. But this is not the whole story, for as Thompson goes on to discuss the role of intersubjectivity is not fully taken into account in this theory. This is where concepts such as the lived-body are useful. Thompson agrees that the ability to put oneself in another's shoes is an important aspect of empathy – he uses the terms 'mimicry' and 'imaginative transposition', which in psychotherapeutic terminology may be similar to the concept of mirroring. However, the important aspect to include here is that the lived-body is open to intersubjective experiences, as this is the means whereby we come to know what it is like to be in a relationship with another body. Empathy and intersubjective understanding can therefore be viewed from the perspective of both therapist and client 'as living bodily subjects or embodied agents, not as inner mental spectators of the outer world' (Thompson 2001: 13).

Empathy as experienced during the therapeutic encounter could be said to be an aspect of intersubjectivity. This is felt in the body and the physical manifestation of it is reported via a range of symptoms, as we shall see in Part 2. This ability to be aware of physical sensations may be due to the peculiar nature of psychotherapy. By this I mean the closeness and intimacy that is often felt by being in a one-to-one relationship with another person. This sets up a common space and as client and therapist also perceive the world through a human body there is an opportunity to share a common perspective of that experience. Thompson (2001: 19) summarises this point by suggesting that 'The intersubjective openness of consciousness and empathy are the preconditions for our experience of inhabiting a common, intersubjective, spatial world'.

Empathy is therefore crucial in enabling us as therapists to gain another perspective, another view of the world – the client's world. The use of bodily phenomena is a significant aspect of this ability. There may be an argument here for choosing a therapist who has had similar experiences to the client, since this may help in matching up similar lived-body experiences. Obvious examples here would be gender and race. This is an important area for further research. However, there is also the counter argument that it would be unlikely that a complete match could be found for everyone.

The most important issue here is that the therapist has the ability to empathise, and that this empathic process is a body-orientated phenomenon. Therefore, my contention would be that as therapists we need to become much more bodily aware and begin to research and use our bodies as a means to understand the intersubjective experience of the therapeutic encounter. In the ensuing chapters I present ways of achieving this via the use of the 'body as receiver' (Chapter 6), 'embodied styles of working' (Chapter 7), and 'body empathy' (Chapter 8).

Empathy is a helpful concept which can guide us through the possibilities of what our physical feelings may mean while working in the therapeutic setting. It must be remembered that empathy 'is not a disembodied and affectless comprehension of the Other, but rather the feeling of being led by another's experience' (Thompson 2001: 23). We are embodied beings and feelings are somatic as well as cognitive processes. Furthermore, feelings can be considered to have significance, and we put value on them because we have feelings in response to events that have meaning for us. Emotions can be said to be our 'value feelings' and as such they 'enact or constitute the world of values'(Thompson 2001: 23). Therefore, as therapists, when we have bodily feelings as a consequence of a therapeutic encounter these must have significance and we need to pay attention to these rather than ignore them. This is of course an interpretation, and it is important that we are clear as to the significance we place on such feelings – I would suggest that it behoves us to be aware of our own value system. Our own values and beliefs are, after all, the results of our experience and must therefore be a part of our lived-body experience, which we bring to the therapeutic encounter.

Summary

In this chapter I have introduced the concepts of embodiment and the lived-body paradigm to provide a conceptual framework for psychotherapeutic embodiment; both of these concepts focus on the body. Psychotherapy literature in general does not address these particular issues. Embodiment is, however, addressed by other disciplines, so I have discussed it in relation to such disciplines. Clearly my intention is to attempt to acquire a space within which to explore psychotherapeutic embodiment and, in order to do this, I have found it necessary to draw on work beyond the boundaries of traditional psychotherapeutic theory. This book can, therefore, be described as a multi-disciplinary work. In one sense this could be considered a weakness, as an exploration of too many theories could lead to a dilution of the core theoretical arguments. However, I think that traditional psychotherapeutic notions of the body have been found inadequate in the conceptualisation of these arguments, and the psychotherapeutic discourses employed to understand embodied phenomena have been found to be insufficient. Therefore I have had to draw on sociological, anthropological and phenomenological theories of the body. I have also introduced a discussion on intersubjectivity and focused on empathy as a means to highlight the important contribution that embodiment can make to psychotherapy practice.

Chapter 4

The narrative turn in psychotherapy

This chapter is divided into three sections: psychotherapeutic discourse, narrative in psychotherapy, and self-disclosure. I discuss psychotherapeutic discourse as a means of providing a context for the use of a narrative approach within psychotherapy. However, the employment of narrative methods necessitates the incorporation of self-disclosure on behalf of the therapist, and this has a long and contentious history within the therapy world. In the context of my argument to bring therapist bodily phenomena into the therapy room, this is an important issue to explore.

Psychotherapeutic discourse

An examination of psychotherapeutic discourse has had a major influence on the study of narrative within the therapeutic encounter. 'Discourse' is a term that describes how certain forms of language and text come to form knowledge within particular professions. Michel Foucault has, for example, studied how medical discourse is constructed. He has critiqued how such knowledge becomes inclusive of the practitioners of its discourse – i.e. the medical profession – and exclusive of the people who are subjected to the practical, sharp end of its discourse – namely the patients (Foucault 1972, 1973). In essence he identified that professions operate a system of power-knowledge which is exercised via their particular discursive practices, the common feature being a knowledge base inclusive to its particular practitioners. This also applies to psychotherapy, which is far from immune from the problem of exercising its power and discourse on unsuspecting clients. Foucault has, therefore, informed the work of many who are looking at narrative methods of working in therapy (see Parker 1999). It would therefore seem appropriate for us to look at some of the key debates relating to psycho-therapy discourse and review some of the current thinking on this issue.

In some ways, unlike professions such as medicine or law, psychotherapy has potentially many, many discourses from which to draw. A look at the literature reveals that there has been a staggering increase in the number of specialist models of therapy on offer: 36 distinct psychotherapy models were identified in 1959, and by 1976 this number had risen to 130 (Prochaska and Norcross 1994). Spinelli

(1994) observed in the early 1990s that there were more than 460-plus diverse forms of therapy, and the number seems to be forever increasing. In itself this raises the question: why so many different forms of therapy? Perhaps this is representative of the diverse nature and complexity of clients' problems presenting for psychotherapeutic treatment. Conversely, it may represent a need for different theories of psychotherapy to maintain their market niche by strongly identifying with a particular model. This would relate to Foucault's notion of power-knowledge whereby professions begin to wield power once they have established a base of knowledge.

To put this in context it must also be realised that psychotherapy is still a relatively young profession, only really being identified as a discrete one at the turn of the twentieth century, and beginning to establish a knowledge base only during the middle of the twentieth century. This knowledge base is supported by the paraphernalia of a profession so that:

> psychotherapy and its multitude of variants (counselling, counselling psychology, clinical social work, clinical theology, self-help groups, bibliotherapy and so on) developed a solid institutional base in professional associations and universities, becoming accessible to significant numbers of people, and taken its place at the heart of modern society.
>
> (McLeod 1997: 1)

It could be then that psychotherapy as a profession has yet to mature and a consequence of this is the proliferation of many forms of therapy which are competing with each other for a particular market.

It is not within the scope of this book to cover the vast range of psychotherapeutic discourses currently used by some 460 models of psychotherapy. However, it is important to acknowledge that some social science researchers have turned their gaze towards psychotherapeutic discourse, resulting in a powerful critique. Kaye (1996: 232) points out that 'most psychotherapies do not merely centre on an *a priori* theoretical narrative, but spell out performative prescriptions: they specify rules for activities whereby change can be induced in another by the specially trained and accredited'.

This provides a rationale for the professionalisation of (and thereby training of) therapists within an accredited programme. It may also explain how some psychotherapeutic discourse becomes acceptable and hence a legitimised form of psychotherapeutic knowledge. This occurs, not by research findings, but by the promotion of ideas within the profession which, in turn, become a means for justifying the position of the profession as a respectable, legitimate form of practice. Kaye continues: 'This in turn perpetuates the concept of the therapist as having privileged knowledge, a socially sanctioned expert who can provide an authoritative true version of a problem and act according to a set of prescribed activities to correct it'. Kaye (1996: 233) sees the imposition of discourse via specialist knowledge as a powerful tool in reconstructing the client's story: 'given the privileged position of the therapist as expert, the therapeutic process proposed in this view is hegemonic and subjugating in that it must inevitably result in the slow but inevitable replacement of the client's story with the therapist's'.

Other authors have written on psychotherapy discourse. Burman (1994) provides a powerful critique of developmental theories in psychology. She observes for example that there are particular discourses for the child, with the result that the child becomes abstracted and something on which research is 'done'. By an analysis of the discourses in operation, she uncovers many gender and cultural assumptions inherent in developmental research. The relevance to this book is that many therapists say that they work with 'developmental issues'. This refers to the early life experience of their clients, and implies that physical and psychological traumas at that time of life have a bearing on the issues which the client brings to therapy.

Parker's (1998: 77) critique of psychotherapy discourse results in the suggestion of linking both social and individual distress: 'a view of relationships which understands the "personal" as "political" without reducing one to the other, and an account of discursive complexes, templates and repertoires as sites for subjectivity'. Parker (1998, 1999) and Kaye (1996) seek a similar path for therapy in calling for a discursive therapy, 'one that privileges an exploration of the discursive regimes by which people are positioned rather than being reproductive of self-interrogative practices' (Kaye 1996: 234).

A consequence of these ideas has been the introduction of narrative approaches to therapy (McLeod 1997; Riikonen and Smith 1997; Etherington 2000). McLeod (2000: 2) has identified three key aspects to this approach when describing a therapist-client encounter: first, it is the manner in which the story of the client's early life is told which is of significance. Second, the cognitive schemas or constructs through which a person makes sense of the world are expressed and structured via stories. Third using 'a radical social constructionist re-definition of therapy in terms of a process of "re-authoring", with attention to narrative and storytelling being placed at the heart of the therapeutic enterprise'.

These approaches view therapy not just as a retelling of a story between client and therapist, but also as a construction of a story between client and therapist and a re-authoring of the client's story. Therapy can be seen as an opportunity for the client to retell their story and reframe the key events of their history through a narrative constructed via a therapeutic relationship.

I have introduced these ideas to enable the reader to appreciate that there is a debate relating to psychotherapy discourse, and that one of the responses to this debate is the employment of narrative methodologies. However, these debates are not widespread within the psychotherapeutic community, and tends to be discussed by those engaged in research. The therapists who took part in the research for this book did not demonstrate an awareness of the critique of psychotherapy discourse, and this is one of the reasons why I have introduced these terms at this juncture.

Narrative in psychotherapy

The employment of narrative approaches to psychotherapy is a relatively recent development in the therapy world (McLeod 1996; Liria 2000). However, it has become an important way of studying people's lives within disciplines such as sociology and anthropology. The increasing use of the narrative approach: 'reverses a strong Platonic tradition of a certain kind of social science summed up by the statement that we think with universals and feel with particulars' (Skultans 2000: 5). Narrative approaches seem to have their origins in the 1950s and 1960s when much work was done on life histories, and as Skultans (2000: 5) observes, this work was done predominantly by women while their 'partners were engaged in the "serious work" of collecting ethnographic data'. However, there are many other influences on narrative methods and, as Speedy (2000: 362) points out, an acknowledgement must also be made of the disciplines of literary theory, cultural psychology, anthropology, philosophy and social theory, and in particular in the world of psychotherapy, the traditions of family therapy. We can see that this is a method with a multi-disciplinary background which eschews the notion of an absolute truth, and within the context of a therapeutic encounter challenges the notion of the therapist as expert. This is a position I particularly favour, as my approach to therapy is one which acknowledges the client's experience as para-mount, *not* the therapist's chosen therapeutic model.

Narrative approaches place much emphasis on the actual lived experience of the client describing their own personal story. A central tenet of this method is the 'bringing of experience to language' (Skultans 2000: 7). Within a psychotherapy setting we can view this process as the client's felt sense becoming verbalised – it is the means whereby a language is put to an experience. Gonçalves and Machado (2000: 252) suggest that 'language serves three interrelated functions: symbolizing the experience; socializing the experience; and liberating the experience'. By viewing this process as a narrative construction, the emotions that are described 'acquire their meanings by being situated within a narrative plot' (Gonçalves and Machado 2000: 252). Such an approach offers the opportunity not only to retell a story but for clients to 're-author their lives'. Narrative events can be seen to comprise of three discrete elements (McLeod and Balamoutsou 1996: 62): 'a wish or intention on the part of the protagonist, followed by a response by another person or persons, and then finally the response or reaction of self'. I would sug-gest that the response of a therapist to their client's story is an embodied one and this is where embodied phenomena which are experienced during therapy could be incorporated into the narrative approach. As McLeod and Balamoutsou go on to suggest, stories have an impact on the audience, and in the therapeutic setting the therapist is the audience. I contend that the therapist's body reacts to the stories told by their clients. It is therefore imperative to bring the therapist's body centre-stage and acknowledge the importance of bodily phenomena, as this could provide crucial information which could then be fed back into a therapeutic narrative. There is not only a client narrative but a co-constructed therapeutic narrative – between client and therapist.

We can see then that personal narratives bring the perspective of the individual experience to a given situation, and also what is given importance is that person's interpretation of their experience (Skultans 2000). This would fit well with many diverse psychotherapy models. In a therapeutic setting, narrative can be seen as 'an attempt to describe a way of working that tries not to privilege specific models, theories or taken-for-granted assumptions about human nature, and remains curious and questioning about how people construct their lives and tell their life stories' (Speedy 2000: 361). This way of viewing therapy therefore allows both client and therapist to construct a form of knowledge that has meaning for that particular therapeutic situation. It therefore becomes less reliant on therapeutic discourse and the interpretation of the therapist, and hence challenges the orthodox position of therapist as expert. In this setting the client is the expert of *their* story, the therapist is the expert of their story and both client *and* therapist construct meaning out of their perception of the therapeutic encounter. This way of viewing therapy uses the therapeutic encounter as a means for clients to re-author their stories within a therapeutic framework. As Gergen and Kaye (1992: 166) point out, 'when people seek psychotherapy they have a story to tell'. The use of narrative has arisen from a critique of scientific methods of attempting to explain the subjective phenomena that arise during therapy. A key issue here has been the growing realisation that therapeutic interpretations were 'heavily laden with the presuppositions of the therapist' (McNamee and Gergen 1992: 3). Instead of the therapist imposing a theoretical metanarrative (e.g. psychoanalytic), those employing narrative methods of therapy see the client's story as the important narrative, and the purpose of therapy to act as a vehicle for examining this narrative and evolving a co-constructed story. Thus therapists bring their own story into the therapy. This is a very different view of therapy and challenges many assumptions about the way therapy operates. It moves away from a theoretical model of practising therapy steeped in the dualism of therapist and client, which has its historical roots in the medical model of the patient and doctor dyad, and towards a more egalitarian view of therapy where the client's story is privileged above therapeutic theory. In a sense the theory arises from the client as their story is told and then alternative perspectives are allowed to be constructed during the therapeutic encounter. I agree with the position of Gergen and Kaye (1992: 174) where they see the use of a narrative approach as 'a strong commitment to viewing the therapeutic encounter as a milieu for the creative generation of meaning'.

It is my contention that as this story is co-constructed the therapist plays a crucial role, and therefore the therapist's body is also of great importance, as it is through our bodies that we perceive our world. Any co-construction of a story therefore occurs via two bodies: that of the client and that of the therapist. This book aims to explore in detail the body of the therapist, and thereby present the therapist's body story or body narrative. This concurs with the position of authors such as Speedy (2000: 365) who emphasise the importance of acknowledging the therapist's part in the therapy, whereas in the past 'therapeutic conversations were undertaken with scant acknowledgement of the therapist's part in the co-construction of such a dialogue'.

It is my contention that our bodies as therapists are a means of acknowledging our part in the therapeutic conversation and the amazing variety of responses that we experience somatically are a way of engaging in a co-constructed therapeutic dialogue. We can also see that narrative and embodiment pose a challenge to psychotherapeutic orthodoxy: '[they undermine] the unquestioned status of the therapist as scientific authority, with privileged knowledge of cause and cure' (Gergen and Kaye 1992: 174). They are heavily influenced by the philosophical movement of constructivism which emphasises how human beings create and construct meaning in their lives. A definition of constructivism is provided by Schwandt (1997: 20): 'constructivists hold that knowledge of the world is not a simple reflection of what there is, but a set of social artefacts; a reflection of what we make of what is there'. Within the world of psychotherapy, clients can be seen to be *culturally embedded*, or as McLeod (1996: 178) puts it, 'people live within cultures, and construct their identities from the symbols and meanings on offer within their culture'. The constructivist argument therefore opens up a different set of possibilities for psychotherapeutic culture. It provides an opportunity to view the therapeutic encounter as a part of cultural practice and not merely as a treatment modality exercised by a therapist on an unsuspecting client. Constructivist ideas can be seen as 'a critical challenge to the subject-object dualism on which the traditional view of the therapist-scientist is based' (McNamee and Gergen 1992: 5).

As McLeod (1996) points out, the basic principles of the narrative approach can be found in many current theories of psychotherapy, (e.g. transactional analysis uses the idea of life scripts and dramatherapy employs many varied ways of bringing stories into the therapeutic arena). The use of stories is not new but the valuing of these subjective phenomena and the reframing of this narrative approach is a novel one for psychotherapy. Within the constructivist framework Guignon (1998: 560) suggests that 'the aim of psychotherapy is to come up with a good story, where the "goodness" of the story consists of not in its being "true" but in its being compelling and useful to the person who hears it'. The aim is not therefore to seek an ultimate truth but rather to focus on the meaning that these stories have for clients. More important is that the stories constructed in a therapeutic setting allow clients access to a variety of perspectives which can help to maintain a distance between the client and an inner disturbance. Within a therapy encounter the story can be used to acknowledge this disturbance and allow time to process the impact of the story (McLeod 1996). Such stories, although they may not be verified in the scientific sense, have much value and 'can be seen as being true in the sense of capturing and remaining faithful to the integrity of the individual's life story' (Guignon 1998: 571).

If we take the view suggested by Gonçalves and Machado (2000: 249) that 'emotions are socially constructed phenomena operating via language and narrative', then it is clear that a narrative perspective on therapy requires an acknowledgement of gender and cultural practices. Also, the idea that emotions are socially constructed has a bearing on the type of feelings that will be expressed in therapy. Gonçalves and Machado (2000: 249) also suggest that 'human knowing is basically tacit, embodied and affective, an understanding of emotional processes seems to be crucial to our understanding of human change processes and psychotherapy'.

We can therefore see that the importance of addressing embodied phenomena has a central role in exploring the intersubjective nature of the therapeutic relationship, and I think there is evidence that this can be achieved via a narrative framework. Therapy itself represents a storytelling process. There is the client's story, but the therapist is also influenced by cultural stories and may find some more compelling than others. An author who acknowledges this aspect is John Gunzburg (1997) who draws heavily on the work of Martin Buber, and shows how not only is there a client story and a therapist story, but that there is a story of the therapy itself. It is in this latter aspect that I think embodied phenomena can be best employed, since the body experience of the therapist is an aspect of the shared therapeutic experience. Therapy is a conversation which reflects the stories and cultures of those involved, or as McLeod (1997: 143) suggests: 'Therapy is a form of conversation, and the therapeutic relationship can be seen as creating the equivalent of an oral microculture between therapist and client'.

Therapy must also be an embodied experience as it is via our bodies that we come to know the world and the culture which we inhabit. Also, when considering therapy as a co-constructed story it is important to realise that the story has an impact on the listener. This aspect has been noted by McLeod (1996: 182): 'Another critical feature of narrative is that it is constructed and embodies an active protagonist'. This brings the therapist's reactions into the story as an essential aspect of the narrative approach. The way that this is usually referred to is via emotional responses and by self-disclosure of personal information. (A thorough and sensitive account of this issue can be found in Etherington 2000, around the issue of sexual abuse where she works within a narrative perspective.) The other way that the therapist's reactions can become part of the therapeutic narrative is via their bodily reactions. From this point of view we can move towards viewing the therapeutic relationship as an embodied experience. The importance of bodily phenomena in this context cannot be overstated. Bodies are imbued with a myriad of cultural symbols and are therefore a rich vein for exploring embodied phenomena in a metaphorical manner. Bodies are our means of communicating, and quite simply we could not convey our personal narrative without one. The centrality of the body in this process is crucial, and makes a study of embodied phenomena an essential task when considering how personal narratives are constructed.

An important issue to remember about the narrative approach is that 'narrative can never represent the world as it is but only as it is experienced' (Skultans 2000: 11). That is, we are dealing with local knowledge that has meaning in that particular situation. This view is echoed by McLeod and Balamoutsou (1996: 74) where they suggest that 'we speak *from* the world of psychotherapy rather than *about* that world. From this perspective, an essential task for research is to capture the meaning of the experience of therapy, for both client and therapist'. It is clearly one of my aims in this book to give space to the therapist's body, which is a much neglected area of psychotherapy, while not forgetting that the client's body can also tell a story. The emphasis of my argument here is to allow the therapist's 'body narrative' some space. In order to use this information as a part of a narrative approach it is important that we now turn our attention to the issues surrounding the topic of self-disclosure.

Self-disclosure

Therapist self-disclosure is one of those contentious issues within psychotherapy that can cause concern, and yet at the same time seems such an apparently normal part of human communication. If viewed from a traditional perspective self-disclosure can be seen as making certain countertransferential phenomena explicit or relaying to the client news of a personal issue for the therapist. Undoubtedly this is a very simplified account of the wide range and variety of self-disclosure, but the attempt here is to convey a spectrum of phenomena. The debate often hinges on the perceived need of the self-disclosure – i.e. whether or not it is the need of the therapist or a valid therapeutic intervention. My aim here is to attempt to address this issue and the significance of self-disclosure within the therapeutic relationship; this is especially important in our discussion of the use of narrative methods of conducting therapy and how to incorporate the therapist's embodied phenomena into the therapeutic encounter.

Self-disclosure is a concept not exclusive to the psychotherapeutic context; it can be seen as a fundamental part of the development and maintenance of relationships (Collins and Miller 1994). There have also been links made between self-disclosure and liking – i.e. self-disclosure is seen as a medium to induce others to like the discloser (Collins and Miller 1994). There may be an implication here for therapists in that self-disclosure behaviour may be motivated by a need to be liked by their clients. However, from a humanistic perspective, self-disclosure may actually demonstrate the therapist's vulnerability with the concomitant risk of being rejected or hurt in some way, a potentially painful experience for the therapist. However, self-disclosure is generally agreed to mediate positive beliefs about the discloser (Harvey *et al.* 1990; Collins and Miller 1994). Also, 'self-disclosure has been an important feature of research and theory on attraction, friendship, intimacy, trust, social support and many other topics in social and personality psychology' (Collins and Miller 1994: 471). Clearly, self-disclosure is an important phenomenon to study when it comes to any therapy which places emphasis on the interpersonal relationship.

Self-disclosure can be associated with the concept of keeping secrets. Kelly & McKillop 1996 challenge the belief that keeping secrets is necessarily detrimental, but also suggest that there are dangers and pitfalls in revealing secrets. It would seem prudent then to explore the potential pitfalls and what sort of information is suitable for self-disclosure.

An interesting way of looking at self-disclosure is via account-making and the personal meaning that is ascribed to self-disclosure (Harvey *et al.* 1990). This ties in well with the narrative view of therapy as a means to construct meaning out of one's experience. In this way the self-disclosure can be seen as a method of informing clients about what it was like for the therapist, who may have had a similar experience. Harvey *et al.* (1990: 56) suggest that this helps to 'motivate others in similar situations and people in general to a fuller realisation of their potential to create meaning and hope and to affect others in positive ways'.

There would appear to be a link here with hope and trust, which have been identified as potential common factors in positive therapeutic outcome (Norcross and Goldfried 1992; Castonguay 1993). It may be that therapist self-disclosure demonstrates how an issue was dealt with, and this could be a valuable role modelling experience for the client. This could also be a means whereby the therapist's lived experience enters into the therapy room, and is one way that embodied phenomena may be used. An example of this could be when a therapist has a particularly strong bodily feeling in response to a client. This bodily information could be disclosed in order to build up a 'body story' within the therapy. Val Wosket (1999: 211) notes from her own practice as a counsellor that 'having a powerful emotional or physical feeling with a client is perhaps the clearest and most immediate way that we can make use of ourselves in our counselling work'. She also suggests that this can become a valuable therapeutic tool when combined with self-disclosure (1999: 53): 'I normally find it useful to disclose something from my response (not necessarily the thing itself, which may be too raw and unprocessed) to my client when this occurs'.

Hence, self-disclosure may come about in the form of storytelling, in itself a powerful medium (Gunzburg 1997; McLeod 1997). Harvey *et al.* (1990: 46) suggest that 'account-making refers to the construction of story-like understandings for events in our lives, with the resultant accounts including attribution, plots, characters, emotional expressions, and behavioural expectations and plans for the future'. So we can see that self-disclosure can be an important and integral part of the therapeutic endeavour. Both client and therapist construct meanings out of the self-disclosure and in so doing enhance the interpersonal encounter. Also, the embodied response of the therapist is a significant aspect of the intersubjective nature of this relationship. It is therefore important to consider how the therapist's embodied reactions can be disclosed during therapy. Harvey *et al.* (1990) go on to suggest that such account-making is related to meaning, hope and generativity. The message for psychotherapists may be that therapy as a social construction has the task of creating meaning out of accounts and, therefore, provides the opportunity for change via the interpersonal experience. This experience can be viewed as another construction alongside previous detrimental constructions about self and other. In this context self-disclosure can be seen as not only important but as an essential part of this process, and may indeed be a common factor necessary for a successful therapeutic outcome.

Lundeen and Schuldt (1992) noted how therapist self-disclosure led to an increase in the willingness of the client to engage in their own self-disclosure. There would seem to be a link here with a build up of trust by using self-disclosure. Indeed, Lundeen and Schuldt go on to suggest that therapist self-disclosure produces for the client a positive attitude towards the therapist. They propose that:

> it is not the therapist's self-disclosure, *per se* that causes an increase in a client's willingness to self-disclose, but that actual self-disclosure by the therapist and the subject's perception of the therapist's self-disclosure affect clients' attitudes toward the therapist and that these attitudes affect the client's willingness to disclose (1992: 11).

This would seem to add weight to the argument of therapy as a narrative construction whereby self-disclosure becomes an integral aspect of mutual creative meaning-making between therapist and client. As such the therapist may have an important contribution to make via the use of sensitive and appropriate self-disclosure, and the therapist's bodily responses are a central aspect of this mechanism.

It is clear from the literature that there are two schools of thought in the psychotherapeutic community on the whole issue of self-disclosure. On the one hand there is the psychoanalytic camp where traditionally self-disclosure was absolutely barred on the grounds that the analyst should be a blank slate or *tabula rasa* (Morrison 1997). Conversely, the humanistic camp would view self-disclosure as a necessary prerequisite to being genuine and present in the therapeutic relationship (Norcross and Goldfried 1992). The therapists who took part in the research for this book come from the humanistic school and favour the latter perspective, practising a relational contact-orientated psychotherapy. However, this is not to exclude the psychoanalytic view which has much to say on this subject. Jacobs (1995: 237) provides a good overview of the traditional psychoanalytic view where self-disclosure was 'generally regarded as a breech of proper technique and, if persistent, an indication of unanalysed character pathology'. This position is well illustrated by Freud himself, who was chronically ill for 17 years with mouth cancer and yet never wrote about the potential effects his ill health may have had on transference (Bram 1995). This is at odds with one of Freud's major insights 'that the unconscious minds of patient and analyst are in constant contact, a situation that gives rise to the continued transmission of covert messages between them' (Jacobs 1995: 238).

It could be argued that self-disclosure is one means of making the unconscious conscious, which could be seen to be a fundamental tenet of psychoanalysis. It is clearly acknowledged among contemporary psychoanalytic authors that the analyst's reactions are useful sources of information (Bram 1995). It can, therefore, also be argued that self-disclosure is a means of exploring insights about unconscious processes (Jacobs 1995). Indeed, Jacobs goes on to suggest that self-disclosure can show a different image of the therapist and that this may help to move the work of therapy on from a point of stagnation. This argument for self-disclosure would not be amiss within the humanistic therapies, and also adds to my argument for incorporating therapist bodily reactions into the therapy.

Bram (1995) makes an interesting point in relation to therapists' ill health and the growing trend to see clients as consumers. The implication here is that self-disclosure of illness, or anything likely to impact on the therapeutic relationship, is necessary in order for clients to be able to make an informed choice about whether to continue with therapy or not. Therapist self-disclosure in this context becomes a professional ethical issue and one where client duty of care is of great significance. Alongside the idea that self-disclosure may have positive effects is the idea that non-disclosure may have negative consequences for the therapeutic relationship (Bram 1995). The essence of the debate here is about withholding important information about the therapist. This ties in with the ethical debate above but may also be repeating a historical developmental pattern for the client. This could be potentially damaging, and may repeat history for those clients who have issues around not being told about important life events. Clearly this could be counter-therapeutic and as Chused (1997: 246) suggests, 'analytic anonymity is deceptive'. The issue of therapist self-disclosure and serious illness is written about with great sensitively by Amy Morrison (1997). She gives an account of her struggle to inform her clients of her terminal illness, and the considerable effort she put into making sure she was not using self-disclosure for her own needs. This is also one of the ways that therapists can raise the issue of their lived experience and thereby incorporate their bodies into the therapeutic work. Morrison (1997: 236) believes that the positive side of 'ordinary self-disclosure, is in its humanising of the relationship'. In doing so she asserts a self-psychology stance which is at odds with traditional psychoanalytic thought, but also makes the point that self-disclosure does not have to be extraordinary to be effective. Self-disclosure of an apparently minor form can show the therapist to be human and fallible – this is a long way from the therapist as *tabula rasa.* Morrison makes many good points about the ramifications of not using self-disclosure. She echoes the point about excluding clients and the potential for repeating the client's history, but also suggests that therapists may not self-disclose about serious illness on the grounds of loss of income. This again would appear to be an issue of professional care and ethics. Morrison also makes the point that self-disclosure may be a part of attunement, and as such reiterates what an important part in therapy self-disclosure may play.

In concluding this section we can see that there is considerable debate around the issue of self-disclosure. It would seem on the one hand to be potentially a major therapeutic intervention, and yet the withholding of information could also be viewed as problematic. As I come from the humanistic school I tend favour the use of self-disclosure and see how tremendous shifts within therapy can occur by its judicious use. However, the psychoanalytic tradition makes a valid point by urging caution, which must be taken into account. There is also the exciting possibility of viewing this concept within a constructivist stance and using a narrative method-ology which would seem to fit well with a mutual therapeutic endeavour and, as Morrison suggested, a 'humanising of the relationship'. I would argue that self-disclosing some of the embodied phenomena which are reported by the therapists in this study is a way of incorporating the therapist's body story into the therapeutic encounter and thereby creating a co-constructed therapeutic narrative between client and therapist. I am not suggesting that we disclose *every* aspect of our physical response but rather, as Wosket (1999: 217) suggests, that we 'embark on a gradient of responding that gradually moves up "through the gears"'.

Summary

In this chapter we have looked at some of the debates around therapeutic discourse and how a critique of this discourse has led to the narrative turn in psychotherapy. This constitutes a challenge to traditional psychotherapeutic orthodoxy by unpacking the assumption that the therapist is the expert, and moreover by putting much emphasis on the storytelling aspect of the therapeutic encounter. We then looked at the thorny issue of therapist self-disclosure and attempted to locate this within a narrative framework. This has given us a basis for incorporating embodied phenomena into the therapeutic encounter.

The next task is to examine the types of embodied phenomena which therapists describe as part and parcel of their everyday practice lives. This will be the focus of the next chapter.

Part 2

Psychotherapists' body narratives

Part 2 focuses on the accounts of therapists and their bodily experiences while working as psychotherapists. Chapter 5 describes the range and variety of physical reactions that therapists experience. In Chapters 6 and 7, I introduce the concepts of 'body as receiver' and 'embodied styles of working'. The chapters in Part 2 explore the actual experience of therapists' bodies and show how the therapist's body is used as a type of receiving device to highlight intersubjective phenomena which occur during therapy. Various strategies and metaphors of the body as a receiver are suggested by therapists which enable them to make sense of their somatic experience, and it is this that I suggest could be described as a body narrative. Chapter 7 explores some practical implications of using and working with embodied phenomena. Again we see therapists adopting a variety of strategies for managing their own bodies, and as a consequence issues of therapist health and managing a practice are discussed.

Chapter 5

Psychotherapists' physical reactions to clients

Therapists' physical reactions

At this point I wish to describe and discuss the range of phenomena that therapists reported in their bodies while engaged in the work of therapy. This will also help us to explore therapists' own accounts of how they use their bodies during the therapeutic encounter. The use of such accounts clearly demonstrates the relevance to practitioners of psychotherapist embodiment. Therefore I will be drawing upon the actual accounts of therapists as they describe various aspects of their body experience while engaging in therapy. This shows how body narratives are already present within the profession, yet also highlights the absence of these phenomena within professional training.

I wish to present the range of therapists' symptomatology in this section, as well as therapists' interpretations of these phenomena. A wide spectrum of responses is presented, from a therapist who reported feeling pregnant to several accounts of how therapists used their bodily phenomena to help them understand issues like sexual abuse. These are presented to show how embodied phenomena can be viewed within a narrative frame of reference.

I have organised the range of responses into the following headings:

- Nausea/sweaty palms
- Gut reaction
- Pregnancy feelings
- Asthma
- Musculo-skeletal pain
- Body mirroring
- Internalisation
- Body reaction linked to abused clients
- Visual disturbance
- Revulsion and closing off
- Smell
- Cold and hot

Each heading represents an example of a physical reaction which was reported by the therapists in this research. The range of therapists' symptomatology is clearly apparent. My aim in this chapter is to try to reflect the variety of phenomena experienced by therapists. In some cases the phenomenon discussed was only experienced by one therapist (e.g. pregnancy and asthma). However, because of the rich textual nature of the responses it seems appropriate at this stage to attempt to depict as much response variety as possible – hence the list of physical reactions presented above. These physical reactions arose because the therapists initially engaged in the interview process by relating how their bodies felt during therapy sessions with their clients. This chapter therefore discusses the most obvious and readily accessible means of locating the therapist's body in the therapy room. I now wish to take each heading in turn. When a quote from a therapist is used a notation will also appear (e.g. 'T1' denotes that the quote comes from Therapist 1 – for more information see Appendix).

Nausea/sweaty palms

An example of this phenomenon was provided by T1 who also works as a trainer of psychotherapists. Here she is relating an episode she experienced while engaged in a group process training session:

> I'm beginning to feel very nauseous, and in fact this did happen while I was training at the weekend . . . and I was aware I actually was feeling . . . feeling my palms were beginning to get sweaty, and I felt very nauseous . . . and it was a nausea that was increasing, and my question to myself was 'am I seeing and or hearing something that is actually a trigger to some unconscious material, or am I picking up something that this client at the moment is actually unaware of?' It's aware in their unconscious but I'm reading the triggers and allowing those triggers to actually alert me to their unconscious material . . .

This therapist's feeling of nausea was taken as a sign that something in the training group was triggering some unconscious 'material'. Here she uses information about a training group she was running. This instance relates to the group process element of that training, where trainees are encouraged to explore their relationships with each other and look at their awareness of unconscious processes. The use of the term 'material' is interesting, somehow implying that there is something tangible in the therapeutic encounter, and that this relates to the client but somehow resonates with the therapist – in this case a bodily reaction of feeling nauseous. This therapist regards the feeling of nausea as something useful, as useful 'material' in the therapeutic encounter (I discuss this notion further in Chapter 9). She goes on to say:

> I worked with it dialogically and found that . . . actually [it] was nothing to do with me but this really was their unconscious material.

The dialogical approach was used to test if the feeling of nausea was originating from the therapist or the client. This approach derives from Gestalt psychotherapy theory (Hycner and Jacobs 1995), which emphasises a way of being and the relational nature of the psychotherapeutic relationship; it is, therefore, existential in nature, and closely related to the humanistic movement. In this instance the therapist was checking out via her bodily sensations whether or not she felt nauseous because of something that might have been going on for her. She does this by asking herself questions about her bodily phenomena, so she is describing an internal dialogue which actually seems at odds with the notion of a dialogic approach (which implies a two-way dialogue between therapist and client). When it became clear to her that this sense of nausea was *not* to do with her, she was able to explain the phenomenon in the following way:

> I would . . . say that I was having a reactive countertransferential response to the client, so I am responding to the unconscious client material at that point.

And she added:

> If it had continued it may have moved into projective identification, and I may have started to act something out . . . you know . . . felt manipulated to respond in a way . . . as it happens I didn't, I was using my thinking simultaneously . . . so that means using egotism at that point . . . you know . . . speculating and spectating . . . so that would be one you know.

She is clearly drawing on notions of countertransference and projective identifica-tion to make sense of these phenomena, which are clear theoretical constructs within psychotherapy and seem helpful in the process of using this 'material'. Nor is this an isolated occurrence for this therapist; when asked whether she had experienced this before she said:

> Yes oh yes, I think it's one of the things I rely on in my practice, to listen to myself very acutely . . .

Far from being an unusual occurrence, listening to what her body is saying is an essential part of her practice, and she assumes that she is accessing the unconscious of her client.

This is echoed by other therapists with some of the other symptoms, (e.g. sweaty palms). T5 works as a dramatherapist[1] and co-facilitates anger therapy groups. At the first meeting of one of these groups she is very aware of feeling scared:

> . . . when you step into the therapy space as a therapist, I often feel kind of very scared and very nervous . . . and I think at the beginning

> of the anger therapy groups . . . there's a communal scaredness really
> . . . when I accept that the actual group are very scared [my] palms
> are very sweaty and [I'm] not feeling particularly grounded and I'm
> working very hard at feeling grounded, and at feeling calm but I know
> I'm kind of combating those, those. . . symptoms in myself.

This therapist is identifying her feelings of fear and nervousness, as manifested physically by sweaty palms, with feelings that she detects within the group, as she goes on to say:

> Yes, and [what] I'm wondering . . . is that you know when we do that
> anger therapy group when we kinda check out at the beginning, 'How
> are you feeling to be here? What's it feel like to be here?' And that
> eases when each group actually owns their own experience, and we
> do sometimes ask them 'What are you feeling in your body? How's
> your body feel to be here?' Not just kinda like, 'How are you feeling
> generally?' So, people will say you know, 'I feel a bit scared. And what
> does that feel like? Well, a bit shaky and palms feel a bit sweaty'. And
> that my symptoms will ease as that's like owned by the group.

Once there is an acknowledgement that the feelings do belong to the group, the symptoms felt by the therapist ease. One of the explanations for this is that some form of transference is in operation. As T5 explained:

> . . . as each person comes into the group I think you know, I get a
> sense of where they are and how they feel . . . and I think there's a
> kind of level of . . . transference going on in that I, you know, that as
> each person walks in . . . it's almost like you get a physical imprint of
> what they're feeling and then another one, and then another one . . .

The idea of physical imprinting is interesting. It is as if this therapist makes some kind of connection with each member of the group, similar to the idea that there is client 'material' present. Again, though this therapist is drawing on theoretical models to help explain how she ends up with sweaty palms, the construct here is of transference – something of the group fear and anxiety is transferred onto her. However, the question arises: how does this therapist know her feelings are not generated from within her own body? She is making an interpretation that her somatic experience is related to some phenomenon within the group. It is curious that these feelings are attributed to the group in this case. One answer to this apparent paradox is that therapists spend a lot of time training and exploring their feelings via personal therapy and supervision of their clinical practice. It is through this highly experiential process of learning that therapists are trained to distinguish their 'material' from the client's 'material'. In a sense therapists become highly attuned to this encounter, and their bodies are a major part of this process.

Gut reaction

There are many references to the 'gut', 'stomach', 'abdomen' and 'tummy'. These different registers may indicate in what way such phenomena are used; the term 'abdomen' would seem to be a more medicalised or professional term compared to 'tummy':

> [T14] . . . especially with clients at certain points where they are very regressed and very small and I'm being . . . sort of nurturing to them somehow, and as I start to think about this it's quite funny, I get a lot of tummy rumbling, yeah a lot of tummy noise.

This therapist made links with her own experience of being a mother and used the term 'tummy' to describe her experience in much the same way that one would talk to a child. It may be that the term used depends upon the type of therapeutic encounter – so 'tummy' is a term that could be used with clients in a regressed state, whereas in the interview set up, which is more of an adult-to-adult consultation, more professionalised words may be used.

This area of the body certainly seems to be very sensitive in the context of the therapeutic encounter, and is frequently used as an example of how the therapist's body becomes involved:

> [T13] Yeah, my gut is my most sensitive part of my body, and a number of organs I guess, but certainly I'm a gut person as opposed to a heart or a head person. I'm using that as an expression . . . I don't know if you've come across the enneagram[2]. . . it's a kind of very old Aramaic kind of personality inventory.

This implies a methodology for registering sensation which is dependent on personality type, in that once a personality is identified it may be possible to focus on an area of the body to provide useful information about the therapeutic encounter. Also of interest here is the borrowing from other cultures of a way of describing the personality with a body type – this is perhaps one way of getting around the mind-body dualism problem.

Another term that is used to describe gut phenomena is 'visceral':

> [T7] Yeah . . . it's really a kind of a felt experience of being in somebody else's world, you know sort of real empathy . . . that's kind of very . . . you know visceral level . . .

This seems to be hinting at a deeper level of connection, almost spiritual in nature, and T7 goes on to describe this visceral feeling as:

> . . . chest, abdomen and . . . the experience of being in somebody else's world or an in-between somewhere, it's like a kind of wavy

> feeling . . . and I might, oh, it's almost like we've landed on another planet or, you know this, oh what's this? . . . and that's where this kind of this sense of spell or having you know, stepped into another realm . . .

This 'sense of spell' is fascinating, almost like a hypnotic trance mediated by body presence and somehow communicated by some bodily phenomenon. The term 'visceral' seems to imply yet another interpretative register, conveying for this therapist a sense of a deeper level of contact with her client, and signals that in some way she is sharing at a deep level something of what it is like to be in the client's world. These descriptions hint at the sharing of bodily experience. Such phenomena have been observed in other cultures, for example the anthropologist Blacking has studied many differing cultural practices and has suggested that language can be very ambiguous when it comes to describing feelings; however, he goes on to suggest that there may be 'shared somatic states' (1977: 9); this is a process which does not require any spoken language. Indeed, as Blacking suggests, this may account for phenomena such as telepathy. It is these sorts of phenomena which appeared as recurring themes throughout the responses given by therapists. A 'sense of spell' is a good example of this as is the next physical reaction which I wish to describe, that of feeling pregnant in response to a client.

Pregnancy feelings

The feeling of being pregnant was described by just one therapist and is a striking example of a bodily reaction in response to a client:

> [T8] Fairly recently within the last month, one of my private clients didn't come to see me and didn't really give a good explanation, so I sent her another appointment and she did phone up and cancel saying that she felt unwell, and at the same time I was off sick with some sort of influenzy type bug, and felt very poorly. But upon actually recovering from this influenzy type bug, people would say to me, 'How do you feel, are you feeling better?' I'd say, well I am, but I feel pregnant . . .

Quite clearly this therapist is stating that she feels pregnant even though it is not possible since she has had a hysterectomy (although she does have four children, so clearly knows what it feels like to be pregnant). She went on to describe this further:

> [T8] And they sort of laugh, because you know I can't be pregnant because I've had a hysterectomy and you know . . . But, because I felt very nauseous, but it wasn't just nauseous, I actually likened it, I actually said deliberately I felt pregnant.

The type of nausea mentioned here seems to have a different quality to that discussed in the previous section. The nausea described here is being attributed to being pregnant:

> [T8] I even said that to my GP recently when I had to take my daughter in for a check-up you know, and he said I looked a bit peaky . . . anyway this client came to see me last week, and she's pregnant. And I can't not connect the two somehow, 'cos I'm very fond of this client.

This was unexpected news for the therapist as the client had not been trying for a baby but, five years previously, the client had lost a newly born child after three weeks:

> . . . but when she said it I smiled because it just automatically . . . clicked into place and I have not felt nauseous since, it's as if I can place where that was now. I mean that's . . . that was very significant because that's happened within the last two or three weeks that I found out.

When I asked T8 what meaning she attributed to this event she replied:

> Well, I . . . I don't know that I sort of have much experience with sort of extrasensory perceptions or . . . you know these sort of sympathy pains that, that a person, people sometimes talk about but that was the connection that I made, that somehow her being [her] psyche had somehow infiltrated through to mine. I was very aware of her not coming to see me and very concerned about her, but as I say I did not expect her to say she was pregnant but that was immediately the connection, I didn't just dismiss it when she was telling me, I'm talking about my experience and think ah well you know; it actually registered. . . and I told her, and she sort of smiled . . .

It is interesting to note that this information was shared with the client:

> I told her that I'd felt pregnant yeah, and I you know, I felt that she was pleased with that somehow . . .

This seems like a very dramatic bodily response, and it is interesting that the physical feelings of being pregnant disappeared so quickly. This also shows how therapist body experience can be shared and builds a body narrative into the therapeutic process:

> [T8] And it's interesting that I have not felt nauseous or pregnant since . . . yeah, since that . . . I can now place that feeling of senses,

those physical sensations with her. So I actually feel quite different in my body having spoken to her.

The disclosure of the therapist's somatic response seemed to be beneficial for the therapeutic relationship, perhaps as a way of really showing empathy for the client. The therapist alludes to sympathy pains or even extrasensory perception (ESP) to help describe this phenomenon. Clearly there is some connection with this client as the therapist talks quite openly that she is fond of the client. It is also interesting that people around her, including her GP, noticed that she looked quite 'peaky' – clearly something was happening in this therapist's body which, unusually for this research, was corroborated by outsiders confirming the therapist's physical demeanour. There was no attempt by this therapist to try and use the constructions of transference or countertransference to explain these feelings; instead use was made of folklore, ESP or sympathy pains, but not because this therapist was unfamiliar with these psychotherapeutic theories, as she used them later on in the interview. One interpretation for using ESP might be that this is a better fit than the notions of countertransference or projective identification. This might help to explain the transfer of information even though client and therapist had not met for several weeks, and it may also indicate that constructs such as countertransference and projective identification are inadequate to describe this sort of phenomenon. This points the way in the search for a fresh way of describing such processes which takes into account a vast range of bodily phenomena and intersubjective processes. It may be that the use of shared somatic states is a better way to describe such feelings. Also, it is becoming clear that the body is far from absent in the therapeutic encounter. Therapists are readily acknowledging their own bodily responses and drawing on professional discourse or, in the case of pregnancy, on folklore to describe such phenomena. It is also clear that many therapists actually share these experiences with their clients and so are already engaged in a body narrative. We can see that therapists' bodies are far from absent in the therapeutic process.

Asthma

This physical experience was mentioned by just one therapist, one of the male contributors, T6. He talked about a client who can induce his asthma. Asthma is a condition that has received some attention in the psychotherapy world over the years; in 1946 Fenichel (1990: 251) described bronchial asthma as: 'a passive-receptive longing for the mother which is expressed in pathological changes of the breathing function'. Alexander (1987: 135) suggests that asthma is related to a history of maternal rejection. George Frankl (1994: 106), a more contemporary author who adopts a psychoanalytic view on asthma, describes a patient: 'who suffered from asthma since childhood, recalled memories of panic, of fears that her mother would disappear, accompanied by breathlessness, which she recognised as "breathless apprehension" of some impending tragedy or loss'.

These authors classify the cause for asthma in their patients as a deprivation of maternal care. Furthermore, according to them, the condition is firmly placed in the body of the patient or client; the therapist's body remains absent. However, T6 quite categorically acknowledged that asthma was *his* condition not his client's:

> There's one client I get who I see and then I end up getting asthma sometimes, which is my condition, I mean she doesn't have asthma but I do and not every time I see her but just sometimes.

I am aware that my background as an osteopath is relevant here, as a funda- mental part of my osteopathic training included the study of pathology and physiology as core elements, and I am therefore very aware of the physiological effects of asthma and that its treatment can involve the use of steroids (e.g. Ventolin inhalers): 'Severe asthma can be fatal and must be treated promptly and energetically' (British National Formulary 1998: 26). Therefore, if it is possible that a client can induce an asthmatic episode, this has the potential for being detri- mental to the therapist's health. This may well link to the idea of 'contagion' (I discuss this in more depth in Chapter 7, where I look at how therapists adopt various strategies for managing their bodies). In this case the therapist noted that, through having therapy himself, his asthma has become much less of a problem. He has monitored his improvement in asthma by noting how many puffs of ventolin inhalers he needed during the day. During the course of his own personal therapy this has reduced from the maximum of eight puffs a day to periods of time of up to 20 months when he didn't need to use any inhalers at all:

> . . . it would go up and down and then gradually through therapy I stopped using my inhaler, and then for a period of 20 months I didn't use it at all, that was almost two years in the end.

He then began to notice his need for inhalers start to gradually increase, not to levels he had used prior to therapy, but nonetheless to a level that began to concern him. He took this issue to his personal therapy and began to uncover a process that was a trigger for him experiencing asthma:

> . . . what it was that triggered it was this process where someone appeared to be present when actually they're absent. So, if my therap- ist was preoccupied in some way then I was very, very sensitive to that, and I'd end up getting asthma and I'd go back next time and say, 'Hey, I got asthma after the last session'. And then she'd then check back to herself and say, 'Yeah, actually I was distracted yeah'. And so between us we began to work out exactly what it was and somehow I learnt to . . . do something other than go into shock, I think shock and asthma for me . . . shock, terror, asthma go together.

Clearly, for this therapist, his own personal therapy has been important in working out why he has asthma attacks, and he attributes his decreased dependency on steroidal treatment to working through issues of childhood in therapy. When one considers the nature of therapy training (that it is a requirement to have therapy as a part of the course), it is not surprising that issues like asthma arise. What is surprising is that therapists, by the very nature of training, have themselves been clients, yet there is very little in the literature discussing the therapist's body; it mainly focuses on the body of the client – as exemplified by the asthma literature where asthma is considered of importance *only* if it occurs in the body of the client. Yet this is a clear example of how important it is to address the therapist's body.

T6 introduced the idea of survival as a means to contextualise his asthma within the therapy setting. It was also important for him to be able to link an emotion with the distressing inability to breathe. The attribution of the emotion of shock helped considerably with his ability to make sense of his asthma:

> Well yes, it's very deeply survival. [What] I could never understand for a long time was, like, asthma is the incapacity to breathe out, and I couldn't work out which emotion that went with, and then I realised it went with shock . . . like intake of breath and hold breath that's a shock reaction, and that's right . . . that really fits for me 'cos I think I was shocked a lot in my childhood . . . I think what I did was learn to watch the other person and sense whether they're present or not . . . and by doing that somehow I could reassure myself and say what if they're not present they're appearing to be present but they're not, and then I didn't get asthma 'cos I was dealing with it out in the open with myself.

The theoretical constructs used in this case could relate to countertransference and relating this to the therapist's earlier experience. Also, this would seem to be a good example of an embodied countertransference response at a profound level of bodily experience. It almost seems like a matter of life and death, the struggle for air being that profound. McDougall suggests that asthma is related to an inability to expel breath (1989: 55), a fear of letting go.

A significant difference with this phenomenon is that the client did not have asthma, so in this instance whatever is being conveyed to the therapist is not a comparable bodily sensation or a shared somatic state in the same way that, say, feeling pregnant was for T8. The sense that T6 makes of this is that his asthma is related to his history, and that it is a history of maternal deprivation that is shared by both the client and the therapist. He goes on to provide a rationale for why this one particular client can spark off an asthma attack in his body:

> I think what is going on is she was left as a very young baby, young child she was left, and no matter how much she screamed out or

reached out the way babies do, then she wasn't responded to. She was on a kind of routine, four-hourly schedule or whatever, feeding schedule and not being responded to, and all that kind of philosophy that was around in the fifties and sixties.

He also describes how this particular client can feel despair very easily when she feels abandoned. This therapist has also seen this client in a group therapy setting as well as in individual therapy and has observed her in the group:

. . . within the group she very easily just cuts off and goes into despair, gives up reaching out, gives up trying to make an impact, so all of that is like evidence, that I think points to in childhood being left and her way of dealing with it is to feel despair . . . gradually she's learning to reach out but she feels her despair very physically . . . now that parallels my history enough so that I, I think I end up feeling asthma which is how I dealt with it as a child.

He goes on to explore this in some depth, not only relating his asthma to the conventional view of deprivation mentioned above, but also to his everyday life and how, when people he is close to appear to be distant, that too can provoke his asthma: if his partner, his therapist or this particular client seem somehow distant or removed from him then this can be a trigger for an asthma attack:

Yeah, it's like my history that is not completely resolved, not com-pletely analysed yet . . . I mean there's still elements of it that can touch me at a level where I can get asthma, and that can happen in my life outside, only with people I'm very close to . . . there's a certain kind of process that happens, usually where they're appearing to be available while they're not available. I think probably the only two people who can do that are my partner and my therapist, they're the only ones that I'm affected by it at a deep enough level to get asthma now, and it used to be I could get affected by loads of people but through therapy I hardly ever get asthma any more. The only person other than my partner and my therapist that I end up getting asthma from contact is with this one client, and I think it's 'cos her issues, experiences are so similar to mine that it triggers off some of my unresolved issues . . . and even with her now I used to get asthma and then it would last for a day and a half and now it's down to until the evening, so it's down to like 12 hours.

He introduces the notion of his history which is not 'completely resolved'. History in this context refers to his past childhood experiences, and he still has to work through such personal issues in therapy. These personal issues relate to why he still suffers from asthma. There appears to be an underlying assumption here – in order to have a 'completely resolved history' the only requirement is to have more analysis. This hints at a belief in the omnipotence of therapy. There is no suggestion that there may be an alternative view of this problem; therapy seems to be viewed as the only viable treatment option.

While this part of T6's history remains unresolved, the client may induce his asthma, so that he needs to use a steroid-based inhaler. The long-term effects of steroid use can include osteoporosis and depletion of the immune system. Clearly, these are serious side-effects and, therefore, the issue arises of potential health implications for this therapist. When I probed this with him, he did say that if his asthma became significantly worse he would stop seeing this client, so he was certainly aware that there was the potential for an assault to his system:

> Well, it's part of the job, I mean if I got chronic asthma acutely every time I saw her then I'd have to stop seeing her, 'cos that's too much of a sacrifice for me to make, but because it's maybe every six weeks, then how I deal with it is to think, OK well it's part of the job, it's some of my unresolved stuff and I'll take it to therapy and that will help me resolve it, so I actually construe it in a positive way, like it's helping me to work through it.

The notion that it is part of the job raises the question of what is reasonably acceptable as a psychotherapist. I was not aware during my training that these issues were dealt with, or even that there is an acknowledgement in the profession in general that there may be an issue on health to be discussed.

It is, of course, worth mentioning here that there would only be health implications if the assumption that therapists are responding to their clients in this way is in fact correct. The quality of this experience is subtly different from those so far discussed in that the issue of asthma is related to the correspondence between the personal history of therapist and client. This I would argue is also a way of incorporating a body narrative into the therapy. T6 has a particular way of dealing with his childhood experience and his client has another way, so perhaps some discussion of these approaches would be useful for the client, who would hear of a different way of dealing, in a physical way, with a similar experience. It is not that one way is better than another but that people can produce different body reactions to a similar experience.

Musculo-skeletal pain

Many therapists experience feeling pain or physical discomfort while working. Again, what we can observe here is that the pain is located within the body of the therapist, not that of the client, and that physical pain becomes a part of the therapy:

> [T1] I do experience things like getting pain across the back of my neck, and across my shoulders, which usually again is to do with the

client beginning to remember, or moving into something that's going to make them tense or scared. You're having to pull against scare . . . it's usually that. The other thing I do experience in working with clients is I have often had tummy pain, I've had stomach pains and that can track back to a variety of things.

This therapist views feeling pain as a trigger to some aspect of the client's experience, and as an important signal that the client is either about to say something or is struggling with difficult memories. Stomach pains are a feature of many other therapists' physical experience of working:

[T10] Yeah, yeah and I know when I have, 'cos I get, you know, incredibly bad stomach pains and I can feel, that's where I hold a lot of my pains in my stomach, in my back for me . . .

T10 was aware that this process occurred both in and out of therapy situations and she linked it to her history. Therapist history seems to be a significant aspect in the meaning-making process; therapists try to relate their physical being in the therapeutic encounter with their own history. This is understandable when we recall that a significant part of therapy training is to undergo personal therapy. This is reiterated by T11:

I made a lot of links between my personal life at that time and my illness and divorce and so on. I think that's more the link really. But I do pick up client material very quickly in my body, I mean that's the other thing, and so that being with this particular client who's very blocked in her body, it was almost like we got very confluent; in other words we were going down the same black hole . . . both of us holding stuff in our bodies.

For both of these therapists, there is a holding process going on whereby their bodies become involved in a storing of information, which they relate to something in the client, but it is felt as a physical discomfort. As T11 puts it:

Oh yes, absolutely I do feel it in my joints and my belly and you know . . . clients may make statements which they feel no feeling for but I can feel like a real pow! In my belly you know a real blow in my belly.

It is as if the client is not expressing the feeling which the therapist is feeling in their body; the therapist is therefore making a claim to feel the pain of her client. Since these phenomena are so powerful there is a tendency to assume that these feelings relate, and somehow correspond, to the client. In a sense this could be seen as a very dogmatic interpretation, since there is no corroboration of T11's assertion that the client is not feeling anything. There is, instead, an assumption that the feeling in the therapist's belly is not just related to the client, but is the client's unexpressed feeling. I think that such assumptions require challenging. It is clear that therapists do feel strong physical reactions, but I would like these to be owned within the therapy and allowed to become part of the therapeutic story.

However, if we take this interpretation at face value, this again raises the issue of acceptable risk for the therapist. Is it reasonable to expect therapists to engage in a profession where they are liable to feel physical discomfort due to the nature of the work? If this is a common occurrence in the profession it would seem wise to address this issue and to inform prospective trainees of the likely risks. These issues were certainly not addressed in my psychotherapy training. If such phenomena are indeed widespread and there is a link with health, then I would suggest it behoves the psychotherapy profession to investigate this further and, if necessary, warn trainees of the potential health dangers.

Body mirroring

'Mirroring' is a term used in psychotherapy to describe a phenomenon whereby the client wishes to mirror something from early childhood within the therapy. This term is used with reference to transference so, for example, in the object relations school of psychotherapy it could be used to describe how a client may, during the course of therapy, develop a mirroring or idealised transference onto the therapist (Cashdan 1988: 22). This is seen as representative of a perfectly normal early developmental stage of life where it was important to believe that the primary caregiver had these qualities of being a 'perfect' or 'ideal' parent. Mirroring is also used to describe how the therapist's face acts as a mirror. In this instance, Winnicott (1971) compares the mother-child relationship to the therapeutic relationship as a mirroring of the therapist's face to that of the client, the therapist occupying the mother position and the client the child. The idea that the face of the therapist is a mirror is built on by the work of Wright (1991) who, heavily influenced by Winnicott, emphasised the importance of the therapist's face in the therapeutic relationship. Perhaps this is one way in which the therapist's body is addressed in therapy; the exposed part of the therapist's body (i.e. the face) is subject to the gaze of the client. The concept of mirroring is not without its problems: Stern (1985: 144–5) suggests that, as a concept, it is used inconsistently and covers three separate processes – namely the behaviour of imitation, a form of empathy and sharing of internal states (which would seem to fit with our earlier discussion on Blacking's shared somatic states – see page 70) and, finally, a verbal mirroring or reinforcement. This concept does address the issue of the therapist's body, albeit in passing, so in the context of this book it is one worth exploring in relation to how therapists describe their somatic experiences.

The way mirroring is described by the therapists interviewed bears little relation to these psychotherapeutic constructs. Mirroring seems to be viewed as more of a systemic bodily process:

[T5] . . . the physical happening in a client, that's where it connects with me often, is either through my breathing or around my heart . . . oh yes and sometimes I can then start actually mirroring what they're doing with their hands . . . then I can say 'I just noticed this, and I'm wondering why this is happening to me and what's happening to you?'

This therapist is not only using the concept of mirroring to explain a phenomenon in the therapy where she physically gets close to her client, but is also using the metaphor of holding the client around her heart and her stomach. The mirroring here is clearly not confined to her face, but has a deep visceral element to it. Internal bodily organs are involved in this mirroring process.

T13 also describes his whole body experience when using the term mirroring – in this example he describes his response to a client who has the disease lupus:

I know I used to like resonate with the rigidity of her body experience, like I just feel my own body mirroring hers . . . yeah, a sense of my own tension, I just noticed as I sat with her . . . I would feel this sense of containment. . . so that was useful information, you know a sense of how . . . you know of how rigidly controlled she was.

This therapist is using the term mirroring to describe how his whole body became tense and rigid, just like his client's body presented to him. We can see that this appears to be the reverse of the process of mirroring which is described in the literature. In this case the therapist's body is a reflection of the client's body; this implies a two-way process. This therapist refers to 'useful information' almost as if there was something tangible in the therapeutic encounter. This evokes the notion 'unconscious material' mentioned earlier by T1.

It is also of note that neither of these therapists refer to their faces being involved in the mirroring process. 'Whole body mirroring' would seem a better way to describe it.

Internalisation

Internalisation is a term from the psychoanalytic literature, in particular the object relations school of thought. It can refer to the way in which a bad experience results in a splitting off of a part of the self; conversely it can refer to the more positive experience of incorporating an enriching experience of the world into the self (Gomez 1997: 78). Johnson (1987) describes techniques for using internalisation in therapy and views the process as a normal feature of everyday life. The therapist models a particular style of behaviour which the client then internalises for use in their own way outside the therapy room. This style of modelling is one used in the training of psychotherapists and perhaps provides a clue to the term 'training', in that training involves the internalisation of the behaviour of the trainers. This has obvious power implications, for it assumes that the trainer has the correct or appropriate behaviour in the first place.

However, the term 'internalisation' is used in a different context in the responses given. T1 uses the term in a way that suggests that internalisation is an active, conscious, body monitoring process, and that there is a choice involved:

> I may make a choice then to work more internally and work more in that person's frame of reference, so that I can get an internal sense of the change that I am seeing. But I may not do that, I may decide to have a discussion with them, it would depend on the focus and the content. I've a number of sort of treatment options, if something was happening countertransferentially I may notice phenomena in my body or in my mind or in my feelings.

T1 clearly links the ideas of countertransference to an internal sense of what she is feeling in her body. At this point she makes a clinical decision to work with this 'felt sense', which she describes as internal. This also sounds similar to the process of mirroring discussed above; in some sense T1 is taking in the client's emotions and internalising them so that she can then decide on what treatment option to take. These decisions are heavily influenced by her bodily felt sense of being at particular moments, which suggests a high level of body awareness.

T8 uses the term 'internalisation' to describe how a client has a bodily impact on her. This is the therapist who felt pregnant which we discussed earlier in the chapter and, in this case, this client is internalised around her heart. The heart, for this therapist, is of considerable importance as she has a heart condition herself.

> Well, I was going to say, well I would carry her in my heart, which is interesting . . . I internalise her. I'm aware I think about her, as part of my professional work she means something to me as a person . . . you know I could say that I love her in a way, and I feel protective and all those sort of things, so I internalise her. I take her with me if you like so that, you know I might flag her up like today, and I didn't think about her coming here but today she, immediately, she would come to mind . . . and she's not the only one obviously but some patients or clients I think you do more than others, I think it depends on the level of, of the depth that you may go into psychotherapeutically.

We can see that this is also a means of using a bodily metaphor. This suggests that this therapist 'carries' the client with her, and internalises an image of this client. Other cultures also use bodily organs as metaphors for emotional states.[3] This therapist seems to be using the heart as a metaphor to explain a phenomenon that makes sense to her within the context of the therapeutic relationship. This metaphor is used with clients with whom she has a particularly deep relationship.

This seems to link with T7 and her use of the term 'visceral' which implied a deep level of connection with her client (see p. 69).

It would seem, though, that the term 'internalisation' is used for the therapist to internalise something of the client, and that this can become a very body-orientated process.

Body reaction linked to abused clients

Another striking feature to emerge from the interviews of therapists was that body response and client 'material' are linked with certain types of client; the one most frequently mentioned was sexually abused clients:

> [T1] . . . it can track back to . . . you know, physical pain, it can track back to abuse, you know I've had very low . . . you know not genitalia pain but just above genitalia pain.

This therapist is actually using her pain as information about her client in a particularly specific manner. She describes in some detail the process whereby pain becomes a signal that the client has been abused:

> This is going back a little while now and I was working with a woman where the material that we were talking about had absolutely nothing to do with abuse at all. I seemed to remember that we were actually talking about school, early school, 5-, 6-, 7-year-old school, as she was talking what I was aware of . . . pains sort of very . . . very low down in my abdomen, and the sort of pain was moving . . . like this thinking, oh I've got wind you know, and then after a bit I thought actually I haven't, it's not me you know I don't . . . but I am feeling something.

T1 is aware of feeling something which somehow does not fit with how she is in herself, and which does not tally with the story that her client is telling her. She makes it clear that because she has undergone a lot of therapy, she can differentiate these bodily sensations:

> . . . I have got a very good body awareness, having done a lot of therapy. I am pretty quick now at tracking, and I do know my own psychological history. So I can listen and think oh that's the memory of, that's the reminder of, but on this occasion you know, I knew it wasn't mine, I also was very clear that it wasn't what I had for lunch.

She clearly disowns her bodily feeling, stating that it is not hers. An aspect of this differentiation process she called 'tracking', as though she monitors her bodily sensations in a methodical way; this body awareness is attributed to having done a lot of therapy work. There would appear to be an inconsistency here in that know-ledge about therapists' bodies is not generally taught on psychotherapy training programmes, and there is a dearth of literature on embodied phenomena in the psychotherapy world. Yet this therapist is stating that, by having been in therapy and thus become aware of her psychological history, she has access to body aware-ness knowledge. The assumption here is that the trainee undergoing personal ther-apy will acquire sufficient information on body awareness which they can then use with clients when they work as psychotherapists. Such a claim to body knowledge seems a little tenuous. First, I was not aware of body awareness being addressed in my training, and second, there was no monitoring of this type of learning in my own therapy. All that was required was that I remain in therapy for the duration of the course. These are fairly standard aspects of training to become a psycho-therapist. Yet, as we can see with this therapist, she is using her body sensations to help her navigate the therapeutic encounter and judge when or when not to employ a therapeutic intervention.

T1 continues her description:

> . . . I think with that client I actually got up and stretched saying I'm feeling uncomfortable and sat down again, and within seconds it was back so I thought this is very interesting, let's listen to this and the pain that I experienced was . . . it was a very tight very unpleasant, quite a sharp . . . as though the sort of bottom of my womb, which actually I haven't got, was really sort of you know, very tightly pulled in. That's the only way I could describe it, that's the best way.

One interpretation here is that she is describing a sophisticated method of checking whether this discomfort relates to herself. By getting up and moving around she is experimenting with her body. However, although she notices the pain in her own body she suggests this is something relating to her *client*. This was clearly an unpleasant experience for the therapist and, in order to try and make sense of it, she tried another experiment:

> Now what I noticed was within ten minutes of her going the pain had gone, and two sessions later the same experience again.

We see here that she was monitoring her body over a period of time, and was able to say clearly that this feeling did not belong to her:

> Now by that time I was much clearer, you know that this was not me this was a phenomena between us. So I worked with saying 'Look I don't understand this but what I do know is that when we talk about things that are around this age I am aware that I had an emotional experience which is that I feel scared, what I also notice is that I'm

getting this very low tummy ache . . . does this mean anything to you?' Now actually it did. It meant a great deal to her and it was the beginning of a good year's work into abuse.

When asked what meaning she attributed to this episode, T1 said:

So what I was doing I think was picking up the unconscious body memory.

At one level we can see how an exploration of the therapist's physical experience has become part of the narrative of the therapy between therapist and client. Clearly the self-disclosure of the therapist had significant meaning for the client and enabled the therapy to move in a different direction. However, there is also another important point to consider when looking at therapists' interpretations of their body experience – namely that therapists are making claims about their own bodies which relate to something in their clients' bodies. I recall during this interview how plausible this sounded, and in no way do I wish to disparage this therapist's account of her work. Rather I wish to highlight a problem which is part of psychotherapeutic culture, of which this therapist and myself are a part. This is the issue of 'the client's unconscious body memory'. On reflection, the claim to feel someone else's body memory is remarkable, especially as this memory is also unconscious. I will return to discuss this in more depth under the theme of professional discourse (see Chapter 9). I introduce this point here to highlight that, although a sophisticated body communication mechanism may well be in operation, there is also a distinct lack of awareness of the consequences of such claims by this therapist. That is, as therapists how can we know that our bodily feelings represent, or somehow correspond to, our client's unconscious body memory? I urge caution when making such interpretations, since there is a problem of implying certainty and dogma to what are essentially subjective phenomena. The physical responses of therapists are an important part of therapy, and feeding these feelings back into the therapy is one way of avoiding the trap of assuming our physical feelings have a causal connection with our client's unconscious body memory.

In fact T1 did just this and self-disclosed her physical reactions in the excerpt above where she asked her client if the tummy ache had any significance for her. This helped build up a body narrative between therapist and client. I continued in the interview with this therapist with an inquiry as to whether or not the client had a similar pain:

Oh yes I mean . . . and that to me is one of the confirming points about it, that after this . . . when she worked on the material she felt pain. If she could remember the pain she could describe it to me, she felt it, it was as though it was there and then.

The fact that the client felt pain confirmed to the therapist that her body feelings were due to the client. In addition, once the client felt the pain the therapist did not:

> Well when she did I had no pain whatsoever, and I would . . . it wasn't just that pain that I've experienced but different sorts of sensations yes, and so I would share them with her.

The sharing of bodily experience was a significant aspect of their work together. It was as if the client somehow implanted in the therapist an experience of pain, and this pain had significant meaning for the client. Once the pain was recognised as being related to the client then the therapist's pain disappeared. My contention is that such phenomena could be shared with the client in a way that allows the therapeutic endeavour to be a mutually co-constructed narrative, since the therapist's bodily experience must arise from the therapist's body, not the client's.

Other therapists mentioned how they experienced physical phenomena which they related to clients who had been sexually abused. A dramatic example is visual disturbance.

Visual disturbance

In this case T4 talks about having blurred vision in response to a particular client:

> I started to get like blurred vision, it was almost like I couldn't see her face clearly . . . and I told her this, I said: 'It's almost like you've got a scarf over your face or something and I can't see you clearly'.

It transpired that the client had been sexually abused and once this information was disclosed the therapist's vision became clearer:

> . . . and when she started to tell me, and she started to reveal to me the details of what had happened it was like gradually . . . I started to see her more clearly.

We can see that this appears to be similar to an embodied metaphor: once the client's secret is out she can be seen more clearly. This really is a striking phenomenon, and may be an indicator of a powerful form of communication that is occurring between therapist and client. The quality of this phenomenon is different to the others described so far: this one is a visual representation, almost a hallucination. Other phenomena have so far been related to physical sensations like pain or feeling pregnant. Also, we can see that this information is put back into the therapeutic arena, thus allowing the therapist's body reaction to become part of a shared therapeutic journey.

Revulsion and closing off

There are other physical expressions felt by therapists which they connect to clients who were sexually abused as children. An example of this is provided by T9 who refers to a generalised distress that she feels in her body, which she terms 'revulsion', almost as if she has closed off something of herself:

> Yes I've experienced, a kind of physical distress or discomfort, particularly the examples that I'm thinking of with clients who have been sexually abused. I haven't experienced it as located in a specific point, I've experienced it as a kind of general distress I suppose . . . it's something that feels like, I'd describe it I think as revulsion . . . to me it's a closing off and backing off, not, not from the client but . . . you know that's the bodily sensation.

A particularly moving account of this sense of revulsion is given another perspective by T10 who reported feeling repelled by her client, who had been sexually abused. This feeling was actually replicated during the interview so that the therapist began to feel repulsion as she spoke:

> . . . in me, a sensation of being physically repulsed, and she was unbounded in her body and everything about her, so she'd spill out and . . . God, I'm feeling sick as I'm saying it, 'cos I'm feeling sad I really do . . . it's somebody I've worked with and it was a very successful therapeutic relationship, but there were times when I, you know, I actually felt that she was leaking her body fluid onto me, or something like that, so I actually felt quite physically repulsed by her. . . snot . . . and you know and just her, I don't know I can't . . . whatever was on the inside was coming out, what I perceived to be coming out on the outside like her skin texture and whatever was . . . that was quite a strong physical pain, which went, eased over time, which didn't, wasn't there all the way through the therapy with her but at times . . . but I can understand that in terms of her history, I can have some explanations for that.

This is a very powerful description and at the time the therapist was visibly moved as she described what she felt. It was also clear how much she admired this client. Her feelings of revulsion are linked with a sense of being contaminated by the client's story of abuse. She introduces the idea of 'leaky boundaries' – as if something of this client's pain was leaking out and covering the therapist. T10's explanation for this feeling was:

> She'd been sexually abused as well, this particular client, and I think that somewhere the kind of . . . physical repulsion, this is my theory

> anyway, that she felt in relationship to the person that abused her. She internalised and then . . . that's what I was responding to.

The therapist's interpretation was that she was responding in a bodily way, in a similar manner to which she imagined her client responded to her abuser. This interpretation had not, however, been corroborated by the client. This type of interpretation is common in the responses given by the therapists interviewed. It hints at the idea of suggestibility, and perhaps we as therapists are particularly open to suggestion and, as a result, do not tend to challenge our own assumptions about therapy and, therefore, do not seek alternative explanations for our bodily phenomena. This is why a narrative approach could prove so helpful in allowing our assumptions to be challenged by our clients, but we can only do this if we share what we are feeling in our bodies, so that these bodily feelings can be incorporated into the therapeutic narrative. Clearly, this is not without its problems and I can readily understand why T10 would have difficulty in disclosing her feeling of repulsion to her client, but this type of response is so powerful that it seems important to incorporate it into the therapy in some way.

Smell

A similar type of response was felt by T11 where smell was considered a very powerful indicator of a sexual abuse:

> . . . clients who have been sexually abused you know, I can pick that up very quickly in my body, and very often clients will show for example, or say I can smell this person . . . and then I can begin to smell something of the smells, I don't know if it's exactly the same, so that my own olfactory system cranks up and begins to sense what is going on . . .

In this case smell seems to be used as confirmation of the client's story, a little like T1 who picked up her client's 'unconscious body memory'.

A possible explanation of these physical reactions is that these therapists are exhibiting a highly sophisticated sense of bodily awareness in response to a particular group of clients. It may be that, with a client who has been sexually abused, the therapist feels a particular attachment. Certainly when these therapists talked about these clients it was with great affection and admiration for the ways in which they had overcome such appalling trauma. Such therapeutic encounters may, therefore, predispose therapists to use their bodies in a particular way. Also, we can see that there is no consensus on how to use these powerful bodily reactions – some therapists will disclose this information to clients whereas others will not. My argument is that a narrative approach frees the therapist to challenge their own assumptions about what their bodily feelings may represent, and in many cases this information is extremely helpful to the client.

Cold and hot

An unexpected topic that was frequently discussed was that therapists felt cold and hot in response to their clients. This was mentioned in 11 of the 14 interviews. Predominantly it was cold that was talked about, and cold and fear were often linked:

> [T1] I might be experiencing myself getting colder; I might be picking up them [clients] getting shocked.

> [T3] I don't know whether it was a tinge of fear, but I felt cold.

> [T6] . . . they'll [clients] be very cold and then we'll help them work through some anger or something, or fear or other things . . .

> [T8] . . . the sense I make of it is fear.

> [T10] There's some link there for me with fear, yeah.

The surprising nature of this phenomenon is that, although mentioned by many of the therapists, there would appear to be no literature on the subject. Even those who have not experienced the phenomenon themselves have heard colleagues talking about it:

> [T13] It's not something that's happened for me, I've heard other therapists talk about that too . . .

Cold is mentioned with reference to particularly horrific stories:

> [T4] I have felt cold if a client's told me something . . . really horrific, like this client who I was telling you about with the blurred vision; it's really when I've had awful things, really, really awful things told to me.

Trauma and cold were linked by T14, where she noticed how her client would warm up:

> I suppose yes he'd been very traumatised . . . he was desensitised much of the time, and when he was desensitised he would be quite white. And when he started to feel he would warm up.

Cold and deadness were frequently linked:

> [T5] . . . what the cold chilled coldness means to me, it's like a kind of you know, the amount of deadness that was around.

[T11] The cold is usually a kind of deadness, some of my clients almost seem like dead babies. Coldness and deadness I think isn't it? That's what I associate with that.

This is a very evocative description which T11 goes on to suggest is due to survival:

. . . as though the paradox of their existence has been that in order to survive they had to be dead.

The meaning here is that by making a part of themselves dead they did not have to feel, a form of splitting of the self. T3 uses an example of a client who had a dream, and of another client who also provoked a sensation of intense cold in the therapist's body:

. . . and it was a dream that had an intense cold . . . and then in the session each of them went into an experience of the body being almost frozen . . . a weird thing because . . . I also felt cold.

He goes on to use Dante's allegory of the descent into hell to make sense of this feeling of cold; we will discuss this in more depth in Chapter 8, where I describe a process of body empathy. This feeling intense cold is an example of this phenomenon, and the use of Dante's allegory is another means of incorporating a narrative approach to therapists' bodily reactions.

T6 makes a link between cold and anger; he uses a description of somebody in a group[4] who was cold:

. . . someone a long long time ago now in a group that I was running with somebody else . . . came in and said, 'Oh my hands and feet are absolutely freezing'. And it was a you know, a kind of an autumn day it wasn't that cold, and so I said, 'Is anyone else cold?' And no, no not really particularly . . . and then during the course of the group session she got really furious about something, and then at the end I just kinda said how are your feet now, and she said, 'Oh, they're boiling'.

For T9 cold is linked to circulation, hinting at a physiological explanation for the phenomenon:

. . . feeling that the circulation's slowing down. I think the hand had got a bit cold 'cos it was draining down.

T10 also uses the image of blood and therefore circulation to make sense of her sense of coldness:

> What I imagine is that the blood drains, goes, from my hands . . .
> yeah, I've got no blood in my hands, yeah, no warmth, no life, no . . .

Heat is mentioned and can be an indicator of an emotion. In this case T10 was feeling nervous about the interview:

> . . . what I can feel often is a sort of . . . like I can feel a flush coming
> up, through my neck, you know, like a heat and . . . I know that if I
> looked in a mirror I probably would have that, I have it now actually
> . . . nervousness, I know that . . . that's the sort of feeling. It's a kind
> of skin . . . a skin feeling.

T11, on the other hand, clearly associates heat with anger:

> . . . hot I normally associate, if I feel something like surging up right
> up here, it's like a volcanic sort of . . . and I associate that with rage.

Not only is cold mentioned as a particular feature of a bodily response to client 'material', but it is attributed to other emotions. The frequency with which it was mentioned was interesting, and indicates that it may be a common occurrence. The various interpretations offered for this phenomenon tended to have an emotional component (e.g. cold and fear). The quality of this experience is different to those we have so far discussed. Here we see body temperature changes. Before, bodily changes were located in particular parts of the body (e.g. heart or gut). A change in body temperature suggests a systemic bodily involvement: the whole body is involved in feeling cold, not just an extremity or an organ; therefore, the body becomes involved in a different sense – it is more of a whole body experience, and the experience itself, whether cold or hot, is a universal feeling. We have all felt hot and cold, whereas we may not experience our bodies as having an 'emotional heart'. In order for a whole body response to occur, some hormonal systemic release must also occur. This is, of course, speculative and this is not the place to launch into detailed physiological argument. However, if there is a different mechanism in operation here, it may suggest a different level of communication is at work in the therapeutic encounter.

Summary

In this chapter we have looked at the physical reactions therapists experience in the course of their therapeutic work. Although not addressed in the training of therapists, except in passing during individual therapy or supervision, these therapists have exhibited no problem with accessing bodily phenomena from their therapeutic practice. The notion of 'client material' is brought into focus as a means of explaining why therapists feel these phenomena, yet it is clear that the therapists are feeling such phenomena in their *own* bodies, and then attributing these feelings to the client.

In order to explain these phenomena, much use has been made of psychoanalytic discourse (e.g. transference, countertransference, etc.). This is intriguing, as most of the therapists interviewed describe themselves as humanistic practitioners, and psychoanalytic discourse would seem at odds with the humanistic movement. Psychoanalysis is perceived by this movement as objectifying people – for example, the use of the term 'patient' in psychoanalysis as opposed to 'client'. This calls into question how psychotherapeutic discourse is employed. The use of psychoanalytic discourse to make sense of their somatic reactions results in the therapists locating their own somatic phenomena into the body of the client. This has echoes of the medical model in the way that the medical encounter of the doctor-patient relationship tends to objectify the patient. This is the very aspect of psychoanalytic theory that the humanistic movement decries.

The types of interpretation offered to explain somatic experience understandably tend to rely on the primary model of therapy in which the therapist was trained. In itself this is not at all surprising, and clearly models of therapy are used to help the therapist navigate the complex and difficult task of engaging in psychotherapy. What is surprising is the tendency towards certainty with which many of the interpretations are offered. An example would be the implied belief by T6 that unresolved history can be resolved by further analysis. There is no suggestion that any alternative to this position is possible. His cure for asthma is simply to seek more therapy. It is almost as though, having trained and then practised as a therapist, then every aspect of life is viewed through a psychotherapeutic lens.

It is, of course, an assumption made by these therapists that the symptoms described in their bodies can be attributed to their clients. One alternative interpretation could be that therapists are highly suggestible people. If this is so, perhaps therapists are simply reacting to their clients' demeanour or behaviour, and to the intersubjective nature of therapy (which we will look at in more detail in the next chapter). As for suggestibility, it has been noted that this appears to change with age, being particularly strong in children and young adults (Sarafino 1994: 159). Because the training of therapists encourages an exploration of psychological history and often provokes a regression to earlier childhood experiences, it may be that a concomitant of training is the acquisition or heightening of suggestibility. This, on the one hand, could increase the therapists' natural tendency to empathise with their clients, but on the other may leave them without the tools to challenge the assumptions upon which they base their interpretations of their somatic sensations. In other words, this could be described as a lack of critical reflection on the interpretations that are made by therapists, in this case in relation to the types of physical phenomena they experience during the therapeutic encounter.

The lack of critical reflexivity demonstrated by these individual therapists is probably symptomatic of the profession as a whole. I am suggesting that, within the psychotherapy culture, there is a collective unwillingness to challenge the basis for psychotherapeutic interpretations and seek alternative explanations for embodied phenomena. It is understandable, then, that the therapists in this study reflect on their experiences through the rather narrow lens offered by psychotherapy discourse. However, what we can also see is that therapists do sometimes disclose their physical reactions to their clients. I believe this is a crucial element to using embodied phenomena within a therapeutic relationship as it opens up the possibility of using the therapist's body narrative as a tool, by creating a co-constructed client-therapist narrative. This must be done with sensitivity and great care, but the ability for the client to challenge or be able to discuss the therapist's embodied reaction at least prevents the therapist from assuming that their feelings are the result of their client's 'unconscious body memory'.

I advocate the narrative approach as a means of making the therapeutic endeavour more egalitarian and freer from traditional therapeutic discourse which has a tendency to locate therapist bodily reactions into the body of the client. Rather than see the embodied phenomena described in this book subsumed into another subsection of transference, I would like to see us, as therapists, own our bodily reactions within the narrative framework, and see them as contributing to the local knowledge that is created between client and therapist.

Chapter 6

Body as receiver

In this chapter we see how therapists talk about the variety of experiences that they feel are communicated to them through their bodies during the therapeutic encounter. The types of phenomena described include how therapists have observed their own bodies changing. This has occurred during their own therapy (some therapists reported feeling freer in their bodies and that some long-term symptoms had disappeared – e.g. eczema). Another example is how therapists describe changes in their body temperature, often becoming colder, while working with clients. These reactions appear to be completely involuntary. In some way the therapist's body becomes attuned to the client and 'picks up' client information. It may well be that these sorts of phenomena are ubiquitous and that, due to their training and perhaps their personal history, therapists are more readily able to sense this type of information, hence using their bodies in a more sensitised manner. The ability to use their bodies as receivers is mentioned by many of the therapists in this study. This suggests that the body as a receiver could be developed into a more widespread technique.

I have organised this chapter into six sections:

- Body as receiver
- Bodily communication
- Therapist history
- Somatisation
- Here and now experience
- Clients' bodies

Each section looks at a particular aspect of how the therapist's body becomes a receiver for information from the client.

Body as receiver

A common strand throughout this chapter is that of 'body as receiver'. This relates to the way that the therapist's body acts as a receiver for information. Communication is therefore clearly involved and takes many forms. The way that therapists refer to their history implies that historical events have a bearing on how they use their bodies in therapy. Sometimes bodily phenomena are of an intense, immediate quality which brings their body into the here and now. The body of the client is brought into the therapy by assumptions and observations that the therapist may make. However, this is predominantly achieved via assumptions the therapist makes about their *own* body i.e. somatic phenomena in the therapist's body are attributed to something occurring in the client's body.

This theme has a passive quality: there is less choice involved. Therapists' bodies receive information whether they like it or not. This is summed up by T9:

> To me this is kind of, it's going on all the time and it's kind of background.

The idea that the therapist's body is some sort of receiving device crops up in several guises, examples including 'body as radar' and 'body as barometer'. Two of the therapists use 'body as radar' as a metaphor to describe how they pick up information in a bodily form:

> [T1] For me it's like using the body as radar. . . those sort of dishes that collect satellite messages and funnel them down, well I see the body in that way . . . that it can actually take experience and then it will funnel, it will track . . . and with good observation and good questioning you can actually follow it through to see what it's about . . . past or present.

This therapist is also claiming that there is a temporal aspect to the information that she receives, i.e. bodily information received from the client can relate to past or present experience. T2 also uses a radar metaphor, and links her ability to react quickly in situations to her past experience of living in a foreign country. She sees her body in the following way:

> So your ears and your eyes are like Jodrell Bank; you're scanning everything . . .

This theme of constant surveillance and of perpetually being vigilant is expressed by T7:

> . . . like a pair of eyes, you know my body was like a pair of eyes if you like . . .

The body appears to be seen as a receiver of information from the client:

> [T6] I mean a lot of the work, working in a Gestalt way, then the first point of awareness is around body sensations, so I think it's very, very important to have as clear a sense as possible about bodily

> information. Sensations which then, we can learn to then make sense of and get awareness and then choose a course of action . . . but it very much starts at the point of the body.

The body for this therapist is almost a gateway, a point of entry in starting the therapeutic process. He states more explicitly later in the interview when talking about his body and the client's body, that his body is:

> . . . a source of information.

This seems to link into the idea of information as 'material' for the therapeutic encounter, and is therefore perceived as extremely helpful by the therapists.

Other metaphors for this process are used – for example, the idea that the body is some sort of barometer:

> [T5] I was holding it in my stomach and it was a lot of kind of tension and, and holding around my stomach and around my heart, like a barometer . . . it is an emotional sense because with that my whole kind of head went kind of fuzzy, and pins and needly . . . and 'cos I can connect to it now, and then kind of the barometer which I used, I use my barometer a lot . . .

T5 sees her body barometer as an indicator of what may be happening for the client at a particular time in therapy. This is similar to the radar metaphors which are used to help track the therapeutic process in the here and now, and therefore help the therapist to decide on clinical interventions. The body as barometer is also mentioned by T10:

> I often use my body process as a barometer, as to what's going on . . . well I think I'm, this is to do with my history, but I think I'm very alert to . . . people's feelings in the room, I think I sort of pick them up, on a kind of physiological level . . . yeah, I don't mean in any psychic sense, I mean if someone's scared or angry, I often feel that first in my body.

This therapist also links her ability to do this with her history. It is as if there may be a predisposition to acquiring this ability and, once learned, it becomes a useful tool in the therapeutic repertoire. Many of the descriptions used seem to draw on the Cartesian 'body as machine' metaphor where the body is perceived as either a radar or barometer, acting to pick up information. Since the Cartesian view of the body is endemic within western culture it is not at all surprising that therapists draw upon the body as machine metaphor.

Bodily communication

The manner in which therapists talk about their bodies is as if they can pick up 'client material'. There are some interesting ways of describing this process. One therapist suggested she was able to utilise this ability as a form of 'body memory bank'. The body is seen as picking up on this 'material', or has symptoms passed on to it. The notion of body as memory bank is mentioned by T2 when discussing how she comes to a diagnosis about a client; her initial feelings about the client are stored in her body memory bank to be used at a later stage to either confirm or disprove a diagnostic hunch:

> . . . I've directed it towards my body for my body to hold it for me, so I'm using my body as a kind of memory bank in that sense rather than having it as a thought . . . my body stores it for me and it . . . the function of it is the tightness in the chest, keeps me focused, keeps me in touch with something . . .

This therapist is using her body as a means to confirm diagnoses about clients. Her bodily experience is important to recall in order to be fair to a client, and it becomes a useful adjunct in her therapeutic repertoire. In this instance the body is used as a store for information which can be drawn upon at a later date.

Other ways that therapists use their bodies in this context are by being aware of bodily tension. So we see that T12 associates bodily tension with something emanating from the client:

> Yes, I suppose it brings up memories of tensions, having tension in my body in different places . . . yes, I can often feel tension in my body that I presume comes from tension in the client, it may also be proactive but it may possibly be reactive, that I'm reacting in a bodily sense to my client.

The use of the words 'proactive', meaning relating to herself, and 'reactive', relating to the client, provide another level of interpretation and allow for the bodily sensation to be attributed to the therapist as well as the client.

It would seem clear, though, that for this group of therapists bodily reactions in response to clients are not unusual and, in the case of T2, a commonplace occurrence in order to help her make a diagnostic decision.

Another aspect of bodily communication that is often referred to is pre-verbal communication. Often therapists would find it difficult to explain, possibly because they were trying to find words to describe a phenomenon which is essentially non-verbal. In general, the term was used to describe times when the therapist considered the client had regressed to an earlier developmental stage in life – i.e. before words:

> [T4] . . . they might be saying you know, I've got this really intense feeling. I believe that the feelings that are pre-verbal are very intense

feelings, because you know the child hasn't had an opportunity if you like to rationalise them or use thought processes to do something different with them so they're experienced as extremely intense emotions, or very intense affect. And so when I, when I see that or when I think my client's experiencing that, then I suppose I judge it to be pre-verbal.

However, descriptions of clients who evoked this phenomenon were frequently the most touching for the therapist and had a profound effect on them. Therapeutic constructs that were frequently used were linked to countertransference. Perhaps in the light of our earlier discussion in Chapter 4 on intersubjectivity and empathy we can view these phenomena in a different way. Such powerful somatic responses are perhaps better described as examples of particular and local inter-actions between therapist and client, and I would suggest are powerful and highly meaningful ways to develop a bespoke narrative. A narrative which has meaning within the confines of that particular therapy, and thereby is a form of local know-ledge between client and therapist.

Therapist history

A central aspect of how the therapist brings their body into the therapeutic encounter is via reference to their own experience of being a client. There seem to be two distinct aspects to this theme: one is the awareness that, through therapy, they have noticed changes in their own body (I have described this as 'therapist body change') and another is an exploration of their life via therapy which has helped them make sense of bodily sensations felt in the therapeutic encounter. The latter phenomenon I have described as 'therapeutic exploration of history'. In each case an exploration of bodily phenomena in their own bodies has helped to inform therapists' practice of psychotherapy.

Therapist body change

Some therapists noted how their own bodies had eased by engaging in their own personal therapy. Terms such as 'I feel freer in my body' and 'my asthma has decreased' (as discussed in Chapter 5) were attributed to their own therapy work. It is perhaps not so strange that these phenomena have been described, because a major part of training in psychotherapy involves the necessity of ongoing personal therapy while in training. What is strange is that such training does not explicitly deal with the 'body', and I would suggest that this is a major oversight when considering the variety of physical responses that therapists experience in their everyday work.

In some cases there have been some major changes in therapists' bodies which are attributed to working through issues in their own personal therapy. A good example of this is T4:

> Since I've been in therapy . . . in individual therapy in the last five years, although I've noticed changes in my emotional self the biggest changes that I've noticed have been in my body, because whereas before I started therapy I had lot of backache, I had a lot of tension in my shoulders, in my neck, I used to have a lot of headaches and a lot of migraines, that I now don't, I just don't have them.

This is quite a dramatic change from feeling physical pain both in the form of backache and migraines, to a state of not having these bodily discomforts any more. These changes are attributed to personal therapy work, and a link is made between working on emotional discomfort and a concomitant decrease in somatic symptoms. This therapist provides a clear rationale that helps her explain how these symptoms have decreased. In order to do so she draws upon her own therapeutic model of Gestalt. There was a particular aspect of the therapy work which was significant for her in decreasing her bodily symptoms:

> . . . and my nails, it's to do with my fingernails because prior to that and all my life as far as I can remember my fingernails have broken off, and been very weak . . . and since I did my cat-work I have not experienced my nails breaking off.

She introduces the term 'cat-work' to describe a process of working on the fragility of her nails:

> My cat-work was being a cat and you know feeling my cat-likeness . . . I really got into it. The other thing is that about, I'd say maybe about mid-nineteen eighties sort of time, which is about sort of 13 years ago, I started to develop eczema. I didn't know it was eczema at the time but I started to develop red blotches on my cheeks, which bothered me quite a lot, and eh . . . to the point where I had to have medication and have hydrocortisone cream, which I was not happy about but as it was itching so much and in fact the whole of my skin was very itchy . . . I had a kind of idealisation transference with my father, I had a very wonderful relationship with my father, and he died when I was 21, so I never kind of saw my father as anything other than wonderful and . . . I was aware I'd done a lot of anger work on my mother, but I had not addressed my anger to do with my father.

In order to understand the 'cat-work' she draws on the psychotherapeutic notions of transference, and some unresolved anger towards her father. She goes on to describe how she does 'anger work' on this issue by using a cushion in place of her father. These types of experimental techniques are a normal feature of Gestalt psychotherapy trainings:

> . . . 'cos I wanted to keep him preserved, this image. But yeah, I knew

> I needed to do that and so when I did eventually get around to doing the anger work on my father, and put a cushion aside for him, the part that I wanted to look after and this part that I wanted to be angry with, and this happened like almost . . . overnight really, that when I'd done this anger work on my father these patches started to disappear.

The eczema disappeared overnight: a dramatic resolution of a long-term symptom which had required a steroid-based cream to manage the condition:

> I mean they can still come up red from time to time, but I've never got itchy with it and nor do I have to put the cream on, and that's like about three years ago now probably. So that's a really important event in my life.

Clearly this was an important and significant event for her. When I asked what meaning she put to it her reply was:

> Well it's like this itchiness . . . I've also had itchy skin and was constantly scratching . . . this involved scratching with my fingernails and . . . the sense I make of it is that, you know it's like . . . retroflection you know 'who do I want to scratch?' you know, when I'm scratching myself . . . and when I'm itching 'who do I want to scratch?' . . . and the sense that I make of it is that it was my father that I wanted to scratch and that you know, irritation which was anger and it was like I couldn't allow myself to have the full-blown anger but I could scratch . . . scratch . . . and it was quite, quite dramatic, whereas other things that happened to me like tension in my shoulders and . . . has gradually gone, but all that was quite dramatic.

The process by which T4 reached this understanding was heavily influenced by her psychotherapeutic training. She was trained in Gestalt psychotherapy which emphasises a creative and experimental way to conduct therapy, thus the use of her 'cat-work' and the use of cushions. In addition, her personal therapy was with a Gestalt psychotherapist. Also, she reflected on the way her bodily symptoms have decreased, and drew some powerful metaphors for why she no longer experienced some of her somatic complaints. For example, her scratching is interpreted as her really wanting to scratch her father but, by a process of retroflection she ends up scratching herself. Retroflection derives from Gestalt psychotherapy discourse (see e.g. Kepner 1993). The dramatic resolution of symptoms is put down to a resolution of emotional conflict and has obviously left a considerable impression on this therapist. It would therefore be understandable for therapists such as T4 to try to incorporate some elements of their personal work into their practice.

Clearly, such dramatic events suggest causal links so, in this case, the therapist is convinced that her 'cat-work' has resulted in a decrease in her eczema. However, there are alternative interpretations: dramatic 'miracle'-type cures of this kind are, of course, not uncommon in any therapeutic situation. I have described this elsewhere in connection with both osteopathic and psychotherapy practice, where I look at how psychoanalytic discourse provides a very useful term to describe such miracle phenomena – 'transference cure' (Shaw 1996a). This is akin to the idea of a placebo effect where physical symptoms apparently vanish for no medically explicable reason. Another perspective on this is provided by Patrick Casement (1985: 174) where he introduces the idea of 'countertransference cure'. He suggests that clients may feel temporarily better as a result of the charismatic influence of their therapist. A therapist, in this instance, may make the client feel worthwhile via a warm, empathic and encouraging demeanour. This may provoke dramatic changes as the client 'gets better' to please the therapist. I introduce these ideas at this point to suggest that there are alternative ways of looking at these phenomena. That the therapist in this case did not seek an alternative interpretation is not surprising, as her explanation is plausible within her own therapeutic frame of reference and therefore she had no need to seek a different explanation. However, the use of psychoanalytic terms like 'transference' is interesting as, although these are used, there is no hint of an acknowledgement of transference or countertransference cure, which also emanate from psychoanalytic discourse. The point here is that, by engaging in one model of therapy, an explanation is sought from that viewpoint *only*. However, other interpretations are possible and this hints at a lack of critical reflexivity when applying interpretations to psychotherapeutic phenomena. This is demonstrated here by the interpretation within the narrow confines of Gestalt psychotherapy discourse.

Another example, albeit not as dramatic, is provided by T14:

> . . . there's been a lot of release of physical tension through some of the work I did . . . so, certainly I've felt my body movement has been much freer, it has become much freer . . . and a lot of that's very directly attributed to certain pieces of work I did where the effect was very obvious, and very immediate but over time as well there's a sort of cumulative effect . . . very freeing.

The quality of what is described here is of interest; T14 describes a sense of being freer in her body as though she has shed a load and can move with more freedom. It is clear again that this bodily sense is directly attributed to her work in therapy.

These are good examples of how therapists come to understand their bodies in the therapeutic encounter. I would suggest that this needs to be acknowledged as a significant aspect of training, and that as therapists we become more body aware.

Therapeutic exploration of history

As well as a decrease in bodily symptoms, therapists' histories help them to make sense of why they became therapists. In this context therapists are referring to history as their biographical history. This has much significance in the arguments I am putting forward about the lived-body, since it is our experience of our lives that gives us our sense of our lived-body, and it is this that we bring to the therapeutic encounter:

> [T12] . . . because my history was to attune to my father, that I very much took that role in my relationship with him, and I would pick up his feelings as a small child, probably as a small child, I would always be aware of his discomfort . . . whatever that was and I think I was, I became very sensitive to that, so I just repeat that with other people and with clients you know . . . it's very easy for me to do that, and it's also very . . . you know something that I'm sort of condemned to do in a way.

The notion of being condemned to be a therapist is an intriguing one, almost as though there is no choice involved, that in some way our experiences in childhood almost condition us to become therapists.

T10 relates her history to an acute sense of being able to pick up people's feelings:

> . . . well I think I'm, this is to do with my history, but I think I'm very alert to . . . people's feelings in the room, I think I sort of pick them up, on a kind of physiological level . . . yeah, I don't mean in any psychic sense, I mean if someone's scared or angry, I often feel that first in my body, that I know.

Both of these therapists suggest that their history somehow predisposes them to working with feelings and, therefore, psychotherapy would seem to suit them well.

T13 relates how his history makes him want to lose his 'boundary' in an effort to get closer to his clients. As a Gestaltist he uses this term to mean his 'contact boundary' which is described by Parlett and Page (1990: 180) as the point where a person engages with his or her environment at a psychological level. If this is disturbed in some way then an interruption to contact occurs, and this is noted by the therapist as not being 'in touch' with the client, or, as T13 describes:

> . . . there's a way in which I'm starting to lose my boundary, I'm starting to think, I've kind of gotta get over there and like work harder, I'm starting to do more than my 50 per cent of the work . . . and my work as a Gestaltist anyway is to come to my, the contact boundary, my contact boundary that's as far as I can go . . . but some-

times I can still find myself, you know kind of willing to go . . . getting
into your world you know, so that's losing my boundary.

He relates doing more than 50 per cent of the therapeutic work to his own past history, which involved a lot of caregiving as a child. Past patterns of behaviour are
played out in the therapy room, not just by the client but by the therapist. This is of
course not unusual and having regular supervision is a means of ensuring that
therapists do not end up repeating patterns which may be detrimental to the client.
However, the use of bodily sensations to monitor this process would seem a useful
way to assess repetitive patterns.

Another method is to have regular therapy. As I have already discussed, it is a
requirement for trainee therapists to undergo their own personal therapy. Many
therapists continue to have therapy after they have trained; indeed, I myself
continued to have therapy for about two years following the end of my training.
Some therapists view having ongoing therapy as an essential adjunct to continuing
to practise as a therapist. An example of this was T6 who asserted this position in
regard to his asthma, and the need to be in therapy to deal with this issue.

An understanding of their own unconscious processes via personal therapy is,
therefore, a concomitant of this element of training. The therapists in this study
draw heavily on their own personal histories, as explored in their own therapy, to
make sense of the therapeutic 'material' presented by clients. They are also
demonstrating links with their history and their bodily reactions. Accordingly, the
body becomes inextricably linked to their history and the client's history as
presented in the therapy room. What appears quite noticeable is how this information is considered part of the therapy process – i.e. the centrality of their bodily
sensations is used to make sense of the therapeutic encounter. The body appears to
be highly significant in constructing meaning out of this encounter, and these
therapists consider this process a normal part of therapy. It is all the more surprising, then, that so little is written on the subject of the therapist's body.

In exploring this theme the therapist's body becomes enmeshed with their own
experience or history, and with that of the client. Here we see that the therapist-
client encounter is embodied by its very nature. The encounter echoes past events
for both therapist and client and becomes a means to explore the lived-experience
of recalled past events. The ability to recall past experience which is related to
the body suggests that this type of information would be useful to explore in
psychotherapy training.

Somatisation

Therapists use the concept of somatisation to describe a bodily phenomenon which
is located in the therapist's body; there are various descriptions of this. T10 links
her somatisation process to her history and makes sense of the phenomenon by
suggesting that she somehow converted what she was feeling on the inside to a
physical complaint:

> . . . That I know, that historically I've had to . . . not show what I was feeling on the outside, and I . . . was often feeling a lot on the inside, so in order to not have that show, I would have to somatise those in some way.

She describes this further by providing an example of the type of pain she would get:

> I get, you know incredibly bad stomach pains and, you know I can feel, that's where I hold a lot of my pains in my stomach, and in my back. I've been aware you know, I'm often aware sometimes when I've been sitting with somebody and you know that will be an indication I've been holding on to stuff, holding back from saying what I might want to say, and sometimes for good reason, but often I can feel . . . 'cos one of the things I do with my own body process is I desensitise around hunger. So I know I can often be hungry and you know, and go into a session and if I somatise, if I'm somatising then I'll lose contact with my hunger.

For this therapist we see that not only does she get physical pain in her stomach, but she has made a further connection to desensitising around hunger. All of this bodily sensation is brought into the therapy room by the process of attributing these sensations to an aspect of the client. When asked if she could provide an example from her caseload, T10 recalled one client in particular:

> Yes I do have a particular client who's extremely wary, and quite paranoid and has been very, very badly abused and actually physically and sexually abused, and being in the room with her is very tense, because she projects a lot onto me and she can become very . . . I mean just a word that I might say or a way of saying something, can evoke in her a sort of scare and wariness, and anger, rage you know, that she holds onto, and sometimes I mirror that in myself you know . . . I'm holding the tension of being there in the room with all her tension, in my stomach . . . it's that, gripping yeah . . . not letting . . . I mean, you know I think it's about not letting anything in, 'cos whatever is going to come in will be toxic . . . that's my body process . . . it's very uncomfortable.

She obviously draws on theoretical constructs like 'projection' and 'mirroring', and it is interesting to note the term 'mirroring' (as mentioned in Chapter 5) again refers to a therapist process, to explain how she feels. The feeling is uncomfortable, and the use of the word 'toxic' suggests dangerous 'material'. (This idea will be developed later in regard to therapist's health.) T10 continues her very full description of her experience by describing what it feels like in her body when the client leaves the session:

> Yeah . . . and sometimes I lay out after she's gone, I mean I'll just go [deep sigh, and expulsion of breath], sort of and . . . and think, 'Cor, bloody hell thank God!' Not that she's . . . I actually enjoy working with her as well . . . but thank God she's gone!!

T10 expresses considerable relief and this gives a flavour of the uncomfortable feeling this therapist experiences with this client. When asked what meaning she made of these phenomena she suggested:

> Well I think it's probably this thing again, I was saying, picking up on somebody else's unexpressed feeling ultimately . . . I mean it's just speculation really, it could be . . . something's happening anyway . . . as soon as she walks in . . . that's quite big.

Again we see that the notion of picking up somebody else's feeling is introduced as a means of interpreting unexpressed feeling on behalf of the client, although in this instance this therapist is clear that this is speculation and, therefore, does not perceive her explanation as immutable, and is open to other interpretations. However, it would seem that she *is* linking her bodily pain to her client.

Similarly, T11 uses the word 'somatise' about her own body and simultaneously makes a connection to her own history:

> Well, I guess it is yeah, somatising the client's material. But then at least I consciously know that, I suppose there's a boundary as well because I also can somatise. I mean my own childhood is where I think in the family dynamics I held so much in my body. My own birth experience was quite dramatic, and therefore, from that I worked a lot on it in therapy. But I think also it enables me to then work at this level, because I know the process . . . I suppose there is like the boundary, whose material is this? And then at that moment it is a shared experience, a profoundly shared experience and . . . in different bodies.

T11 also makes a link with shared experience – i.e. a bodily experience that both therapist and client share. It is as if her experience of somatising, and the therapy work she has done herself, enable her to work with clients who may be presenting with a similar process. This suggests a form of bodily communication. She goes on to provide an explanation for this process, putting it firmly in the body of the client:

> . . . I suppose my main understanding of the need to somatise in clients is because there's nowhere else for the feeling to go, or the feelings are so overwhelming inside them, or the experience is so overwhelming that the only place for what is happening is to go into our bodies . . . and therefore . . . the unresolved material is held somatically.

These are points where I think therapeutic discourse becomes problematic. I can understand the essence of what this therapist is saying, that she experiences strong bodily feelings and this has something to do with unresolved issues relating to her client. But it does sound as though the therapist is directly feeling the client's un-expressed emotion. It is this issue which needs untangling. Bearing in mind my earlier discussion on empathy and intersubjectivity I think we need to be clear that, as therapists, what we feel in our bodies must be our affect not our client's experi-ence of that emotion. This is not to say that our feelings are not of importance at this juncture – far from it. I would argue that they are highly important. What I wish to emphasise is that these feelings relate to the intersubjective nature of the thera-peutic relationship and therefore need to be incorporated into the therapeutic narrative.

Another example of how therapists draw upon their history is provided by T8, who also makes the link between her past and how she somatises now:

> On somatisation. Well I have actually quite strong views on that. I have a heart problem, and I am quite convinced in my mind that if I can get my emotional heart, you know resolved . . . because I have had a lot of emotional trauma as a child . . . I'm quite sure that I would go as far as to say 70 per cent of my physical condition would be improved.

Not only is this therapist using the term 'somatisation' to express some of her own somatic discomfort but she is incorporating the term 'emotional heart' to convey further a sense of her emotional history to explain why she currently has a heart condition. This puts her in the unusual position of claiming the word 'somatisa-tion' in a non-pejorative manner to help her make sense of her particular condition. The construction of her 'emotional heart' helps her in an understanding of her own emotional life. The use of the term 'emotional heart' is reminiscent of the use of 'squeezing of the heart' (Craig and Boardman 1990), the 'angry liver' and the 'melancholy spleen' (Ots 1990), as discussed in Chapter 1. I would suggest that it is terms like 'emotional heart' that would be helpful when constructing a thera-peutic narrative, rather than attempting to describe these phenomena in terms of countertransference and projective identification. Such terms lack the meaning of a co-constructed therapeutic narrative, whereas 'emotional heart' conveys a mean-ing that is inclusive of this therapist's emotional life. T8 goes on to describe the importance of this term for her, clearly differentiating between emotional and physical pain:

> I really made that connection and if . . . emotionally I'm in a great deal of pain, I always somatise it around my heart, I may not recognise it immediately . . . but I will feel ill, physically ill . . . and somatise around my heart condition. It's not the same as if I walked up a steep hill and got pain, that's a direct physical cause and effect condition, but if I

don't walk up a steep hill but emotionally walk up a steep hill, I'd still get the same sort of pain. That's my personal experience.

T8 makes no claim to feel her 'emotional heart' during therapy sessions, but the use of the term 'somatise' in conjunction with psychotherapeutic discourse is helpful for this therapist in understanding her heart condition.

Other ways of incorporating somatisation are by using clients' accounts of physical discomfort. T9 provides a methodology whereby she observes or uses physical symptoms in her clients and checks out what her own body is telling her:

> That's how I always or very often work, with the physical symptoms that clients talk about. I would be seeing it in terms of, what is the meaning of this for the client, and does it in any way connect with . . . their experiencing of their life or what's happened to them. So is it located in a part of the body that has experienced some trauma? Or you know, where does it locate in the body and is there any reason, any possible reason for that?

The area of the client's body can become important in this process. The questioning of meaning is an opportunity to explore the client's experience of their body:

> [T9] I mean I see feelings as located in the gut, so . . . or arising from that part of the body. So, my experience is that somatising would kind of start there . . . I often work with that with clients because I'll ask them, you know, whatever they're talking about I might ask them where they feel that in their body. Yeah, so yes I mean, yeah I guess, that would be where I would pick it up I would guess.

Once an area of the client's body has been identified, the therapist uses her own somatic response as a form of confirmation. This is quite a common occurrence in her practice:

> Well I don't think there's any other part of my . . . for me it would be the main part . . . I mean I would see certain feelings might locate in the shoulders for me, possibly in the neck and shoulders but generally in this part of the body [indicates stomach], so yeah . . . so if I feel feelings that, that would be where I feel them I think . . .

Although she may experience feelings elsewhere in her body, it is her stomach that is the main source for this somatising information.

The term 'somatisation' derives from medical discourse (see Chapter 1) and as such it needs to be put in context in terms of the manner in which therapists employ the concept. Somatisation is used to describe a process which occurs not only in the client's body, which is the traditional way to use the term but also in the therapist's body. The use of the term in the medical literature does not convey the same meaning. Medicalised terminology has a history within psychotherapy, probably due to the close links between medicine and psychoanalysis. However, by using the term somatisation there would appear to be a tension: as a medical term it originates from a discourse which is antithetical to the humanistic tradition espoused by the therapists in this book. Somatisation is predominantly used within medicine to categorise a particular class of 'difficult' patient – therefore, it comes with a pejorative label and is used as a means of categorising and pathologising human behaviour. This would suggest that a different term might be useful along the lines of *leib*, as Ots (1990) suggests: a pre-dichotomatic term which incorporates a sense of body, mind and soul (see Chapter 1).

This also highlights the use of language and raises the question of why psychotherapy models use terminology from other discourses. It may be that there are clear historical precedents. Freud was, after all, a trained medical doctor. However, there may be other reasons: one could be a means of acquiring some sense of professional credibility by using quasi-scientific language to describe phenomena, and thereby appearing to be a part of the wider scientific community. Such use of language could then be perceived as lending a certain gravitas to psychotherapeutic theoretical constructs.

Here and now experience

A very interesting phenomenon sometimes occurred while I was conducting the interviews. Some therapists actually felt somatic phenomena in their bodies which they attributed to what they were describing *in that moment of the interview*. It was as if the memory of the event brought up a bodily correspondence with the phenomena being described. This ties in very well with the idea of the lived-body, so that in this case the therapeutic encounter can be considered to leave an imprint on our lived-bodies.

An example of this is provided by T8, who experienced a drop in body temperature during the interview:

> I can think of a client, but it's not so much with sadness, it's as if I feel angry with him, and this is a man who I feel very angry . . . sometimes, about his behaviour towards others and again my breathing would become quite shallow, and my body, I have no doubt my body temperature would drop, and it's as if I am somehow containing . . . it feels as I am speaking now and trying to get into visualising this person, like a survival mechanism that's shut down, and you become very compact and you know, that sort of experience. And I'm actually experiencing it a bit now; I feel that my body temperature has dropped, yeah it's strange.

This temperature change is associated with one particular client who is recalled in the interview: on visualising this client, T8 reports that her body temperature drops. The process of recalling this client has an effect on her immediate bodily experience; it is as though there is a conscious memory and concomitant body memory – in this case, a drop in body temperature.

When asked what sense she made of this experience, T8 replied:

> The sense I make of it is fear. When I'm thinking of this person and . . . his behaviour towards others and how fearful his . . . I nearly said victims but I mean the people who would have experienced his behaviour, may well have felt that, so that actually comes in on another level, it's like a third dimension there. Yeah, I'm thinking that, I'm thinking on my feet there because I've . . . you know provoked those thoughts. Well, I'm feeling for a third person almost.

The connections she is making here are novel, as she says 'I'm thinking on my feet'; she has not really thought through what meanings might be involved. One of her explanations is that she is picking up feelings not from the client but from other people who may experience fear with this client. This appears to be yet another level of bodily communication. The feeling of cold felt in the therapist's body does not relate to the therapist's history, nor does she employ therapeutic discourse and explain this feeling in terms of her countertransferential response to the client, but to how a third party might experience her client. She continues:

> And I'm sensing the potential with this particular person, the potential the destructive potential that he has, although I can't say I actually ever feel fearful of him, I don't . . . I have actually, I have gone quite cold there thinking about him.

The experience of cold has been discussed earlier (see Chapter 5) and is referred to later in the story of Dante's journey into hell where there is a link made between cold and fear (see Chapter 8). However, a significant aspect here is the immediacy of the feeling of cold. It seems to take T8 by surprise. It is as if the lived-body memory of this client could be brought back in the interview situation.

When asked whether she felt the cold was her 'material' or the client's, T8 replied:

> I find that quite hard to answer. I would say my immediate response would be to say that that's mine, but it's possible that he has not a coldness, but a detachment to his behaviour, and you know I'm not sure whether that's, you know, could be mirrored. I can't say he's a cold person you see, he's quite a warm person and quite jolly and . . . but he has this detachment to what his behaviour may you know, inflict on others.

There is some ambivalence about the source of this sensation, and an interpretation that the coldness may represent a detachment in the client's behaviour. It seems that T8's sense of this phenomenon is related to how the client is perceived by other people. In effect this therapist is putting herself in the position of a third party, and her bodily feelings convey a sense of what it feels like to be experiencing the client from this perspective, so in a sense this could be seen as another form of empathy.

T10 reported feeling physically sick when recalling a client during the interview:

> I was thinking, it was a client I had who . . . there was a sort of, I think what she induced was a kind of . . . a sensation of being physically repulsed, and . . . she was unbounded in her body and everything about her, so she'd spill out and . . . God, I'm feeling sick as I'm saying it, 'cos I'm feeling sad I really do.

The client meant a lot to this therapist, and the concomitant feeling of sadness conveyed how moved she was by her client. Here, though, the therapist's reaction appears to be in relation to the story that the client is telling and the therapist's sense that she is being invaded by unpleasant 'material'. So vivid is this recollection that she feels sick as she talks about it.

This phenomenon points to how vivid somatic reactions can be and indicates that this could be a way of exploring these feelings in a supervision setting. If it was possible for therapists to evoke such strong responses in a research interview setting, I would suggest that in clinical supervision this information could be used to explore what these bodily feelings mean for the therapist and the client, thereby, building up a picture of the body narrative within the therapy.

Clients' bodies

So far I have focused on the therapist's body. Clearly the therapeutic encounter requires two bodies and, it is not surprising that the client's body was often mentioned by the therapists who took part in this research. T14 noticed how her client's body changed in colour in response to working on touch in the therapy:

> Yes, a male client who used to . . . actually change colour . . . parts of him would be quite red and other bits white, and when I did work with him on touch and to start with his hands were very white, and cold and he had very little sensation, but as we worked on that he became more able to . . . and felt safer with touch, the circulation responded to that and his hands became warmer and he could feel the comforting touch, and it was quite dramatic as well, you could actually see the changes going on.

This therapist is making a link between using touch in the therapy and the change in colour and temperature that she witnessed in the client. She suggests that this is a process related to a change in circulation and, therefore, evokes a physiological explanation for this dramatic change. Even though the touch work focused on his hands, his face was also affected:

> Well, the touch work was with his hands but the changes in colour affected his face as well, frozen . . . I suppose yes he'd been very traumatised, he'd been sexually abused and he was, he was desensitised much of the time he was desensitised, and when he was desensitised he would be quite white. And then he started to feel, so he would start to warm up.

A link is made here with the client's traumatic childhood and the apparently simple touch of his hands by the therapist had a profound effect on him, as though he was beginning to thaw. The meaning attributed to this encounter involved a recollection by the therapist of how her own body used to feel very cold. She also recalls how this was similar to her own process of feeling freer in her body (see p. 99):

> Well, I mean it relates a bit to the freeing up of bodies, funnily enough I was thinking then, certainly when I was young I felt terrible cold a lot of the time, my hands used to get poor circulation and . . . and again I think part of my freeing up, I don't experience that in the same way now, that does relate to the freeing up of body process and circulation. It's hard to respond to that, I don't know medically how to describe that but again it's a very real phenomenon you know, this was a very obvious phenomenon as the changes in colour were so marked, so dramatic I don't know how it works, but you can actually see . . . as he became able to feel you could actually see the change.

T14 made the link in the interview, and relates the idea of becoming warmer to a notion she introduced earlier about the freeing up of bodies in therapy. The idea of freeing up she has attributed to herself and her own therapy, and her circulation is seen as becoming freer and, as a consequence, it warms up her client and, she realises, may have warmed up her own body. These expressive and descriptive terms are I think very rich in meaning and are a way of incorporating a different type of discourse into therapy – a language that has significance for both parties.

Another way that the client's body is referred to is via the presentation of bodies. An example of this would be the way that some clients have their bodies pierced. T12 works a lot with young people in a student counsellor setting.

> It's interesting about body piercing isn't it? Because it seems to be some sort of cultural phenomenon, and perhaps reflects the wish to

self-harm, I really don't know . . . like tattooing . . . yes I have lots of clients who self-harm, who cut themselves, I have had lots of clients who have cut themselves who . . . I'm doing it myself, I've got this sort of whitlow thing on my thumb which I can't leave alone and it's uncomfortable and at the moment I have a client who tears little bits of skin all around her fingers. She doesn't bite her nails but she bites the pieces of skin and tears them off, and it can become very, very painful and raw . . . and she also does it to her lips, so she will tear off skin all around her lips, she can't stop it and . . . she says that it corresponds to internal feelings of stress, as she calls it stress . . . so it sounds to me as if, I mean this is the theory isn't it? That it is more, it is easier to harm yourself physically that to tolerate certain internal feelings.

This therapist describes several phenomena here related to client's bodies. First, there is the more obvious manifestation of body piercing which she locates as a cultural phenomenon. However, she goes further and suggests that this process may be a method of self-harm; she therefore interprets body piercing through a psychotherapeutic lens. When she describes a client who is actually self-harming to the extent that she is tearing the skin off her fingers and lips, the therapist makes a connection with a similar process in her own body with her whitlow. In a way this seems like a form of psychotherapeutic solipsism, where every somatic complaint is identified with at some level by the therapist. In this instance, this therapist feels that she is drawn to be a therapist because 'I'm sort of condemned to in a way'. It may not be surprising, then, that therapists tend to overidentify with their clients. They are, perhaps, always 'condemned' to see the others' points of view, to such an extent that phenomena in therapy are reflected back into their own bodies. This represents the form of reflexivity with which therapists are familiar. However, this is a rather contained notion of reflexivity, focusing on a therapeutic frame of reference with no regard to external influences. It is therefore inherently lacking in awareness of sociological perspectives and gives the impression of being always inward-looking, as though the answers are always within the confines of the therapy hour, and the therapy room.

Summary

This chapter has looked at the way the therapist's body becomes a type of receiving device. This is a passive process. There does not seem to be a choice involved, it just happens. In some way the therapist's body becomes attuned to the client and 'picks up' client information. It may well be that these sorts of phenomena are ubiquitous and that, due to their training and perhaps their personal history, therapists are more readily able to sense this type of information and hence use their bodies in a more sensitised manner. Frequently the interpretations for this ability are made through the traditional psychotherapeutic lens. This is not surprising bearing in mind therapists are drawing upon the tools of language which are available to them. The use of medical terminology is sometimes employed in explanations (e.g. somatisation), and we have seen how the use of this term is problematic from the humanistic standpoint advocated by the therapists in this study. The ability to use their bodies as receivers is mentioned by many of the therapists, and suggests that the 'body as a receiver' could be developed into a more widespread technique.

However, we have seen that traditional psychotherapeutic discourse may not be the best way to describe these phenomena, as this leads therapists to imply that they are feeling their client's feelings. The suggestion I am putting forward is that these sensations would be better located within a narrative framework. In this way the therapist's lived-body could be incorporated into the therapeutic encounter. By adopting such an approach it would be possible for therapist and client to develop an embodied discourse which was specific and compatible with each therapeutic situation. Indeed, an incorporation of the ideas of the narrative movement and the lived-body paradigm would broaden out the possibilities for sharing these phenomena within the therapeutic encounter.

Chapter 7

Embodied styles of working

I now wish to introduce some of the variety of ways in which therapists manage their own bodies during the therapeutic encounter. I have called this 'embodied styles of working', since many of the techniques that therapists employ derive from their own sense of embodiment.

A significant feature of this chapter is that we can begin to see how traditional therapeutic discourse is not necessarily employed by therapists to discuss and make sense of bodily phenomena. It is here that we see therapists seeking explanations further afield from traditional psychotherapeutic discourse, and attempting to develop strategies to cope with the somatic demands of their profession. Many therapists draw upon eastern philosophies of thought to help them in their everyday practice lives, so we see that meditative practices or the use of Buddhist or other eastern philosophies are common. The manner in which therapists manage their bodies is brought into focus in this chapter. An example of this is the use of touch, which is seen as contentious and highly problematic, yet the benefits of this technique seem to outweigh the potential pitfalls of its use. We will also look in some detail at the issue of therapist health, and see that some therapists have frank opinions on this subject. There is a strong suggestion that there is a health implication to working as a therapist. These effects can be both positive and negative. It would seem an important part of training that health, and strategies to cope with the symptoms of 'burnout', should be addressed. As for touch, it would seem that clearer guidelines need to be given about the possible repercussions of using this technique, and perhaps about seeking informed consent from clients.

These issues demonstrate that the method of training may need to be critiqued, so that trainee therapists are sent out into private practice properly equipped with suitable strategies. This would seem essential so that they are not left exposed and vulnerable by the form of therapy which has been modelled to them during their training.

I have organised this chapter into four sections which use verbatim accounts from therapists and draw together the theme of this chapter:

- Cultural perspectives
- Touch

- Management of the therapeutic encounter
- Therapist health

These four sections explore the styles and techniques which therapists use to bring the body into the therapy. From our discussion to date we can see that it is increasingly clear that the therapist's body is very present in the therapy room. Chapters 5 and 6 focused predominantly on how the therapist's body is implicated in this process. This chapter also builds on this debate, but also starts to look at some other aspects of the body in therapy – for example, how the client's body is perceived and some of the strategies adopted by therapists to counteract the perceived dangers of therapy.

Cultural perspectives

The therapists in this study seem to draw on cultures other than their own western culture to help them manage themselves and the therapeutic encounter, and the most frequent way mentioned is the use of meditation or yoga. T5 uses yoga as a means to prepare herself for group work. Prior to meeting a new group of clients she first of all finds a quiet place where she can be alone and acknowledges any feelings within her body. Frequently when meeting a new group she feels scared and she actually works on her own body at that moment:

> I will stretch or I'll do some brief yoga exercises . . . or I'll kinda walk round the space, and work out how I'm feeling in different parts of the space.

In order to be emotionally as well as physically prepared, this therapist obtains benefit from yoga. This idea is mentioned by other therapists – for example, many refer to the importance of meditation in their lives. T13 provides a good example of this:

> I think about my Buddhist kind of leanings and beliefs in my regular meditation practice and those kind of things which support me being in touch with my body experience, bringing me into my present experience.

The use of meditation clearly helps T13 with his bodily sense. It is almost as if meditative practices are used to cleanse the body, to clear it of 'client material'. Other therapists seem aware that not to engage in some form of other practice would be detrimental to their health. T6 is very aware that dealing with a lot of emotional negativity and trauma can have an effect on his well-being, and he even goes so far as to liken it to the suicide rates in other professions:

> Well I think that, I mean statistically the highest suicide rate is among psychiatrists followed by GPs . . . I think it is, and I'm not surprised

> by that given the amount of emotional negativity or painful experi-
> ence or trauma that I'm in contact with, then I can end up picking it
> up and end up feeling it myself yeah . . .

This therapist is drawing comparisons with medical practitioners and seems to be learning a lesson that it is important to look after yourself as a psychotherapy practitioner. This is the therapist who mentioned that sometimes he has asthma when in contact with a particular client. He is probably acutely aware of the physical effects of therapy on his health, and one of the ways he combats this is to stay in regular psychotherapy and also to have regular shiatsu sessions. Both these activities are a crucial aspect of his support system and allow him to maintain a psychotherapy practice. For this therapist shiatsu is important in dealing in a more direct manner with what he terms his 'energy flow'. It is the use of these non-western terms that is interesting; the therapists in this study are borrowing from an eastern way of viewing health care, and yet they themselves are steeped in the traditional western mode of healing or treatment. Psychotherapy, after all, evolved from psychoanalytic thought which was itself a product of medical discourse. Hence, terms such as 'diagnosis' and 'patient' abound in the psychoanalytic literature. Perhaps this group of therapists who are trained in the humanistic school are trying to redress the balance of medical discourse by incorporating eastern health care ideals into their philosophy of health care.

Some therapists have taken on board cultural metaphors which help them with their understanding of their practice life and its effects on them and their bodies. T11 replied to a question I asked about how she used her body in therapy, and she remembered a particular metaphor:

> I don't know but as soon as you said that I went back to a Japanese
> name that a Japanese girl gave me, years ago, she explained the
> origin, what my name meant in Japanese and she said [name of
> therapist], and she drew the characters out. It was this [draws out
> symbol], and it comes from the Chinese characters, this is like the
> salmon's eye and this is kind of a character from a vessel so a real
> eye, a true eye . . . overflowing vessel, and that's the sort of image
> that I have of this work, is that I am the containing vessel of this
> work.

What we see here is the use of metaphors from other cultures, and the importance that they are given by therapists. The idea of a containing vessel is a good image for what we do as therapists and uses an image to symbolise an aspect of the therapeutic task. I would suggest that this is a good use of narrative, a way of using an image which has meaning for this therapist. It may not have meaning for other therapists but for this therapist it clearly is of significance and helps her to make a symbolic representation of her body in therapy. One of the strategies this therapist adopts as a part of her practice life is to take regular holidays and to experience other cultures. This seems like an excellent way of exposing oneself to different ways of perceiving the world, and also to other cultural narratives. I am not advocating here that we all need to go on exotic holidays but that different therapists should seek out their own particular way of incorporating alternative methods of looking at their practice.

These other cultural expressions help inform these therapists about their work, and in some cases are an important aspect of remaining healthy. Not all of the therapists in this study use meditation, but perhaps the significant aspect here is that many do, and that when they do this has a positive impact on their practice lives.

Touch

One method by which the body can be directly introduced into therapy is via touch. Within the humanistic school of psychotherapy touch is an acceptable therapeutic intervention, as opposed to the view held in the psychoanalytic movement where touch is considered a taboo. Therefore, since the majority of my interviewees came from the humanistic school of psychotherapy, touch was not as contentious an issue as it could have been. However, having said that, it was clearly regarded as problematic and generally thought of as highly significant with certain clients. T1 values touch very highly but is more circumspect about its use, and tends to use it very sparingly. She bases her use of touch on her ability to judge where the client is in a developmental sense, what particular issues are predominant and which developmental issues the client is wishing to explore. So, for example, if the client had in the past been inappropriately touched this therapist would explore the particular need of the client and might well use gentle touching techniques like hand holding to introduce the client to a different form of touch. On the other hand, if the client had been 'over touched' in childhood then:

> I would appropriately withhold from touching, despite their request, so we've kind of got a multitude of ways of going with it.

This therapist clearly sees touch as a useful clinical tool, yet is aware of the potential pitfalls and therefore uses it sparingly. She also provides a glimpse of how touch is managed in her practice, and how her judgements are affected by the needs of the client.

The absence of touch is also a technique, so we see a spectrum of interventions from touch to no touch. The hint of the danger of touch is picked up by other therapists:

> [T2] I'm much more cautious than I used to be about touch. I wait until people ask me. Some people say they'd like to be hugged, I'll hug them quite happily . . . or they will put out a hand and signal in their distress that they want their hand held, and I will do that . . .

This therapist actually refers to the type of touch she would use, but the sense here is of caution, and this has arisen from an occasion when her touch was misinterpreted and a complaint was made against her. This was a really bad experience in the use of touch. She was engaged in couples work with a husband and wife, and after a particularly distressing session, as the couple were leaving, and began to put their coats on, the therapist noticed that the husband's coat was slipping down his back. At this moment T2 moved forward to help him on with his coat:

> . . . so I lifted the coat up behind him and put it on him, and left one arm around his shoulders and said 'This has been hard going hasn't it?', and sort of half gave him a hug with one hand, and his wife went absolutely berserk and she said 'Oh, she's a tart!', and then went to complain to the GP[1] that I was unprofessional so I . . . I don't help anybody with their coats now.

This episode was clearly distressing for T2, and shows how an apparently innocuous gesture can be interpreted to the detriment of the therapist. This also highlights the vulnerability that therapists have to live with and the potential that their actions may hold for interpretation in a negative manner. One of the possible outcomes of the complaint mentioned above was that the therapist could have lost her job; this did not happen but the complaint in itself was a very uncomfortable experience for the therapist.

Touch is clearly seen as important and the debates on the use of touch and the psychoanalytic arguments are well-known to this group of therapists. The use of touch was linked to particular theoretical constructs, typically to meeting a developmental need. The therapists viewed touch as providing a level of developmental support that was lacking at a particular time in the client's childhood. The suggestion was that if this need was not met in the therapy then this could actually evoke trauma. There was also an acknowledgement that the therapeutic relationship itself could provide a contained environment which could offer the necessary support.

Therapists are recognising in the client a developmental deficit in childhood, in that they had not been touched, and so via the therapeutic relationship this need may be met by touching. This recognition process provides a justification for the use of touch in therapy. This justification is further underlined by the suggestion that not to touch in certain circumstances may re-traumatise the client. This would appear to be a very difficult decision to make, and the possibility of re-traumatising the client puts a lot of pressure on the therapist to make the right intervention at the right time. The therapeutic use of touch is also linked to particular stages of therapy that the client has reached. The onus on the therapist is to make a clinical judgement about whether to provide touch, which as we can see is quite a complex issue and requires a high degree of clinical judgement. This seems like a high-risk strategy since, if they get it wrong, there is the potential for complaints to be made which could affect their livelihood. As they become more experienced, therapists seem to use touch less often:

[T8] Well, I think touch has to be used quite sparingly. But I think that it has to be very carefully censored, and that using touch may evoke your sense of privacy or the client's sense of privacy and . . . even if you check it out with them, in my experience I've found that even if they say yes, which is usually to please you I think, their body language shows that they didn't mean yes.

This therapist is reiterating the idea of using touch sparingly and introduces the notion of censoring the use of touch. She is aware that clients may say they want to be touched simply to please the therapist. This adds another dimension to when and why to touch. T8 goes on to explain that an intuitive sense governs her interventions on touch, so that her most effective use of touch has occurred when she has not been consciously aware of why she has done so – in effect she just finds herself sitting next to a client and holding them. Again this appears to be another high-risk strategy. It calls into question what therapists are expected to do and what risks they are expected to take. Therapists are trained to use their intuition but if this leads to a touch which is deemed inappropriate by the client complaints and professional sanctions could be the legal consequence.

T10 looks back and sees how her attitude to touch has changed, starting from when she trained:

Well, I think my attitude towards touch has changed since I trained. Because when I trained, in terms of what we were modelled if you like, by the trainers, was that . . . this was the more negative aspect of it, there's loads of positive stuff as well, in terms of you know, that you held people, unless somebody was sort of in a heap on the floor and you were scooping them up, that therapy wasn't happening.

Here the term 'modelling' arises, and it seems a very powerful way to demonstrate how to behave professionally, yet here it is potentially dangerous and encouraging a non-reflexive attitude to touch. This therapist is aware that her training led her to go out as a novice therapist and use touch in an indiscriminate manner. The only issue around touch that she recalls was that with people who had been sexually abused it was advised not to touch if the client was in a regressed state. The worrying aspect of this was that she was left feeling that she had to find out about touch on a trial and error basis, and to use her words at the beginning of her practice life:

I was a lot more available in that way perhaps . . . over available in that way, and I've pulled back a lot since then. The way I offer touch and the way I make myself available for touch is very different now I'd say.

It would seem that this therapist was unprepared for using touch in practice and had to learn by experience; for such a contentious issue this would seem a rather cavalier way in which to train therapists. With some experience T10 came to the realisation that it would be a good idea to back off a little from the model she had been exposed to in training. This highlights a pitfall of the modelling approach to training. The model of touch as an intervention in the training group is a relatively safe technique, but if that technique is transferred to a private practice setting then the therapist is put in a very vulnerable position. T10 went on to explain that she was fearful for her own safety when using touch, and that as she has matured as a practitioner she finds that the therapeutic relationship acts as a container and touch is not so important. She is aware of the importance of being able to provide touch but, at the same time, is careful of her own professional safety. With experience she has developed ways of metaphorically holding clients in the relationship without the use of touch. This has a clear resonance with the psychoanalytic argument which views the therapeutic relationship as a container which symboli-cally holds the client. This would seem to echo the ideas of psychoanalysis where touch is frowned upon, and it appears that experienced practitioners in the humanistic therapies view touch in a similar way to psychoanalytic practitioners, with the one exception that touch may be useful in certain circumstances.

A major issue to arise from this discussion is the vulnerability of the therapist. Bearing in mind that there are alternative methods of containing the client which do not require a physical holding, in this context it seems surprising that any therapist would even entertain the notion of touching. There is a tension here in that touch for these therapists is considered important, albeit fraught with hazards. The intuitive nature of providing touch is a powerful therapeutic tool but it leaves the therapist very vulnerable to complaints and, in the increasing atmos-phere of litigation in professional practice therapists may be risking their very livelihood.

Management of the therapeutic encounter

There were many occasions when the body was described in a particular way which helped to manage the therapeutic encounter. It could be argued that touch was a means of introducing a body-orientated technique, but I have treated touch as a discrete theme because of its contentious nature and its peculiar properties within psychotherapy. By focusing on 'management of the therapeutic encounter' I am intending to provide a flavour of the rich and varied nature of the body in therapy, and convey some of the creative ways which therapists use to bring the body into the therapy session.

T5, who works as a dramatherapist, used many creative techniques to introduce the body into therapy, and one example was by focusing on the hands of the client. The therapist directs the client to feel what is happening in their hands and then lets their hands be symbolic of how their body is feeling at that time. This work is usually done in a group setting and then the therapist may ask the clients to explore their feelings further by using words or, for example, by inviting them to hit out at cushions if their emotions are related to anger. T5 also employs techniques of guided imagery, using writing or drawing to enable clients to express their bodily feelings.

The focus of this piece of work is the encouragement of the client to explore their bodily sensation and use the feelings engendered to express themselves via their hands. The body talked about here is that of the client. I was interested to know what was happening in the therapist's body. T5 was readily able to make a connection with her own body sensation and was able to make connections with the group experience. One of the ways that she did this was by being aware of her breathing and holding her body in a similar way to the client's body. In a sense this would seem like trying to feel what it is like in another person's body, a way to empathise in a very body-orientated fashion. She used a particular phrase which was very evocative of this process:

> . . . where it connects with me is around my heart, the physical happening in a client, that's where it connects with me often.

She was also keenly aware when working in this way that she can find herself copying what her clients are doing with her own hands:

> . . . sometimes I can then start actually mirroring what they're doing with their hands . . . then I can say 'I just noticed this, and I'm wondering why this is happening to me and what's happening to you?'

This therapist has an acute awareness of some of her bodily processes; she locates these feelings around her heart, reminiscent of T8 who referred to her emotional heart in Chapter 6. The therapist then interprets these somatic sensations and feeds them back to the client by a process of mirroring (as discussed in Chapter 4). The therapist manages the process by picking up cues from the client and by being aware of how her own body is feeling.

There is a suggestion of a two-way bodily communication here, which is similar to a phenomenon described by other therapists – for example, T12, who is aware that she reacts in a bodily manner to her clients:

> I often notice that I'm inclined to keep my hand across myself like that [her hand lies across her abdomen], and then if I notice I make myself do this [she uncloses herself by removing her hand].

T12 is suggesting that her client's tension is reflected in her own body and that this awareness can make her want to lay her hand across her abdomen. However, the interesting point to note here is that the therapist is using the information provided by her own bodily tension consciously to make her body appear less tense. She goes on to describe how this can have an impact on the client, in that the client will copy the therapist's posture. T12 then makes a conscious decision to change her posture. In order not to appear tense to her client by holding her hand protectively across her abdomen, the therapist decides to hold her hands together in a non-defensive posture. What ensues is a therapeutic dance whereby the client mirrors the therapist's body. A two-way process of bodily communication is being described here: the client is picking up cues from the therapist who, in the first place, decided to change her body posture in response to her bodily tension which was attributed to the client.

Some therapists are aware of how they can override bodily responses. This technique is important in cases where the impact of the client's story is so strong that to feel their physical reaction at that time would be unhelpful in a therapeutic context. The ability to override these bodily sensations is important for the therapist in enabling them to stay with their client and not be overwhelmed by physical sensations. T9 describes how she manages this particular aspect of her practice and for her it is a way that the client can feel accepted. Also, for this therapist this is very much a gut reaction: the initial reaction is felt as a gut reaction and the secondary response is to override this sensation. The important feature for her is that she can soothe this initial reaction:

> So, in a way I'm kind of overriding the initial impact, which is a bit of a gut reaction . . . so it kind of involves me having to soothe, soothe the initial reaction, so it's quite difficult to identify it because what I'm actually doing may be counter to what the impact is . . .

It is almost as though T9 can somehow pigeon-hole her somatic response and put it to one side. By doing this she is then able to 'get alongside the client' and therefore work with the client. It is as if the therapist's physical response would be a hindrance to working effectively at that moment. This would seem to require a high degree of bodily awareness in order to make a clinical judgement at this juncture.

Therapist health

A striking feature to arise from interviewing therapists about their bodily experiences is that there seems to be a health cost to therapy. Although there are rewards and many therapists really enjoyed their work and were very fulfilled, there may also be dangers. Several therapists mentioned that they knew of colleagues, who were practising therapists or in training, who were suffering from serious illnesses and had had to give up work or finish their training. The types of illness people referred to were clinical depression, chronic fatigue syndrome and instances of terminal cancer. Clearly, these were anecdotal accounts and it must be remembered that the majority of people who train to be psychotherapists in the UK do so having been in another career, so the therapist population is likely to be older post-training than other vocational occupations, and therefore, possibly more likely in any event to be suffering from chronic and/or serious illnesses. However, the opinions of the therapists in the study implied that there could be a health cost to either practising or training as a psychotherapist. The issue I wish to highlight here is that psychotherapeutic work has a clear impact on the bodies of psychotherapists. There are a variety of ways in which this can occur and it is important to examine the nature of this phenomenon and look at any potential long-term effects on the health of therapists. I wish to explore some of the health effects in this section. In the interviews I conducted it emerged that clients who have had particularly unpleasant experiences evoke powerful bodily responses. For example, one client was tortured and her therapist had a nightmare that corresponded to the client's experience. The therapist did not normally have nightmares but:

> [T14] . . . one night I had woken up after this absolutely horrendous nightmare and it took me some time to realise . . . I thought I've never had anything like that in my life, I suddenly realised that this was exactly the sort of nightmare that she describes . . . so it was you know it wasn't the same story but it was just like the quality of nightmare, so that was quite a scary experience really.

When I asked what explanation T14 had for this she made a link in that she had a very deep connection with this particular client, and somehow the dream was a form of pre-verbal communication, because this client was unable to put her feelings into words. The client became absolutely stuck to the point of not being able to say anything, therefore the nightmare somehow became a means of communicating:

> I sort of pick up, she's needing to communicate something to me but she can't do it through words, she becomes completely traumatised, she can't speak.

The deep level of connection is of significance here, and the explanation is that communication is occurring at a pre-verbal level, at a level where there are no words. McDougall (1989) talks about dreams as a psychosomatic experience *par excellence*. However, disturbance of sleep has clear health implications and if clients can have this effect on our sleep this is likely to affect how we work.

T5, the dramatherapist, talks of feeling physically sick after hearing about a client who suffered a brutal attack. T5 also mentioned going off sex after hearing stories relating to child sex abuse. In particular she noticed how she needed to protect herself around her womb and her stomach:

> I get a real physical connection, of you know my womb and my stomach, and of needing to protect that space and close up completely. And it did have an effect on my sex life as well, that kind of reclaiming of a woman's space and you know not being penetrable or anything. A kind of completely closing up, it left quite an imprint on me emotionally and physically.

T5 was deeply affected in a very physical way and she talks about the need to protect herself, a concomitant of this being that her sex life is affected, which could impact on her relationship with her partner.

The impact of a therapist's work is considered by many of the therapists in this study, who talk about a 'cost of therapy'. T7 draws upon Cashdan's notion of 'stepping into the countertransference' (Cashdan 1988). She describes the way she works as relational, meaning that the relationship that evolves between herself and her clients is a crucial part of her work. It is by 'stepping into the counter-transference' that she is then able to sense what it is like to be in another's world. This has clear links to our earlier discussion on empathy and intersubjectivity, and this concept of being in another's world is a central part of this process. However, the consequence is to allow the client to have an impact on us:

> [T7] . . . to allow myself to be so impacted by somebody, to allow myself to know somebody to that degree and therefore, know myself to that degree, I mean there's wonderful rewards as well . . . but there's a real cost . . .

'Cost' in this context seems to refer to a process in which the therapist allows herself to feel the impact of a 'client's material'. The sequelae to this can be a very uncomfortable bodily feeling as well as the potential for discovering aspects of the self which were hidden. T7 felt that this was a costly way to make a living, and experienced the growing realisation that it was important for her to strike a balance in her work. Once she had finished her training she decided to take a year off to travel and see the world. She emphasised the need to redress the balance in her life and this is a key feature of her practice life now – she is very aware of balancing the demands of her job with her social life.

This idea that there is a social consequence to therapy work was mentioned by other therapists. The therapist who described the metaphor of the vessel has made some conscious decisions about the company she keeps:

> [T11] I think there's a cost in terms of friends that I feel I can no longer mix with, because their lack of awareness or you know the kind of jokeyness around that and I really don't want to be with that. I've chosen to minimise my contact with people who kind of make sexist jokes or jokes about women. I don't want to spend the time of day with people who actually, who are jokey or abusive. I think the unconscious kind of aggression and abuse behind some jokeyness, I don't want to be around.

This suggests that another cost of therapy is a reduction of social contact, by making the decision not to be in the company of people with bigoted opinions. An understandable result of listening to stories of abuse at work is that to hear these issues talked about in a frivolous manner is offensive.

Several other therapists acknowledged that their work had a negative impact on their social lives. T12 describes herself as becoming a 'bit phobic, a bit allergic to social life, social contact', and the thought of phoning a friend in the evening having heard many distressing stories from clients during the day becomes an onerous task. The thought crosses her mind that a friend may be demanding, which is the last thing she needs, as she feels she has no resources left. She ends up in a dilemma, as not phoning could result in a loss of social contact, which she does need, and a feeling of guilt for damaging the friendship. But if she does phone then she may not have enough energy to be available for that friendship. The very fact that in order to work as a therapist it is important to listen means that it sometimes becomes a problem when friends want to make demands. As a result there is the danger of losing friendships and becoming isolated. The issue of isolation has been identified as one of the problems of health and burnout in the psychotherapy profession (Grosch and Olsen 1994; Sussman 1995). There is a 'high incidence of mental illness (especially depression), drugs and alcohol abuse, sexual acting out and suicide among therapists' (Sussman 1995: 1). Some of the main factors associated with these problems are linked to social isolation, and relationship problems in marriage or with children. It would seem clear that therapy carries a risk to health.

However, as has been discussed, in many ways therapists appear deeply touched by their exposure to clients and this is represented in a bodily form. A good example of this is the therapist who had an asthma attack (T6) with one client, whom he identified as being very close to him. He also recognised that other people could induce this feeling, but they were all people who had a very special meaning for him. This may say something about the danger of therapy and it is important to consider the health implications of, for example, having a client who sparks off an asthma attack. As we have discussed previously in relation to asthma there can be long-term consequences to taking steroids to treat this condition. The question arises as to the cost of the physical and mental health to therapists: what is an acceptable risk in the therapy setting? One way to address this question is to look at training. Generally, issues such as health risk are not addressed in the training of therapists (Sussman 1995). The therapists in this study seem to be recounting similar stories about the effects of therapy on their lives as other groups of therapists (Sussman 1995).

We now come to the notion of 'shared affective experience' (Chayes 1988: 83) which evokes a sense of contamination or contagion. This links well to our earlier discussion on empathy and intersubjectivity. There is a blurring of the distinction between therapist and client. 'Contamination' in this context is the 'client's material' somehow provoking a bodily response in the therapist. This has parallels with the idea of human biological material being dangerous within the medical field; in this case the human body is viewed as hazardous and the harbinger of dangerous pathogens, material in this context referring to microbes or infectious agents. One suggestion arising from the interviews is of another form of contamination, one that is mediated not via a microscopic agent that can be viewed by the medical gaze, but via the relationship between the therapist and the client, in the intersubjective space. Indeed, T11 uses the term 'contamination' to describe the process whereby her clients, and then herself, are affected by 'inappropriate human contact':

> I see my clients as being contaminated by the most inappropriate human contact, and obviously they can communicate that to me, so it's almost like sharing the experience. I know it's theirs, and there-fore, in honouring my own body I choose not to poison it further with all the things that I know are not good for me.

When she refers to poisoning she is talking about taking in alcohol and eating unhealthy foods; this is almost as a counterbalance to taking in toxic 'material' from clients. This was the therapist who earlier in this chapter described the Japanese symbol of the 'salmon's eye' as a metaphor for a container to help describe how overfull she can become with 'client material':

> Yeah, overflowing with the wrong stuff I guess, at that point over-flowing, and I see the vessel it is really overflowing in different ways now, creatively . . . but yes there is a cost to that and those things I choose not to do actively.

She makes choices about her life – not to drink alcohol and to adopt a mainly vegetarian diet, and not to mix socially with people that she now finds offensive. These are in effect positive aspects of working as a therapist whereby a healthy lifestyle choice is made. Another example of this is T7 who is aware how her use of alcohol has changed:

> before I used to drink quite a lot of alcohol and that's one way of unwinding but I have thought about this quite a lot really, what an unhealthy process that was . . . seeing lots of clients, working for social services with people that were very damaged as well, and my way of letting go was to retroflect basically. I mean that's not good, that's not healthy . . . now I don't drink any alcohol at all.

These life choices are taken as a response to practice life, not as a response to training. The whole process of training to become a therapist and then practising has inherent problems. There are undoubtedly costs involved in becoming, and then working as, a therapist. For example, the large amount of time and commit-ment required during the training process, and the total immersion in the subject that is needed to meet the rigorous requirements of the course. As T10 puts it when describing what it was like to complete her training and set up a private practice:

Yes, and it's, I think that feeling, when I was saying to you I became tired all the time, I know that was to do with having done a case study and getting all that stuff done as well, it was actually trying to keep a practice going. It felt like everything was therapy, every weekend I was doing something to do with it, it took over my life. So, if I'd carried on like that I'd've had a limited life definitely.

T10 introduces the idea of a limited life, referring to her practice life as a therapist. Rather surprisingly, it has been noted that the average practice life of a therapist is only ten years (Grosch and Olsen 1994). Issues such as burnout are mentioned by some interviewees and an example is provided by T12:

That part of our training is to become sensitised to the other person, that we could end up carrying tensions that are malign for us. Well, you know a very passive-aggressive client for example could leave us feeling seething with rage and needing to do something with it, if we don't do something with it and we retroflect that back into ourselves that could go into our muscle tone and our internal organs and become ME^2 and something like that. It might sound a bit melodramatic to put it like that, but it is certainly possible isn't it? To become burnt-out.

Interestingly this therapist actually makes links with specific diseases like ME. Other authors who have looked at the notion that therapy can be detrimental to health include McCann and Pearlman (1990). They describe some of the consequences of listening to traumatic 'material' which includes the notion of burnout.[3] They state quite categorically that: 'exposure to the traumatic experiences of victims may be hazardous to the mental health of people close to the victim, including therapists involved in the victim's healing process' (1990: 135).

There would seem to be a health risk for psychotherapists who are witness to the stories of abused clients. In some cases therapists give a graphic description of how this feels for them (e.g. T10 talked about leaking boundaries) (see also Chapter 5), almost as though there was a blurred boundary between therapist and client:

[T10] I actually felt that she was leaking her body fluid that was on to me, or something like that, so I actually felt quite physically repulsed by her.

This therapist is implying a different quality to the term 'boundary'. In a psychotherapy setting, boundaries are normally taken to mean keeping the time for an appointment, payment of fees and not transgressing with techniques such as touch etc. These have a substantive quality to them and are familiar within other professions; in my osteopathic training we were introduced to professional boundaries – for example, we had to wear a white clinic coat when working in the public osteopathic clinic. Clearly, professional boundaries are important for maintaining a particular identity. Such boundaries also help the practitioner to distance themselves from the client and, in effect, protect themselves. However, it is very difficult to protect oneself if one is not prepared, and this notion of leaky boundaries seems to fit into this category. T10 is not prepared for what the client is going to say, nor for the effect on her body. Therefore it becomes very difficult for her to maintain a distance and hence she feels a sense of being invaded; her boundaries have been breached.

While doing these interviews, I have been aware how some of the issues which have arisen may be related to my own practice – in particular, how therapists develop strategies to avoid leaky boundaries infiltrating their everyday lives. I was very struck by one therapist who, after seeing one client, felt that she needed some time on her own to just walk very slowly and put one foot in front of the other:

> [T11] . . . and I take moments out during the day when I can just put one foot in front to the other, and just kind of be with myself or ground myself again.

This is a really simple remedy which somehow brings one back to earth again, being almost meditative in quality. Another strategy for therapeutic survival was the structured use of time; by this I mean therapists were very disciplined about how long they would see clients, and those that had been in practice for some time seemed to make an effort to ensure they took time off for holidays. It was noticeable that therapists who engaged in this structuring of time, or developed strategies, were those who had been in practice for some years.

The therapists in this study seem to be aware of the potential for their health to be affected by the work that they do. It is therefore all the more surprising that this is not addressed in the training of therapists. This raises the issue of informed consent of students training to become therapists, and also that of the lack of general discussion of health issues within the profession. Perhaps one of the problems is that working as a therapist has a cumulative effect on health, as suggested by Sussman (1995: 2): 'most of the occupational hazards are cumulative, only surfacing over extended periods of practice'. He also suggests that there is a taboo on talking about illness within the profession. It is difficult to know exactly why this taboo exists, but an acknowledgement of the fallibility of therapists may provide a clue. Sussman (1995: 4) makes an excellent point by suggesting that: 'throughout the history of psychotherapy, the personhood of the practitioner has been all but ignored'. The culture of the profession has tended to focus on the client and not on the therapist. Clearly there are good reasons for this, in that it is the client that therapists are trying to help, not themselves; also, the psychoanalytic tradition has been for the therapist to be a blank screen onto which the client can project their 'material'. One of the consequences of this culture is that often clients will view their therapist as the perfect being, or they will have an idealised transference onto the therapist. This is a notion echoed in the training where modelling is a process often used to convey how best to behave in the therapy situation. The fact that therapists do succumb to illness does not fit in with this superhuman notion. The Greek myth of Chiron the 'wounded healer' may illustrate the point. Chiron was a master of medicine and a skilled healer, yet he himself had an incurable disease which he could not alleviate. He was thus able to heal others but not himself (Grant and Hazel 1993). This myth was introduced to me during my osteopathic training as a way of assessing why we were training to be osteopaths. It is also used in other complementary medicine disciplines: Danciger (1993), a homeopath, uses the Chiron story to explore why it is that people seek an occupation that involves the healing of others' suffering. This legend is therefore a metaphor for understanding someone else's suffering based on one's own experience. Many therapists, myself included, enter the therapy world to work on aspects of themselves and *then* become therapists. As Sussman (1995: 4) describes:

> Many therapists, for example, grew up playing the role of caretaker, go-between, parentified child, or burden-bearer within their families of origin. Having learned at an early age to attune themselves to others, therapists often have great difficulty attending to their own emotional needs.

The personal therapy aspect of psychotherapy training is crucial in this respect. The assumption made within training is that a therapist cannot possibly practise safely unless that therapist has worked out his or her own psychological history and come to terms with it. The implication of not undertaking this task is that therapists will use their clients as a means of working out their own unresolved issues. Personal therapy is therefore understandably given considerable importance within the training regime, and the rationale for this appears logical and professionally sound.

T12 relates her history of having to look after her father and provides a graphic description of being 'condemned' to be a therapist:

> Because my history was to attune to my father, I very much took that role in my relationship with him, and I would pick up his feelings as a small child. I would always be aware of his discomfort whatever that was, and I became very sensitive to that, so I just repeat that with other people and with clients you know . . . it's very easy for me to do that, and it's also very . . . something that I'm sort of condemned to do in a way.

Although 'condemned' sounds like a strong term, it could be reframed as a term which suggests a predisposition to become a therapist. Maybe the role we take on in earlier years is the beginning of our training, and in the context of this book, this is where we learn to be sensitive to other people's needs, attune to subtle cues and begin to recognise these feelings in our lived-body. After all, it is biographical experience which enables us to differentiate many aspects of our everyday lives so this important stage of our lives I would suggest is where we start to learn how to empathically attune via our bodies.

I wish to return to the limited life of the therapist and try to link together our discussion in this section. T10 wonders about the practice life and suggests that there is an emotional drain over time. She has noticed, by talking to colleagues, that therapists' priorities change over time. One reason for this is that personal therapy is not so important. The significant issues that brought T10 into the therapy world have been 'worked through', and a part of her 'process' was to become immersed in therapy to the point of living, eating and sleeping it. Now, this is not so important:

> It's not that I'm not interested in being a therapist, but I'm not interested necessarily in therapy as part of my personal journey now. I want to find something else you know, finding ways now to bring things back into my life which I had put to one side . . . to do this, and I think this is going to be really important for me in sustaining this career.

These are important choices and are echoed by other therapists in this study. There is a need to see beyond the therapy world and experience other aspects of living. It is as if a realisation dawns on therapists in the post-training phase:

> [T10] I notice when people get to a certain point they say, 'Therapy's not everything, you know'. There's got to be something else, you've got to get a balance, and 'cos you know dealing with people's distress you know hour after hour is you know . . . and working self-employed I think that's part of it too, although I work within an institute . . . I work for myself, there's no one there in terms of institution that holds you or says you've got to have a break now or you can be sick now or you can do this now. You know, I have to look to myself.

Having been immersed in therapy T10 now sees that there is a world beyond, one that has also been recognised by her colleagues. She raises another important issue about self-employment: along with the stresses of working as a therapist are the demands of building and maintaining a practice. There is the potential for this to be a very hard, difficult and lonely business. She is also recognising that looking outside therapy for support is important to achieve some balance in her life. The therapists mentioned here have all recognised that there are potential health hazards to being a therapist and have devised strategies for helping them cope with the demands placed upon them. The search for something outside the therapy world to sustain practitioners' mental as well as physical well-being is, I would suggest, of vital importance. Some means of addressing the demands of therapy and how to cope with them should be an integral part of training and, up to now, this has been omitted. These are issues which really need to be addressed in a very serious manner during the training of therapists.

Often therapists will receive support by continuing to have personal therapy, but there may be problems with this approach. As Seligman (1995: 55) suggests, there is a quest for 'a magical perfect cure that lies at the end of a rainbow called "enough therapy"'. This seems to echo T6 and T8, who implied that their respective health problems of asthma and heart disease could be 'cured' by more of the 'right type of therapy'. At times it is almost as if the only way of viewing any particular aspect of life is through a psychotherapeutic lens – that there is some 'holy grail' of 'enough therapy'. We could see this as a form of psychotherapeutic solipsism which appears endemic within psychotherapy culture. However, in this chapter we have seen therapists attempt to use other cultural practices to help them navigate the complexities of their bodily experience. Perhaps one of the reasons for trying to see all phenomena through a psychotherapeutic lens is that therapists have invested much of themselves in their chosen model of therapy. In fact this is so important for some therapists that they have made a conscious decision to choose a particular therapeutic model because it fits with their particular personality and the way they wish to conduct their everyday lives. An example of this was provided by T1. When discussing the issue of touch she was very aware that its use was part of her personality so that:

> In terms of my personality I work that way, it would actually cause me a compromise to my integrity to withhold [touch] and I think it's extremely important that we work congruently and that our personality is congruent to our therapeutic discipline.

In some cases it is clear that therapists' lifestyle embodies their chosen therapeutic model. In other cases therapists have chosen a particular model of therapy because it best fits with their own values and beliefs. Such an awareness would seem essential when looking at embodied phenomena from a narrative perspective. An acknowledgement of the power dynamics in the therapeutic relationship is a significant part of the narrative movement. Therefore, a therapist's decision to choose a particular model (and thus lifestyle) could have an impact on the type of therapy they offer. There has been some discussion of this issue in the literature. Spinelli and Marshall (2001:6) have put together a fascinating compilation of experienced therapists' accounts of how 'they can be a living expression, or embodiment of his or her chosen theoretical model'. Their analysis highlights the significance that the model has for each particular therapist, and how this relates inextricably to therapists' personal systems of values and beliefs. We can see then that the actual choice of therapeutic model is one that has a basis in the embodiment of that model in our practice and everyday lives.

Summary

This chapter has explored embodied styles of working. It is here that we see therapists seeking explanations further afield, attempting to develop strategies for coping with the somatic demands of being a therapist, and attempting to make sense of the intersubjective nature of the therapeutic encounter. Many therapists draw upon eastern ways of thinking to help them in their everyday practice life, so we see that meditative practices or the use of Buddhist or other eastern philosophies are common. The management of the therapist's body is brought into focus in this chapter, and we can see that therapists employ varying strategies to look at embodied phenomena. The employment of touch is seen as contentious and highly problematic, yet the benefits of this technique seem to outweigh the potential pitfalls of its use for this group of therapists. The issue of therapist health has been discussed and some candid opinions have been offered by the therapists. The health implications and the issue of touch relate to the training of these therapists.

It would seem an important part of training that health, and strategies to cope with the symptoms of burnout, should be addressed. As for touch, it would seem that clearer guidelines need to be given about the possible repercussions of using this technique, and perhaps about seeking informed consent from clients. These issues demonstrate that the method of training may need to be critiqued, so that trainee therapists are sent out into private practice properly equipped with suitable strategies. This is essential so that they are not left exposed and made vulnerable by the form of therapy which has been modelled to them during their training.

This chapter brings to a close Part 2 of this book, in which we have looked at how therapists actually describe their physical responses to their clients, seen how therapists use their body as a receiver, and explored different ways that therapists manage their bodies during the therapeutic encounter. By drawing upon our earlier discussion in Part 1 we can now see that it is possible to view therapists' embodied experience within a narrative perspective. By integrating these notions into the actual lived experience of therapists in the therapeutic encounter we can see that what is emerging is a method for using bodily phenomena. One of these is the 'body as receiver', and we have seen how therapists use this as a metaphor in their work by using terms like 'emotional heart'. We have also seen how a therapist's personal history is an important factor in how they interpret their embodied phenomena, and that this ties in with the ideas from the lived-body paradigm in acknowledging that therapy is a lived experience. Not only do therapists experience a wide range of physical phenomena but they employ a range of methods of working with the body.

In the final part of this book I wish to discuss the idea of body empathy and how we can employ a narrative approach to psychotherapist embodiment.

Part 3

The embodied psychotherapist

In Part 3 I bring together the arguments we have previously explored in relation to embodiment and how therapists experience their bodies while working with clients. Chapter 8 summarises the types of bodily phenomena that therapists frequently experience. I also introduce the idea of body empathy as a different means of describing these feelings, and as a means of incorporating the ideas of the lived-body into the therapy room. This, I suggest, has the added advantage of moving away from traditional discourse and incorporating the more egalitarian values of the narrative approach. It is also interesting to observe that therapists are in any event drawing upon cultural stories when describing their bodily feelings. An example of this is T3 who draws upon Dante's *Divine Comedy* to explain a particularly profound bodily experience. In Chapter 8 I also describe physical reactions which I have experienced while working as a psychotherapist; these too can be framed within the notion of body empathy. In the final chapter we examine the implications for psychotherapy practice of adopting an embodied narrative approach and I suggest how this may be achieved.

Chapter 8

Body empathy

When therapists describe bodily phenomena it is often but not exclusively with clients who have made a profound connection with the therapist, and this response may be positive or negative. The therapists' responses in these instances seem to have a significant bodily element. There is also the sense that the therapist is 'tuning in' to their client in some way, and that this is related to the intersubjective experience of being in therapy – hence the notion of 'body empathy'. The use of the term links to our earlier discussion on how embodied phenomena can be viewed as a significant aspect of the intersubjective nature of the therapeutic relationship. I am hoping to convey here a sense that body empathy is more of an active process compared to my earlier description of 'the body as receiver' where there seems little choice and which is a much more passive process. Body empathy has a more active quality about it and there are clear links with the other bodily phenomena presented in this book in Chapters 5, 6 and 7. Another significant aspect of body empathy is that it enables therapists to draw upon their own lived experience and that this starts to build up a body story that is related to the therapists' experience. This implies that such phenomena could be used as a form of self-disclosure, and I would argue that this is important in allowing the client to also build up their body story of the therapy.

There are two examples of body empathy that I wish to discuss at this juncture. This is not to imply that there are merely two examples but that these examples are good illustrations of this particular notion of body empathy. The first relates to a feeling of 'spell' and the second to 'the journey into hell'. As we shall see, these are predominantly body-orientated methods by which therapists incorporate their bodies into therapy, and it is the therapist's body which mediates this process. Another crucial aspect of body empathy is the often intensely personal nature of the phenomena described, and that frequently the clients that evoke such phenomena have a special connection with the therapist. These clients will often have been significant in that they present with unusual and often horrific stories, or will have evoked in the therapist much compassion and admiration for the way the client has managed to overcome and work therapeutically with an appalling personal history. The story of 'the journey into hell' is representative of this phenomenon. In this case the therapist evokes Dante's *Divine Comedy* to help explain a feeling of 'existential cold' which occurs in response to particular clients. This use of Dante's allegory is interesting in the light of the narrative turn explored in this book. Therapists also report strong bodily feelings with clients with whom they have a particularly difficult therapeutic relationship; an example of this is provided by the therapist who described the feeling of being in a 'spell'.

Spell

T7 used the word 'spell'. She introduced the idea of being in a spell with a particular client, with whom she had had a very difficult therapeutic relationship. For reasons of confidentiality it is not possible to provide details of this relationship, but suffice it to say that it had been a medium-term psychotherapeutic relationship where the therapist had found the client to be very demanding and had unfortunately ended acrimoniously. There was something almost hypnotic in the description of being in a spell, and the sense was that this feeling evoked a semblance of what it was like to inhabit her client's world. She first talked about the spell being broken with the client once she began to talk and enquire into how the client was feeling. The sensation of being in a spell was present most times with this client, and T7 made an interpretation of this feeling being about the client being scared. She would ask her client:

'Are you feeling scared at the moment?' Then she'd kind of, then she'd start to move and kinda come to life a bit and say, 'Yes, I'm feeling very scared'. And the spell would be broken, we would never stay with it for very long, her scare.

The term 'being in a spell' was one T7 used to describe other clients, but was a term she had not used until I interviewed her:

No, that's not something that I've used before, no that's something today.

It was interesting that this term arose from being interviewed – in effect T7 was thinking on her feet, and she then drew on some theoretical constructs to help develop this theme:

Well that profound, I mean you know that's part of what motivates me with my own research . . . is that profound, kind of . . . it's like an interface where . . . I think it is connected to . . . my notion of you know, profound interdependency . . .

T7 is struggling at this point to try to put words to an elusive feeling that seems to govern her life in general, and not just the therapeutic world in particular. This also highlights some of the difficulty in trying to pin down a bodily feeling with words – sometimes the correspondence between words and feelings is not good enough:

> Yes, it's a philosophy of life, yes it's something I believe to be, it's also a real kind of . . . felt experience sometimes, and some people talk about these strange and lyrical moments, that we would burn up in if we were to stay there for too long. You know I think that something happens when I have surrendered, and the other person has also and it's something that's created, and I think what we touch is God and what touch is . . . just some kind of immensely powerful source.

This sounds spiritual in nature, and T7 seems to be grappling with a profound sense that the therapeutic encounter can provoke a deep sense of God within her, and both therapist and client surrender to the relationship that they have created. For this therapist the experience is deeply rooted in her body, and she describes this further:

> . . . chest, abdomen and . . . the experience of being in somebody else's world or an in-between somewhere . . . it's like a kind of wavy feeling . . . and I might . . . Oh, it's almost like we've landed on another planet or, oh what's this? . . . And that's where this kind of this sense of spell or having, stepped into another realm . . .

This sense of spell is like another world; it has a hypnotic quality about it, a timelessness, all of which is a lived-body experience. This therapist is providing a graphic description of her lived-body experience at these moments of being in a spell:

> Yeah . . . it's really a kind of a felt experience of being in somebody else's world, you know sort of real empathy . . . that's kind of . . . you know visceral level . . .

T7 uses 'empathy' in conjunction with 'visceral', which seems to intimate a deep personal connection felt in her body. The description of felt experience would seem to fit well with the phenomenological lived-body paradigm, and for this therapist her bodily experience was a significant contribution to her therapeutic work. We can see that for T7, although the term 'spell' was a new one for her, a description of spell is a way to link a profound sense of connectedness to her clients. She clearly owns these feelings, since for her they are at a deep visceral level, which is also a deeply inscribed bodily metaphor.

We can see that such notions link well to our earlier discussion on empathy and intersubjectivity – in this instance the feeling of spell conveys a sense of the intersubjective relationship between client and therapist. To reiterate what Cole (2001: 66) suggests when talking about emotional contagion:

I may not be able to feel your pain, that most private of feelings, but I can share your suffering. It is through behaviour that this is possible, through the embodiment of inner states in a way which leads us to them being available for others to see and then more, for by taking them into themselves they can then be felt and are used to motivate another.

The idea of spell seems to fit well with this and also with Blacking's (1977) notion of shared somatic states. The client and the therapist are sharing an intimate and profound moment. This I would conjecture can only occur when the therapist is open and receptive to the impact of body empathy. Another example of this deep bodily connection is used by T3 in his description of the journey into hell.

The journey into hell

This story was related by T3 in order to make sense of an experience of feeling cold while working with clients. The bodily sensation of cold was, for him, of a particular nature, and he noted that the room temperature had nothing to do with his feeling of being cold:

> . . . this seemed to be something quite different, I would say it was a sort of an existential cold, rather than a temperature cold . . .

The use of the term 'existential cold' suggests a profound feeling, and it was clearly memorable from the times that he recalled experiencing it. This striking phenomenon had happened twice in this T3's 35-year career, and initially perplexed him; he could not make sense out of feeling intensely cold while at the same time the ambient temperature of the room was warm. The phenomenon was initially felt by his clients, and then he too felt cold:

> . . . and then in the session each of them went into an experience of the body being almost frozen, a weird thing because I also felt the cold.

He also made a link with the language of his work setting. At that time he was working as a padre in the army. The first client who evoked this response was a soldier:

> . . . and I became aware of how much the language that was used in the barrack room was the language of coldness, of freezing out, of being given a cold glance or cold shoulder, or if a soldier had made a request to authority and it had been turned down the soldier might say: 'Padre, I've got the order of the frozen mitt'.

In order to help with his understanding T3 recalled reading Dante's *Divine*

Comedy[1] (the particular edition to which he refers is Dorothy Sayers' 1949 translation):

> . . . and I can remember now with this excitement with which I realised . . . I'd forgotten, I used to carry this Dante's, this Dorothy Sayers around with me ever since I'd read it when I was at university, that the ultimate circles of hell were underneath a frozen lake.

The second time he experienced this existential cold was 30 years later, with a client who had described some dream work. His client described how he'd emerged from a tower and found to his surprise that there was a drawbridge that he could go over to escape from the tower. The therapist made the interpretation that this was the client wishing to rejoin the world. During a subsequent session the therapist used this dream to encourage the client to explore what it would be like to walk across the bridge in a guided fantasy:

> But as he was walking across the bridge, in the fantasy journey, he fell in the water, and went down, and down and down, and he said 'It's freezing, God it's freezing!', and 30 years later we were there again . . . he was frozen, he said 'I can't move', and once again just a tinge I don't know whether it was a tinge of fear, but I felt cold.

In both cases the therapist has this sense of feeling cold and the use of Dante's story helps him to make sense of what is happening in his body. Dante's story not only describes the phenomenon of the existential cold, but also provides an allegory of the therapeutic journey. At the beginning of the *Divine Comedy* Dante finds himself lost in a dark wood and is helped by the Roman poet Virgil to find the entrance into hell as a means of escaping the dark wood and finding a way out of his current predicament. This seems to mirror the beginning stage of therapy where clients seek help to extricate themselves from their own dark wood and the therapeutic journey requires a descent into their own hell with the help of a guide. In Dante's case this was Virgil; in the therapeutic scenario Dante is the client and Virgil the therapist. The two poets then embark on the descent into the circles of hell:

> [T3] It was Dante that taught me the absolute necessity that you cannot go through the therapy process on your own, if you do you get involved, 'cos the nearer you get to yourself on your own, the nearer you get totally involved and you just get caught back in the circle again . . . this is the function of the therapist, not to know more, or supply an answer, but to keep your head above water.

As the two poets descend the circles of hell they encounter various scenes. Each circle depicts a punishment which is commensurate with the sins that have been committed in the mortal world. For example, in the second circle 'the souls of the Lustful are tossed for ever upon a howling wind'(Sayers 1949: 97). The deeper the poets delve, the worse the punishments become, and the journey becomes more perilous and more frightening. Eventually they reach the frozen depths and the last circle of hell, the ninth, which is reserved for the souls of traitors, who are totally immersed in ice. It is here that the two poets come across the terrifying figure of Dis, who in Dante's story is analogous with the devil:

> [T3] He [Virgil] guides Dante, and keeps him going and they have to crawl over this figure of Dis before coming out and into the light, and this was fascinating, I would now be quite sure that that horrible figure of Dis . . . is the self, the repressed self.

This story provides a powerful metaphor for the psychotherapeutic concept of repression, and an explanation for the behaviour of clients when they access the repressed parts of themselves:

> [T3] In the modern terminology you have to come to terms with yourself, frozen in the depths, fascinating. That when Dante gets near the frozen . . . he starts to behave in a very cruel and sadistic manner kicking at the lost souls that are frozen in this depth.

The power of this metaphor is in capturing something of the therapeutic encounter between the therapist and client when the realisation of the repressed parts of ourselves becomes conscious. The client's response is then to lash out and try to run away. The significance of the therapist/Virgil position is that the client/Dante is compelled to stay with this repressed self and face the darkest parts of the self. Clearly, for T3, this story has had a big impact:

> I've learnt more of this function of the therapist from rereading Dante's journey through hell and the significance of Virgil, than from any book of psychodynamics.

This is quite a statement from a therapist who has been working for more than 35 years and who has studied the psychodynamic approach in some considerable depth. Again, body empathy would seem to be a means of describing this particular phenomenon and T3 goes on to link this concept with Dante's story by suggesting:

> You see, if there is in the literature anything relating to coldness, I don't know about it . . . the only sort of explanation that makes any sense, you know, Virgil actually goes with Dante through the depths of hell and the frozen depths so he gets bloody cold with it.

T3 goes on to ask a fascinating question, and to put forward a rationale for the origins of Dante's story:

> And the extraordinary thing is a question, where the hell did Dante get these images from; they are unique in Christian iconography, absolutely unique. Where did he get them from? I can only [think] that he had had such similar experience himself.

One of the ways T3 makes sense of this phenomenon is to suggest that an empathic bond has been established:

> I was with someone, that there was an empathic bond.

This would suggest that a connection at a profound level had been made between the client and the therapist, and just like the description of the spell above, T3 believed he had entered into their world. This is again evocative of shared somatic states and links the importance of these phenomena when looking at the inter-subjective experience of therapy.

These experiences have clearly had a significant impact on these therapists, and the body empathy seems to have deepened their connection with their clients. Overall, body empathy seems to be an active process, a form of heightened body awareness. It is active in that the therapist seems to be making choices to become involved in a complex communication process which is body mediated. The information arising from this process is used to help in an understanding of the therapeutic encounter for both therapist and client. The use of Dante's allegory is interesting in that it suggests a non-psychotherapeutic model to describe the phenomenon of cold. This has echoes of the movement to narrative ways of looking at therapy discussed earlier although clearly, in this instance, the story is neither the client's nor the therapist's. It is noteworthy, however, that other modes of thought are introduced to try and explain bodily phenomena. This suggests that classical psychotherapeutic theoretical models like countertransference may be inadequate when addressing these profound bodily phenomena. I would suggest that such phenomena are too important to ignore, and that to consider them a sub-category of countertransference or a part of projective identification does them a disservice. Rather I would prefer that we use these phenomena as part of a narrative framework. Therapists are already employing stories and metaphors within their work, and if this can be linked to the ideas put forward in this book on embodiment then I believe a rich vein of possibilities can be opened up for the psychotherapeutic community. Clearly this will need some considerable thought, but the synthesis of embodiment and narrative methods which are discussed in this book could provide a powerful, challenging and more egalitarian discourse for psychotherapy.

Practice experience

I am aware that as a practising psychotherapist I have also experienced significant and at times powerful somatic reactions when working with clients and would at this juncture like to describe some of these phenomena. These descriptions also show how the phenomena may be described as body empathy. Another reason to do this is to put my experiences alongside those of the therapists who have taken part in this study. Also, as I am making an argument that embodiment is central to the therapeutic endeavour, in a sense my embodied experience permeates the whole of my research. It seems only reasonable then to describe how I, too, have been affected. These examples are also linked to the idea of body empathy since my body was reacting to the intersubjective nature of the therapeutic relationship, and in the examples I describe I had a close therapeutic bond with my clients. In fact, in some cases I have experienced some of the phenomena described by the therapists in this study. One example of this was a visual phenomenon I experienced where my client appeared to be getting smaller and smaller. This happened on several occasions and I took it to supervision. On exploring it, I made a link with my brother who had died aged 7, when I was 4. My supervisor interpreted this phenomenon as being representative of this client's relationship with me evoking aspects of my relationship with my brother, to whom I had been very close. My client and I were engaged in a long-term psychotherapeutic relationship, and there was a close bond between us which was enhanced by us both having been to the same university at about the same time, and sharing a similar sense of humour. My supervisor's interpretation was, therefore, to link my sense of my client becoming smaller to the time when my brother was alive. I remember that at the time this interpretation was very helpful, and seemed to make sense of the therapeutic relationship with my client. It does, though, demonstrate that interpretations are linked to historical anecdotes, and it is noteworthy that I sought no alternative explanation. I would still have difficulty explaining this phenomenon, and it has not happened since with this or any other client.

Another client who had a history of sexual abuse provoked in me a profound sense of revulsion. This manifested in my body as a feeling of nausea. I have written about this client elsewhere (Shaw 1998).[2] In supervision I explored this sensation of nausea as it was a frequent occurrence. Again, my bodily response was attributed to how it must have felt for my client when she was abused. The psychotherapeutic interpretation was that I was experiencing a form of counter-transference, that my feeling of nausea was representative of what my client was feeling at that time in the therapy session. This was helpful at the time, but does seem to miss another, perhaps obvious, interpretation – hearing stories of abuse is very unpleasant, and perhaps it is a perfectly normal reaction to simply feel sick when confronted with a particularly horrific story. Thus, this is not so much a countertransferential response, but more of a shared experience when hearing about a particular aspect of someone's story. In this instance I was able to confirm with my client that she, too, felt nauseous at the same time that I experienced nausea. Perhaps we were both reacting in a similar way to the retelling of her story.

I offer these cases as examples of the types of physical response that I have felt, and to show that these are similar to the types of response reported by the therapists in this book. Also, I realised after the first few interviews that I, too, was experiencing physical phenomena, some of which seemed to bear some relation to the subject matter of the interview. The most striking of these occurred with T14 where she described a nightmare:

> I've had on one occasion, I had a dream which was her [she is refer-
> ring to her client at this point] dream it wasn't mine, it didn't fit into
> my dreams at all . . . I mean she's tortured by these sort of terrible
> nightmares . . . which at times she's described and they were so
> horrific and like it's hard to, it sounds a bit like a screenplay for a
> horror movie or whatever, I haven't sort of felt too much in those
> but one night I had woke up after this absolutely horrendous
> nightmare and it took me some time to realise . . . I thought I've
> never had anything like that in my life, I suddenly realised that this
> was exactly the sort of nightmare that she describes . . . so it was you
> know it wasn't the same story but it was just like the quality of
> nightmare, so that was quite a scary experience really.

This was a very vivid description, and the note I made to myself after this interview was as follows:

> I had a dream last night, almost a nightmarish dream, very unlike me.
> I almost never have nightmares, in fact I can't remember the last time
> I did. Someone was in the house, a white shadowy figure. I woke up
> feeling very scared and my heart was racing. Has this something to
> do with the interview?

It was almost as if I was repeating the behaviour of the therapist with her client. Although I knew the therapist, as we had been on some workshops together, I had no information about this particular client, and it was a surprise to me during the interview when she recounted her dream experience.

I had another experience in this interview where my bodily reaction resembled that of the therapist:

> [T14] One of the bodily responses that I get which I'm starting to see
> as significant is that, especially with clients at certain points where
> they are very regressed and very small and I'm being . . . sort of
> nurturing to them somehow, and as I start to think about this it's
> quite funny, I get a lot of tummy rumbling, yeah a lot of tummy noise,
> yeah, it's starting now as I begin to talk about it . . .

I made a note during the interview: 'I felt still and my stomach rumbled'. This happened at the same time that the therapist felt her tummy rumbling.

I certainly did not have such experiences with all the interviewees and some of my physical reactions were quite vague – for example, having a headache after some interviews. The examples described are mentioned because they seem to relate to the interview and correspond to the bodily sensations felt by the therapists. It could, of course, have been coincidence that I happened to feel these sensations at the same time. I am, though, a psychotherapist and these phenomena are experienced by psychotherapists, so it is likely that I will be open to receiving information in the same way that my interviewees describe.

This may also be a process which we all use but, as therapists are trained to be receptive or condemned to be listeners (T12), it is not surprising that such bodily phenomena are so apparent among members of the interview group. Also, as I am trained in this way of working I, too, am sensitised to receiving such information. I may also be as suggestible as the therapists in this study, since I have undergone a similar induction into the psychotherapy profession.

Within the literature on the supervision of therapists there is the notion of 'parallel process' which provides a psychotherapeutic perspective on the phenomenon of body empathy. In a relationship with the supervisor, the supervisee may re-enact an aspect of the therapist-client relationship: 'Parallel process occurs when the central dynamic process of the counselling relationship is unconsciously acted out by the trainee in the supervision relationship' (Holloway 1995: 98). The interviews in this research have similarities to a supervision session in that there is a therapist talking about a client, and I am in the position of the supervisor (while clearly not engaging in supervision). As will be clear from my developing critique of psychotherapeutic discourse, I see the description of this phenomenon as problematic in purely psychodynamic terminology. The supervisory relationship, like all other therapeutic relationships, is embodied. I am advocating a deeper exploration of these embodied states by suggesting that, in the long term, it will be more fruitful for the psychotherapy profession to engage in a wider perspective on embodiment than to attempt to seek yet more psychotherapeutic rationales for somatic experience.

Summary

In this chapter we have focused on the notion of body empathy. This concept provides an opportunity to view the physical reactions we feel as therapists in a different light, away from the traditional psychotherapeutic spotlight. Body empathy is more of an active process when compared to our earlier discussion on 'the body as receiver', and has the potential for understanding physical feelings that occur within the therapeutic encounter. Often when therapists describe their physical experiences it is with clients who have made a strong impact on them, and a strong empathic bond has been established; hence the term 'body empathy' has been suggested to convey something of the intersubjective nature of this profound experience.

Chapter 9

Psychotherapist embodiment and narrative

In this chapter I summarise the main arguments put forward and discussed on embodiment and narrative. One of the consequences of conducting the research for this book has been a realisation that the type of language we use to interpret our clients' narrative is sometimes inadequate. This will be discussed in a section entitled 'Professional and personal discourse'. The result of raising these issues has been the growing realisation that we need to take a good hard look at therapeutic discourse, so within this chapter there is also a section entitled 'Towards a critical psychotherapy' which addresses this particular issue.

Throughout this book the central argument I have put forward is that the therapeutic encounter is embodied, and the therapist's body is therefore a vital part of this encounter. Therapists may well be suggestible to embodied states of being due to the nature of therapy, a peculiarly intense and intimate relationship unlike other adult relationships common in western society. Also, the manner of psychotherapy training, within the humanistic tradition, places considerable emphasis on experiential learning; this unwittingly sensitises therapists to tune into this aspect of themselves. The embodied nature of the relationship probably echoes an aspect of therapists' lives and, therefore, they feel this in their bodies.

Throughout this book therapists' bodily phenomena can be seen to be helpful in constructing a therapeutic narrative. The therapist's body can be seen as a vehicle for conveying something of the intersubjective nature of the therapeutic relationship. If this is done via a narrative framework, issues of self-disclosure arise. However if, as narrative methodology suggests, the primary purpose of therapy is the telling of the client's story, and the therapist reacts in a physical way to this story, it would seem imperative that this bodily information is used within the therapeutic relationship in order to help listen to the client's story. It is the type of information which could become part of a co-constructed, shared therapeutic narrative, and become a crucial aspect of therapy. There are two quotes that for me highlight the importance of psychotherapist embodiment, and emphasise how central our bodies are in the therapeutic encounter:

> [T13] . . . often what I am doing when I'm with clients or when I'm in any situation I suppose, is like coming back home, it's the sense like that my body is my home, I come back home to it.

[T11] I mean, I live in my body, I would have nowhere else to live if I didn't have a body, so yes I am embodied.

Both these therapists see their bodily sense as central: T13 sees himself as coming back to his body in the sense that it is his home; T11 states clearly that she is embodied, which is the essence of this book – she is an embodied psychotherapist. In particular, psychotherapist embodiment relates to the way that therapists talk about and refer to their bodies during the therapeutic encounter, and how this then becomes a body narrative.

One of the features when researching this book was that it has become important to address some of the emerging problems involved in using language to describe bodily phenomena. In particular, it seemed important to include something of the nature of psychotherapeutic interpretations and the basis for the use of such language. We can see clearly that therapists use their bodies in a rich and varied manner, at times borrowing from other cultures to help them understand some of these bodily phenomena. It is almost as if therapists have an ability to resonate with their clients, and that this is a highly intuitive process. This process seemed to be replicated in my own body and this is why I have described some of my own bodily phenomena, both as therapist and researcher (see Chapter 8). In the therapeutic encounter the body becomes highly important in terms of the ability of therapists to empathise at a somatic level with their clients. This somatic resonance I would argue is a crucial aspect of the therapeutic encounter. T11 sums this up beautifully when describing a poignant moment with a client which was physically painful for both:

. . . and then at that moment it is a shared experience, a profoundly shared experience and . . . in different bodies.

It is this ability to feel body empathy which I would suggest has great relevance to psychotherapy, and this is a profoundly embodied experience. I am not at all keen that such experiences should be regarded merely as a sub-section of counter-transference, but as a significant aspect of the embodied encounter between therapist and client. It is for this reason that I am suggesting such phenomena be framed within a narrative perspective. The notion of using a narrative methodology arose from an analysis of the types of discourse that therapists used to describe their physical responses. These were drawn from both personal and professional worlds. I would therefore like to turn our attention to this issue.

Professional and personal discourse

There are many examples of discourse employed in this study. For the purposes of this discussion I wish to concentrate on the term 'material', which is used by several of the interviewees. This term acts as a means of focusing on an aspect of psychotherapeutic discourse which permeates the language used by psychotherapists in this study. I have also chosen this term as it acts as a pivot around which other discourses have been employed.

T11 discusses at some length the usage of this term in the therapeutic context:

> I made a lot of links between my personal life at that time and my illness and divorce and so on yeah . . . yeah, I think that's more the link really. But I do pick up client material very quickly in my body.

She provides a link here with her personal life and thereby connects the importance of her personal history to her ability to pick up 'client material'. The process of picking up client material appears to be mediated via her body. This material seemed to be located in the client's body, and thereby evoked the medical discourse of 'clinical material' and of contagion – i.e. this material is the substance which can be worked with therapeutically:

> Yeah, I can, I mean I can think about one particular client whose mother was also always ill, you know that was the theme . . . and it really took a long time for her to be able to really engage with me again, because she feared that her material would contaminate me even further . . . and you know, therefore, the transference was really powerful and you know, the maternal transference was really powerful.

She points out that the client's material could contaminate her and therefore further evokes medical discourse around bodies and notions of clinical or bodily waste. It is as if the client material may be toxic. This has similarities to T10 who referred to her client with 'leaky boundaries'. There is clearly a sense here that there is something which can transfer from the client to the therapist. 'Transference' is used in a very particular way here, as maternal transference, and the interpretation is clear at this point, as the therapist is stating unequivocally that her bodily experience is related to the client's experience of her mother (i.e. the client's mother):

> [T11] Well, she was projecting mother on me, and also, therefore, in Gestalt terms retroflecting a lot of her own stuff, and holding on in her own body . . . you know the material that needed to be out there between us really.

T11 is describing a complex phenomenon here; not only is the client projecting mother on to her, but the client is taking back or retroflecting (a Gestalt term which describes a process whereby clients defend themselves against external agents), material into her own body. 'Material' in this context seems to refer to phenomena put into the therapist and, at the same time, retained or reclaimed into the client's body. A further explanation is provided by T11:

> Yes, holding on in her own body the impulse to drive out and put it out there, either to be angry or be sad or . . . you know feeling it in

> your own body, but not being able to do anything with it, but for fear that she would contaminate me, my body even more with her material. It was a very powerful, blocked effect that it had.

The idea of contamination arises again in T11's account, and she hints at this material being somehow real and tangible, as if it could physically enter the therapist's body:

> I made a lot of links between my personal life at that time and my illness and divorce and so on yeah, I think that's more the link really. But I do pick up client material very quickly in my body, I mean that's the other thing, and so that being with this particular client who's very blocked in her body, it was almost like we got very confluent, in other words we were going down the same black hole . . . both of us holding stuff in our bodies.

T11 introduces the idea that she is confluent,[1] a notion derived from Gestalt discourse. In this process boundaries are blurred and there is a merging of the experiences of client and therapist. In this instance, the therapist is using the term to denote a merging of body experience, mediated in part by this therapist's ability to pick up material easily in her body. This suggests a sophisticated form of body communication and, because the therapist is sensitive to picking up this information, it can be used within the therapeutic encounter.

T1 provides another example of how material is used:

> I would say that I was having a reactive countertransferential response to the client, so I am responding to the unconscious client material at that point. If it had continued it may have moved into projective identification, and I may have started to act something out you know . . . felt manipulated to respond in a way, as it happens I didn't.

There is no doubt for this therapist that her response, which she describes in terms of countertransference, is a result of client material. This material is also unconscious at this point. Clearly, this is only one interpretation of what is occurring at this moment; since the material is unconscious there must be some debate about what is being felt by the therapist. However, the therapist is adamant that her bodily feelings are caused by some unconscious material in the client. T1 goes on to suggest that this could have moved into projective identification, which would seem to suggest a further interpretative layer upon the notion of the client's unconscious material.

I think it must be strongly debated whether or not therapists 'pick up' their client's symptoms or material; I would suggest it is more likely that the embodied nature of the relationship echoes an aspect of the therapists' lives, or their lived experience, and therefore they feel this in their bodies. The therapists in this study have, after all, discussed aspects of themselves which they consider important, (e.g. asthma or being 'condemned' to work as a therapist). Clearly a therapist is encouraged to look at their past life through a psychotherapeutic lens via their own therapy. It is not surprising, then, that somatic phenomena come to be viewed through the same lens. We can also see that there is a link between personal and professional discourse (as seen above with T11) and, since therapists are required to undergo their own therapy, this is not surprising. However, this does pose the question: with what authority do therapists make their interpretations? Does it derive from professional discursive practices or from personal experience? The most likely answer to this is that there is a merging of these discourses. One of the problems of adopting this particular interpretative methodology is that subjective phenomena tend to be described as 'real', sounding like something substantial and concrete, and this suggests that there is a reification of subjective experience. T3 was actually aware of this problem when describing how therapeutic theories were in his opinion employed:

> I prefer the mythological images of the water to the id, they are more vivid and also less modern and less abstract, the chaos of the waters, 'Where are you, what does this mean for you?' Whereas concepts like the id, fine it helps us to focus down, but it goes dangerously towards what bedevils central psychotherapy and its theories and that is reification.

This therapist prefers to draw upon images from mythology, and used Dante's allegory of hell in our earlier discussion on body empathy in Chapter 8. The use of mythological images and stories would, in some ways, seem to be a better fit with an exploration of subjective experience, and a move away from dogmatic theoretical constructs and the reification of subjectivity prevalent within psychotherapy. I would suggest that this is another compelling reason to adopt a narrative methodology for psychotherapy, since this may offer a way forward in exploring subjective phenomena in a non-reified manner. Psychotherapy thus becomes a means to explore narrative, rather than impose a rigid psychotherapeutic theoretical construct onto an unsuspecting client. In some ways the approach of dramatherapy is already achieving this by incorporating a wide variety of methods to explore clients' stories (e.g. role playing, mask making, etc.). Indeed, as Jennings (1998: 37) points out when critiquing the psychoanalytic approaches of Freud, Jung and the more recent object-relations school: '[they] attach reductionistic meanings to observed phenomena. This "meaning", if it is never challenged becomes a closed system of thought, a *reduction* of understanding'.

Perhaps one of the problems in the psychotherapeutic exploration of subjective experience is related to its historical roots in medicine, leading to reductive mechanistic discourses becoming pervasive in the language of the therapist.

'Material' is just one example of this problem. Clearly it is important for therapists to have a means of describing subjective experience, but there is a tendency to reify this experience. It has been suggested that reification may be useful for psychotherapists: 'reification may be extremely helpful from the point of view of description' (Sandler 1988: 1). However, it is important for us to remember that it is *only description*, although the impression is sometimes given that descriptions are actual examples of reality. This is, perhaps, a problem of the original training experience where therapists are expected to imbibe information with little questioning. The concept of 'material' would seem to fit into this category. The pitfalls here are that therapists trained with such notions come to believe that subjective material is 'real' or reified. They slip back into the Cartesian dualistic discourse (see our earlier discussion in Chapter 1). There is perhaps a more insidious consequence – that of using such theoretical constructions to exert power in the therapeutic relationship. If countertransferential responses are believed to be real, in the hands of an unscrupulous therapist this information could be used on a vulnerable client to meet the needs, not of the client, but of the therapist (Jehu 1994; Heath 2000). It is here that the importance of challenging psychotherapeutic theories is crucial, and as therapists it behoves us to be aware of the type of language we use in our interpretations. By adopting a critical stance to the language of psychotherapy, we would be able to uncover and understand the inherent power dynamics prevalent within the language used in our own particular model of therapy.

Psychotherapist embodiment

The vast majority of the literature which examines either the body or embodiment focuses on the client's body. However, by its very nature, psychotherapy requires a relationship which has been clearly identified as a common factor (Norcross and Goldfried 1992). It is important to remember that there are two bodies present in the therapy room. This study has examined how therapists view their own bodies in the therapeutic encounter, and, far from being absent, the body is very present. We have observed that not only is the therapist's body present, but the therapists in this study use their bodies in a highly intuitive way to help manage the therapeutic process. They also manage their own bodies in response to potential health implications, and have devised complex theoretical constructs to help explain the nature of some of the bizarre phenomena reported.

Psychotherapist embodiment suggests that a potential starting point for acquiring knowledge about the therapeutic encounter is an understanding of embodiment. As Merleau-Ponty (1962: 203) suggests: 'The theory of the body is already a theory of perception'. The phenomena described by the therapists in this book arise from experiences within their own bodies, not their clients' bodies. It is by interpreting their own lived experience through a psychotherapeutic lens that therapists produce claims to knowledge about their clients. This is clearly problematic, as in the case of 'client material' and the reification of subjective experience. These somatic phenomena are therapist responses which, through a layer of psychotherapeutic interpretation, become located within the body of the client. However, what is possible is an exploration of therapist embodiment; this may have something to say about the therapeutic encounter, and I am sure that it is of importance in the process of a therapeutic relationship, and has a bearing on the intersubjective nature of such a relationship. It can though, unless discussed with the client, only ever mean anything to the therapist.

Body perception is an intensely personal experience. Therapists must realise that theories about their bodies relate to their perceptions of the therapeutic encounter, not necessarily their clients' perceptions. I, therefore, echo the sentiments of Halling and Goldfarb (1991: 328) and urge the psychotherapy profession to reconsider its position regarding the use of psychotherapy discourse to describe somatic phenomena:

> To take embodiment seriously is to take seriously how one speaks and how one listens to self and other. The recognition that one is an embodied being includes the acknowledgement that even in a situation of being an observer one is an involved observer – someone who is being affected by and is affecting what is taking place. Being a researcher or a therapist requires that one become fully and thoughtfully involved. It is as if one is engaged in a dance moving forward and moving back: one steps closer and steps away, has an effect and is affected, all as an embodied being.

In our everyday work as therapists we deal with embodied phenomena. The body is far too important a subject for the profession not to take seriously. My contention is that we currently do not have the language to express and explore a phenomenon like embodiment. There is a need for the psychotherapy profession to drop its inward-looking attitude to its discourse, and embrace the wider anthropological, philosophical and sociological concepts of embodiment. This would inevitably require a critique of current psychotherapeutic discursive practices. The presentation of psychotherapist embodiment in this book, I suggest, offers a starting point for this critique. The types of discourse employed by therapists to describe their bodies have demonstrated a general lack of critical reflexivity and the use of unchallenged concepts from a variety of psychotherapeutic theoretical models. The lack of critical reflexivity has uncovered potential problems around power in the therapeutic encounter, and therapists' bodies may become involved in this process. This may happen initially via assumptions about their own somatic states during their work with clients, which remain unchallenged. It must also be remembered from the literature that the therapist's body could be seen as a fertile ground for abusive practices from inappropriate touch to more serious sexual abuses. At the same time the exploration of embodiment has suggested that working as a psychotherapist may involve a risk to health.

A key feature that cannot be ignored is how we as therapists use language to describe our sense of embodiment. Throughout the research for this book it has become clear to me that there are problems with the language we use to describe somatic feelings. My assertion at this juncture is that my research has revealed deficiencies and inadequacies within the discourses employed by therapists to describe embodied phenomena; in particular, the nature of psychotherapeutic interpretation has been shown to lack a critical reflexivity. It is clear that the therapist's body is used as a means for monitoring the psychotherapeutic process. One aspect of this may be an intuitive process of empathising somatically with the client – or 'body empathy' as I described it in Chapter 8. This process of body-orientated communication would seem to be an important area to research and incorporate within psychotherapy training, but this would need to be investigated in a rigorous and critical fashion. I am not convinced that we can class such phenomena as merely aspects of countertransference. Indeed, the employment of this type of psychotherapeutic discourse would seem inappropriate to use in the context of the findings that I have presented in this book. The types of phenomena described would seem to represent a profound connection between therapist and client, and are informative of the embodied therapeutic relationship, highlighting the intersubjective nature of therapy. I would suggest that psychotherapy in general needs to embrace other disciplines in order to investigate and theorise about these phenomena. This is perhaps where qualitative approaches to research are well suited, where it is the *process* rather than the *outcome* of psychotherapy which is investigated. Indeed, this was the approach I used in the study presented in this book. Such research values the subjective experience of its participants. Instead of engaging in psychotherapeutic-centred discourse, and continually attempting to see all phenomena within one frame of reference (namely a psychotherapeutic model), I am advocating embracing the challenges of critical reflexivity. This would necessitate viewing embodied phenomena through a wider lens, and incorporating the traditions of, for example, the lived-body paradigm. This is likely to be an uncomfortable process, as it would require an analysis of the discourse currently used within the profession and, by implication, necessitate a thorough critique of psychotherapy training regimes. The importance to psychotherapy of this project is clear since, if these somatic phenomena are commonplace, as is suggested by the literature and my research, then they are far too important to ignore, and potentially represent a different way of viewing the therapeutic encounter.

The arguments I am putting forward in this book have addressed one of the issues within the therapy world – i.e. much is written about the client's body but little has been written about the therapist's body. The therapists in this research have used their somatic experiences to help them navigate the complexities of the therapeutic encounter. In doing so they are emphasising the importance of their bodily perceptions. This clearly links with the ideas on the lived-body paradigm discussed earlier. We have seen how the lived-body experience of therapists has been important for them in making interpretations about the therapeutic encounter. The source of this knowledge is the therapist's body. Therefore, the interpretations offered in this research can be seen to be embodied therapeutic knowledge. It must be stressed that this knowledge is 'local' – i.e. it relates to particular instances between the therapist and the client, and no generalisations can necessarily be drawn from it.

The theme of psychotherapist embodiment also suggests that the body is very present in the therapy room. The therapists in this study tended to report bodily sensations that were uncomfortable, and hence their bodily state was more noticeable. As Leder (1990: 160) suggests: 'The body stands out at times of dysfunction only because its usual state is to be lost in the world'. Thus, far from the body receding into the background, it was felt as present and, in some cases, this brought with it considerable somatic discomfort. Often, when clients invoked in the therapist some bodily phenomenon, that client had a strong connection in some way to the therapist. It was almost as if the more emotionally involved the therapist was with their client, the more significant bodily phenomena appeared.

The importance of the work presented here is that knowledge of the therapeutic encounter can be acquired somatically by psychotherapists. This knowledge can make a significant contribution to the therapeutic encounter. It is therefore an important, though not easy, task for therapists to acknowledge their bodily contribution: 'The body is never a simple presence, but that which is away from itself, a being of difference and absence' (Leder 1990: 103).

The description of bodily sensations with words is also problematic. It is impossible to check the correspondence of a word to a bodily feeling as this represents a translation of a somatic experience into a verbal one. Although it is true that verbal experience is also somatic experience, it is different in quality to, for example, feeling asthmatic or feeling pregnant, which were just two of the somatic experiences reported by therapists in this research. Therefore, the use of words to convey these experiences is difficult and further confused by the psychotherapeutic interpretations offered to explain these phenomena. A significant feature to emerge from the exploration of embodiment was that therapists seemed to receive all sorts of bodily information, and acted upon this within therapy, yet this way of working was not addressed in the training of therapists. This would seem to be an omission, and, I would suggest that there is a need to include teaching on this in psychotherapy training. Possibly this could be done by exploring the nature of embodiment, and also by looking at some of the management strategies employed by therapists in their practice lives. In this book, Chapters 6, 7 and 8 could provide a basis for a body curriculum for psychotherapy training.

It seems that, within the profession itself, there is a tacit acceptance of the need to look after oneself as a practitioner. However, this is not an explicit aspect of training either, and tends to be learned in an *ad hoc* fashion after training. If there are health implications for working as a therapist, it would seem an important area to address; it also indicates another avenue for further research. As discussed earlier, there is a literature on burnout, and it would seem that work could be done to link the ideas presented here with health management and styles of working. There are also potential positive benefits to health: some therapists in this study reported changes in their eczema, asthma and lifestyle changes which are all considered by the therapists concerned to be related to their own personal therapy, and to have enhanced their state of well-being.

Clearly the emphasis of this book is on psychotherapy, and I am also a practising psychotherapist, and have been through the training required to be on the UKCP register. I am also a BACP registered practitioner. I am, therefore, bringing to this research a knowledge of psychotherapy culture. In order to bring to this research a reflexive attitude it has been important to acknowledge my experience as a practitioner of psychotherapy as well as a researcher. At times this has been an uncomfortable process for me, and at other times it has been enlightening. I am very aware that, as a psychotherapist, I have had my successes and failures. My work has provided me with many rewarding experiences, but the theoretical constructs I learned during training do not seem to do justice to some of the work that my clients and I have completed. Nevertheless, concepts such as transference and countertransference have been useful in my work. I have come to realise that they can only be used as metaphors, and that an open mind in such work is essential. The exploration of reification, which is apparently endemic in the practice of psychotherapy, has been a challenge to my practice, and the exploration of discourse has challenged my mode of working as well as my own assumptions about how psychotherapy functions. By engaging in reflexivity at this level I have had to confront the discourses that I use in my psychotherapy practice. This has been a considerable challenge and has at times made me very confused regarding how I practise psychotherapy.

I have also questioned the model of therapy in which I was trained. I have had to challenge the claims to knowledge that I make as a therapist and, as a concomitant, I have questioned my psychotherapeutic interpretations. At times while I was conducting my research it was very difficult for me to practise as a psychotherapist. I am, though, convinced that psychotherapy can make a significant and important contribution to people's lives in a very positive sense. I will practise in future with much more awareness of the issues of power and discourse which operate in the therapy room, as well as of my own embodied state. I now work in a way that acknowledges my embodied experience, and am more aware of how my physical reactions can be used within the therapeutic encounter. This increased awareness of embodiment has enhanced my practice life and has helped me to integrate my lived-body experience into the therapy room with my clients; I, too, am an embodied psychotherapist.

Narrative

In this book I have also explored the potential links with embodiment and the narrative way of looking at therapy, since as Boothe *et al.* (1999: 258) suggest: 'Everyday narratives refer to events, but the act of narrating does not serve merely to retell facts. Instead, in narrating, we recount personal experience. We do this suggestively, attempting to involve the listener emotionally'. I would suggest that the emotional involvement of the listener is an embodied response, and that psychotherapist embodiment encapsulates this ability to listen and become involved in a client's story. This relates to our earlier discussion on narrative where McLeod (1996: 182) has observed: 'Another critical feature of narrative is that it is constructed and embodies an active protagonist'.

Two examples from my practice may help to illustrate this point. I was invited to run a workshop in Oslo (Shaw 2000b) which related to the client I mentioned earlier (see p. 140). I invited my client to write a contribution I could take with me to present at the workshop. A quote from her piece sums up the importance of being heard: 'I was given the chance to say what I thought as an adult, but best of all was that I was not just listened to but actually *heard* by someone that did not give up on me'. When therapy finished with the client who had appeared to be getting smaller and smaller, I received a card a few days later which simply said: 'Thanks for your ears over the last three years! Glad we got through it together'. Both of these comments suggest the importance of being able to listen, and become involved in someone else's story. These abilities are, I suggest, important in constructing meaning within the therapeutic encounter, for both client and therapist. Listening and involvement in this context are, by their very nature, bodily phenomena, and thus constitute a form of local psychotherapeutic embodied knowledge. The therapists in this research use various examples of embodied phenomena to make meaning out of the therapeutic encounter (e.g. gut reactions, visual experiences etc.).

The importance of this to psychotherapy is clear: the therapeutic encounter is inherently an embodied experience and the research presented in this book opens up an avenue for deepening the understanding of psychotherapist embodiment. However, this requires an acceptance that current psychotherapeutic constructs to describe such phenomena may need to be changed. I would suggest that psychotherapy examine its training regimes, and adopt the position put forward by Jennings (1998: 139) when discussing the training of dramatherapists:

> You will need to have a basic working knowledge of social anthropology, both to understand people in their social and cultural contexts as well as a range of rituals, symbols and myths in their cultural context. Anthropological understanding will at least guard against using a myth, for example, purely from a psychoanalytic perspective or as a way of reinforcing this narrow view of human nature.

One of my key points is that the embodied knowledge presented in this book needs examining through a wider lens and the narrative movement is one means of achieving a broader perspective on the therapeutic encounter. This, as we have already discussed, necessitates a critique of psychotherapeutic discourse, and it is to this issue that I now wish to turn.

Towards a critical psychotherapy

I have taken a quote from the flyleaf of Spinelli's book *Demystifying Therapy* (1994) to begin this section: 'Spinelli has become aware increasingly of the philosophical naiveté of many therapists – their unnecessary and artificial reliance on "techniques" and their abuse of power bestowed on them in the therapeutic relationship'.

During the course of my research it became clear as I analysed the interviews that I needed to look carefully at the way therapists interpreted their bodily phenomena. I remember vividly that initially I had great difficulty with looking at psychotherapy discourse. One reason for this was my use of this same discourse in my practice – for example, I would have used terms like 'client material' in the same way my interviewees had employed them. I noticed in myself an unwillingness to challenge the assumptions upon which I based my psychotherapeutic interpretations, and thereby my practice as a psychotherapist. In other words, I had to face up to my own philosophical naiveté as regards my practice. However, it was by engaging in an analysis of psychotherapy culture, and looking at the type of language that I and the interviewees used to describe bodily phenomena, that it became clear that I could not avoid a critique of psychotherapy discourse.

One of the consequences of this critique was that I came to view one of the concepts of somatisation in a different way. I began my research journey fascinated by this term which was largely a legacy of the time when I worked predominantly as an osteopath. I had the idea that an exploration of this term could somehow integrate my two professional lives, that of osteopath and psychotherapist, and that I would be able to operate as a truly holistic practitioner. I now know this is not possible because both disciplines operate from a dualistic perspective and people who come to see an osteopath have very different expectations to those who seek out the services of a psychotherapist. I do realise that there is some transferability of skills between the two and for me my practice as psychotherapist and osteopath has been enhanced by undertaking this research. But it is now clearer to me that firm boundaries need to be in place, so for example I will not treat any of my psychotherapy clients osteopathically due to the contentious nature of touch within the psychotherapy setting. However, an enlightening moment for me arose when I realised that using the concepts of embodiment that I have described in this book it is possible to bring the body into therapy.

An analysis of somatisation did, however, produce a useful avenue of study: the types of discourse used by therapists. This was not the original intention of my research, but there are clear implications here for psychotherapy. Although the types of discourse which therapists use will be influenced by their training model, there would appear to be a need for some clarification. With so many different forms of therapy, there is a concomitant number of discourses; underlying this is the problem of correspondence of words to subjective phenomena. We have already highlighted the problem of reification within psychotherapeutic discourse (e.g. the use of the term 'client material' to suggest something substantive which is subjective). I would suggest that in order to be clearer about our knowledge base we need to address our use of discourse, and examine the reasons for the existence of large numbers of single-school psychotherapies. It could be argued that the integrative psychotherapy movement is already undertaking this task, but I am advocating a thorough discourse analysis of psychotherapeutic language and practice. A potential way forward in this enterprise is an exploration of narrative forms of therapy (McLeod 1997). The narrative movement explicitly examines discourse and the power relationship between therapist and client: 'Narrative theory reminds us that there are many cultural dominant discourses about therapy and therapists that place the therapist in a privileged position relative to the client' (Richert 1999: 276).

If we can assume that psychotherapy is a discipline which aims to explore subjective experience, it is vital that the language used in this endeavour undergoes a critique. Since at best language can only be an attempt at describing subjectivity, it is important for the psychotherapy community to be honest about this and accept that its theoretical constructs are metaphors for subjective experience, and not 'real things' in themselves. For example, transference does not exist *per se* – you cannot pick it up and physically hold it in your hands. It is a Freudian theoretical construct, albeit a very useful idea, and it exists, if it exists at all, in the minds of therapists who happen to use the term. Clients may use different terminology to describe transference, but they may experience something akin to the therapist's notion of it. This in itself does not make the phenomenon 'transference', rather it demon-strates that there are different ways of experiencing and describing this particular phenomenon. Human subjectivity is by its very nature different from person to person. This basic philosophical position needs to be conveyed in the training of therapists which, as we have seen, is inherently problematic. If the people responsible for training are unaware of or, more disturbingly, not willing to analyse their own rhetoric, then it could prove difficult to change the culture and practice of current psychotherapeutic discourse. The dogma of single-school therapies does, after all, justify an adherence to a particular model and thereby promote a tendency to resist a critique of its entrenched position.

I would suggest that embodiment could also prove a useful means of addressing the philosophical naiveté highlighted by Spinelli, since there are definite links with the phenomenological movement via the lived-body paradigm. Therapists are very sensitive to their own embodied state and the spectrum of physical feelings explored in this book shows that this is a strikingly consistent theme. Therapists are also readily able to access this information about their embodied selves in the therapeutic encounter. I would suggest that psychotherapeutic discourse becomes the subject of rigorous critical scrutiny. This would not be with the aim of looking for a replacement discourse for, as Kaye (1996: 235–6) points out: 'no discourse is inherently liberating or oppressive, it behoves all of us practitioners not to follow blindly (or merely seek to refine) practice prescriptions, but rather to scrutinise the institutional and disciplinary knowledge by which we are positioned'. The aim is to challenge psychotherapeutic models and generally adopt a critical view to theory construction. If an exploration of subjectivity is the main aim of psychotherapy, then a study of embodiment could provide a means of moving towards a different method of creating knowledge for psychotherapy. That is to say, a study of the lived experience of the therapeutic encounter could be a means of acquiring psychotherapeutic knowledge. I hope that throughout our discussion on embodiment I have contributed to this project by exploring and analysing the problems of psychotherapeutic discourse when trying to describe embodied experience.

Conclusion

In order to capture the essence of the experience of the therapist's body in the therapeutic encounter I have coined the term 'psychotherapist embodiment'. This is a complex subject and I have tried to tackle the issue of mind-body dualism which is inherent in our western society. In a sense embodiment is an attempt to address this mind-body dualism and introduce a holistic method for viewing the therapeutic relationship – or put another way, my research has from a clinical theoretical point of view tried to collapse the mind-body dualism present within psychotherapy culture. I am aware, too, that an inextricable aspect of this work has been the necessity to look at language and the types of interpretation we as therapists use to describe the variety of physical reactions we feel while working within the therapeutic relationship. This has been challenging for me and I suspect for the reader. My solution to this particular language problem has been to advocate the incorporation of narrative methods into the therapeutic relationship. This at least allows for psychotherapist embodiment to become an overt part of the relationship, and not become hidden in the murky waters of countertransference, a term which I do not think captures the essence of psychotherapeutic embodiment.

We are embodied beings who happen to be therapists. Whether we are 'condemned' to be therapists, as suggested by T12, is open to debate, but our past experiences clearly have an impact on how we perceive the world, and inevitably on how we perceive the therapeutic encounter. Our ability to draw upon our lived experience helps us to use our sense of embodiment during our therapy work. By being aware of what our bodies are saying to us while working therapeutically, and with the ability to use this information in an overt manner, it is possible to contribute to the intersubjective nature of therapy. Our embodied sense is a means of contributing to a therapeutic story that is co-constructed by client and therapist.

Appendix: summary of interviewees

Therapist number and gender (f/m)		Professional affiliation	Years of practice experience	Practice type
T1	f	B, U	15–20	Integrative
T2	f	B, U	15–20	Integrative
T3	m	B	30–35	Eclectic including clinical theology, psychodynamic and humanistic
T4	f	B, U	5–10	Gestalt
T5	f	D	5–10	Dramatherapy, psychodynamic
T6	m	B, U	5–10	Gestalt and integrative
T7	f	B, U	5–10	Gestalt
T8	f	B, U	5–10	Person-centred and integrative
T9	f	B	5–10	Integrative
T10	f	U	5–10	Integrative and gestalt
T11	f	U	10–15	Integrative
T12	f	B, U	15–20	Integrative, psychodynamic and person-centred
T13	m	NZ	20–25	Gestalt and person-centred
T14	f	U	5–10	Gestalt, cognitive-behavioural

B = BACP (British Association of Counselling and Psychotherapy)
D = British Association for Dramatherapists
NZ = New Zealand Association of Counsellors
U = UKCP (United Kingdom Council for Psychotherapy)
(humanistic and integrative psychotherapy section)

Notes

Introduction

1 'Client' is a term used throughout this book to denote the person who seeks therapy and is a term used by both psychotherapists and counsellors. Psychoanalytic therapists often use the term 'patient'.
2 For a full account of the methodology and data analysis used in the original research see Shaw (2000a).
3 Those who belonged to the UKCP were registered under the Humanistic and Integrative Psychotherapy Section (HIPS) of the Council.
4 This is just a brief description of some of the ethical issues. As a member of the BACP and the UKCP, I have also been directed by their respective research guidelines which I have used throughout this research. For a more in-depth discussion of ethical issues relating to this research, including power issues within the interview, please see McLeod (1994), Mason (1996) and Shaw (2000a).

Chapter 1

1 An earlier version of this discussion was published in the *British Osteopathic Journal* (Shaw, 1995).
2 Seltzer (1992) provides a good examination of the link between scientific discourse and the representation of the body as a machine.

Chapter 3

1 'Cartesian' relates to the work of René Descartes, and in this context refers to the debate on mind-body dualism discussed in Chapter 1.
2 A good example of this is provided by Heath (2000) who critiques Roberts' (1999) paper.
3 I am of course making an assumption that most psychotherapy occurs via a relationship between two people physically present in the same room. I do want to acknowledge that there are other forms of therapy which do not require this – i.e. telephone and online therapy. The issues of embodiment would be interesting to explore in these contexts, but this is not within the scope of this book.

Chapter 5

1 Dramatherapy is a discrete profession and has its own state registered body, the British Association for Dramatherapists. Dramatherapy incorporates the body into its work in many ways by the use of movement, voice, dance, theatre games, role-play, improvisation, puppets and masks (Jennings 1998: 12). Dramatherapy is very different to traditional

psychoanalytic psychotherapy which, as Jennings (1998: 39) points out: 'relies upon verbal exposition. The body is kept as still as possible while either in a prone or sitting position and words are the main content of the analysis'. Such body stillness is antithetical to the active roles that dramatherapists use to bring the body into therapy.

2 'Enneagram' is a term not used in conventional psychotherapy theory. It derives from ancient eastern culture and is used to differentiate personality types. People are distinguished as either head, heart or gut people. The inference is that, when under stress or when feeling lots of emotion, depending on your personality, you will experience somatic discomfort in one of these three areas.

3 In other cultures there is an attempt to link affect to bodily organs; an example here is how Afghanis refer to a 'squeezing of the heart' to denote sadness or depression (Craig and Boardman 1990), which is discussed in Chapter 1. Ots (1990), in his discussion of traditional Chinese medicine, looks at how organs are used to link affect – for example, 'the angry liver', 'the melancholy spleen' and 'the anxious heart'.

4 In this context 'group' refers to a therapy group. This is a common method of receiving therapy. Instead of individual one-to-one therapy, the group meets every week and works on individual as well as interpersonal issues within the group.

Chapter 7

1 Many GPs now employ counsellors within their practices. In the interview sample four of the therapists earned their living primarily through working in a general practice setting.

2 ME refers to myalgic encephalomyelitis, which is described by Martin (1990: 447) as 'A muscular disorder characterised by muscular fatigue and pain, slow movements, lack of concentration, memory loss, and extreme tiredness'.

3 Other professions are aware of this problem. For example, osteopaths can call on COSSET (Confidential Osteopathic Support Service for Emotional Traumas) if they have a problem of a professional or personal nature.

Chapter 8

1 The original work by Dante Alighieri (1265–1321) was started around 1308, and was written in colloquial Italian not in Latin so that it could be more widely read.

2 Our therapy work spanned six years and initially I saw this client as an osteopathic patient. This work is published (Shaw 1998) and describes the various phases of our work, from osteopathic treatment to psychotherapy. A most significant aspect of this paper is that this client has written a response at the end. Although I did not realise it at the time, this represents a narrative approach to therapy where, in this case, the client puts her side of the therapy story.

Chapter 9

1 Clarkson (1989: 55) describes confluence as the 'condition where the organism and environment are not differentiated from each other. The boundaries are blurred as between mother and foetus'. In this case the therapist is describing a process where she acknowledges that her experience and her client's are so similar that the therapist is in danger of overidentifying with her client.

References

Achterberg, J. (1985) *Imagery in Healing*. Boston, MA: Shambala.

Alexander, F. (1987) *Psychosomatic Medicine its Principles and Applications*. New York: W. W. Norton.

Alyn, J. (1988) The Politics of Touch in Therapy: A Response to Willison and Masson, *Journal Of Counselling And Development*, 66(9): 432–3.

American Psychiatric Association (1987) *Diagnostic and Statistical Manual of Mental Disorders*, 3rd edn, DSM III. Washington, DC: American Psychiatric Association.

American Psychiatric Association (1995) *Diagnostic and Statistical Manual of Mental Disorders*, 4th edn, DSM IV. Washington, DC: American Psychiatric Association.

Armstrong, D. (1989) *An Outline of Sociology as Applied to Medicine*. London: Wright.

Armstrong, D. (1993) Public Health Spaces and the Fabrication of Identity, *Sociology*, 27(3): 383–410.

Arthern, J. and Madill, A. (1999) How do Transitional Objects Work? The Therapist's View, *British Journal of Psychology*, 72(1): 1–22.

BACP (British Association of Counselling) (2000) *Research Department Statistics*. Rugby: BACP.

Badaracco, J. E. G. (1997) The Body in Psychotherapy, in J. Guimón (ed.) *The Body in Psychotherapy*. Basel: Karger.

Balint, M. (1955) The Doctor, His Patient, and The Illness, *The Lancet*, 2 April: 683–8.

Barsky, A. J. (1992) Amplification, Somatization and the Somatoform Disorders, *Psychosomatics,* 33(1): 28–34.

Bayer, B. M. and Malone, K. R. (1998) Feminism, Psychology and Matters of the Body, in H. J. Stam (ed.) *The Body and Psychology*. London: Sage.

Blacking, J. (1977) Towards an Anthropology of the Body, in J. Blacking (ed.) *The Anthropology of the Body*. New York: Academic Press.

Bloom, F. E., Lazerson, A. and Hofstadter, L. (1985) *Brain, Mind and Behaviour*. New York: W. H. Freeman & Co.

Boadella, D. (1988) Biosynthesis, in J. Rowan and W. Dryden (eds) *Innovative Therapy in Britain*. Buckingham: Open University Press.

Boadella, D. (1997) Embodiment in the Therapeutic Relationship: main speech at the First Congress of the World Congress of the World Council of Psychotherapy, Vienna 1–5 July, *International Journal of Psychotherapy,* 2(1): 31–44.

Boothe, B., von Wyl, A. and Wepfer, R. (1999) Narrative Dynamics and Psychodynamics, *Psychotherapy Research*, 9(3): 258–73.

Boyne, R. (1990) *Foucault and Derrida*. London: Unwin Hyman.

Bram, A. D. (1995) The Physically Ill or Dying Psychotherapist: A Review of Ethical and Clinical Considerations, *Psychotherapy*, 32(4): 568–80.

Briggs, J. P. and Peat, F. D. (1984) *Looking Glass Universe*. London: Fontana.

British National Formulary (1998) *British Medical Association and Royal Pharmaceutical Society of Great Britain* (no. 35). London: The Pharmaceutical Press.

Burman, E. (1994) *Deconstructing Developmental Psychology*. London: Routledge.

Busby, H. (1996) Alternative Medicines/Alternative Knowledges: Putting Flesh on the Bones (Using Traditional Chinese Approaches to Healing), in S. Cant and U. Sharma (eds) *Complementary and Alternative Medicines: Knowledge in Practice*. London: Free Association Books.

Capra, F. (1975) *The Tao of Physics*. London: Fontana

Capra, F. (1982) *The Turning Point*. London: Wildwood House.

Casement, P. (1985) *On Learning from the Patient*. London: Routledge.

Cashdan, S. (1988) *Object Relations Therapy*. New York: W. W. Norton.

Castonguay, L. G. (1993) Common Factors and Non Specific Variables: Clarification of the Two Concepts and Recommendations for Research, *Journal of Psychotherapy Integration*, 3(3): 267–86.

Chayes, M. (1988) Discussion of Joseph, in J. Sandler (ed.) *Projection, Identification, Projective Identification*. London: Karnac Books.

Chiron (2002) The Chiron Centre for Body Psychotherapy, www.chiron.org, accessed 10 January 2002.

Chused, J. F. (1997) The Patient's Perception of the Analyst's Self-Disclosure: Commentary on Amy Lichtblau Morrison's Paper, *Psychoanalytic Dialogues*, 7(2): 242–56.

Clarkson, P. (1989) *Gestalt Counselling in Action*. London: Sage.

Coen, S. J. and Sarno, J. E. (1989) Psychosomatic Avoidance of Conflict in Back Pain, *Journal Of The American Academy Of Psychoanalysis*, 17(3): 359–76.

Cole, J. (2001) Empathy Needs a Face, *Journal of Consciousness Studies*, 8(5–7): 51–68.

Collins, N. L. and Miller, L. C. (1994) Self-Disclosure and Liking: A Meta-Analytic Review, *Psychological Bulletin*, 116(3): 457–75.

Cooper, A. M. (1985) Will Neurobiology Influence Psychoanalysis? *American Journal Of Psychiatry*, 142(12): 1395–402.

Cottingham, J. (1997) *Descartes*. London: Orion Publishing.

Craig, T. K. J. and Boardman, A. P. (1990) Somatization in Primary Care Settings, in C. Bass (ed.) *Somatization: Physical Symptoms and Psychological Illness*. Oxford: Blackwell Scientific.

Craig, T. K. J., Boardman, A. P., Mills, K., Daly-Jones, O. and Drake, H. (1993) The South London Somatisation Study 1: Longitudinal Course and the Influence of Early Life Experiences, *The British Journal Of Psychiatry*, 163: 579–88.

Crossley, N. (1995) Merleau-Ponty: The Elusive Body and Carnal Society, *Body and Society*, 1(1): 43–63.

Csordas, T. J. (1990) Embodiment as a Paradigm for Anthropology, *Ethos*, 18: 5–47.

Danciger, E. (1993) The Wounded Healer, *The Homeopath*, 51: 130–2.

Delozier, P. P. (1994) Therapist Sexual Misconduct (special issue Bringing Ethics Alive: Feminist Ethics in Psychotherapy Practice), *Women and Therapy*, 15(1): 55–67.

Depraz, N. (2001) The Husserlian Theory of Intersubjectivity as Alterology: Emergent Theories and Wisdom Traditions in the Light of Genetic Phenomenology, *Journal of Consciousness Studies*, 8(5–7): 169–78.

Edward Mann, W. and Hoffman, E. (1980) *Wilhelm Reich: the Man Who Dreamed of Tomorrow*. Wellingborough: Crucible.

Ellis, C. and Flaherty, M. G. (eds) (1992) *Investigating Subjectivity*. Newbury Park, CA: Sage.

Etherington, K. (2000) *Narrative Approaches to Working with Adult Male Survivors of Child Sexual Abuse: the Client's, the Counsellor's and the Researcher's Story*. London: Jessica Kingsley.

Evans, P. (1993) Mind and Body: From Anecdote to Evidence, *Journal of The Royal Society For Arts*, CXLI(5436): 127–41.

Fagan, J. and Silverthorn, A. S. (1998) Research on Communication by Touch, in E. W. L. Smith, P. R. Clance and S. Imes (eds) *Touch in Psychotherapy: Theory, Research and Practice*. New York: The Guilford Press.

Fasal, J. and Edwardes, M. (1993) Heart to Heart, *Changes*, 11(1): 20–4.

Featherstone, M., Hepworth, M. and Turner, B. S. (eds) (1991) *The Body: Social Process and Cultural Theory*. London: Sage.

Fenichel, O. (1990) *The Psychoanalytic Theory of Neuroses* (first published 1946). London: Routledge.

Field, N. (1989) Listening with the Body: An Exploration in the Countertransference, *British Journal of Psychotherapy*, 5(4): 512–22.

Fisch, R. Z. (1987) Masked Depression: Its Interrelations with Somatization, Hypochondriasis and Conversion, *International Journal of Psychiatry in Medicine*, 17(4): 367–79.

Ford, C. V. (1986) The Somatizing Disorders, *Psychosomatics*, 27(5): 327–37.

Foucault, M. (1972) *The Archaeology of Knowledge*. London: Tavistock.

Foucault, M. (1973) *The Birth of The Clinic*. London: Tavistock.

Fox, N. J. (1993) *Postmodernism, Sociology and Health*. Buckingham: Open University Press.

Frankl, G. (1990) *The Unknown Self*. London: Open Gate Press.

Frankl, G. (1994) *Exploring the Unconscious*. London: Open Gate Press.

Freud, S. (1905) Three Essays on the Theory of Sexuality, in *On Sexuality*. Harmondsworth: Pelican.

Freud, S. (1923) The Ego and the Id, in *On Metapsychology: The Theory of Psychoanalysis*. Harmondsworth: Pelican.

Gergen, K. J. and Kaye, J. (1992) Beyond Narrative in the Negotiation of Therapeutic Meaning, In S. McNamee and K. J. Gergen (eds) *Therapy as Social Construction*. London: Sage.

Glickauf-Hughes, C. and Chance, S. (1998) An Individualized and Interactive Object Relations Perspective on the Use of Touch in Psychotherapy, in E. W. L. Smith, P. R. Clance and S. Imes (eds) *Touch in Psychotherapy: Theory, Research and Practice*. New York: The Guilford Press.

Goldberg, D. P. and Bridges, K. (1988) Somatic Presentations Of Psychiatric Illness In Primary Care Settings, *Journal Of Psychosomatic Research*, 32(2): 137–44.

Gomez, L. (1997) *An Introduction to Object Relations*. London: Free Association Press.

Goncalves, O. F. and Machado, P. P. P. (2000) Emotions, Narrative and Change, *European Journal of Psychotherapy and Health*, 3(3): 249–60.

Goodman, M. and Teicher, A. (1988) To Touch, or Not to Touch, *Psychotherapy*, 25(4): 492–500.

Gordon, H. H. (1983) The Doctor-Patient Relationship, *The Journal of Medicine and Philosophy*, 8(3): 243–55.

Gothill, M. and Armstrong, D. (1999) Dr No-body: the Construction of the Doctor as an Embodied Subject in British General Practice 1955–97, *Sociology of Health and Illness*, 21(1): 1–12.

Grant, M. and Hazel, J. (1993) *Who's Who in Classical Mythology?* London: Dent.

Grosch, W. N. and Olsen, D. C. (1994) *When Healing Starts to Hurt*. New York: W. W. Norton.

Guignon, C. (1998) Narrative Explanation in Psychotherapy, *American Behavioral Scientist*, 41(4): 558–77.

Gunzburg, J. C. (1997) *Healing Through Meeting*. London: Jessica Kingsley.

Halbrook, B. and Duplechin, R. (1994) Rethinking Touch in Psychotherapy: Guidelines for Practitioners, *Psychotherapy in Private Practice*, 13(3): 43–53.

Halling, S. and Goldfarb, M. (1991) Grounding Truth in the Body: Therapy and Research Renewed, *The Humanistic Psychologist*, 19(3): 313–30.

Hannay, D. R. (1980) The 'Iceberg' of Illness and 'Trivial' Consultations, *Journal Of The Royal College Of General Practitioners*, 30: 551–54.

Harvey, J. H., Orbuch, T. L. and Fink, K. (1990) The Social Psychology of Account-Making: Meaning, Hope and Generativity, *New Zealand Journal of Psychology*, 19(2): 46–57.

Heath, G. (2000) A Constructivist Attempt to Talk to the Field, *International Journal of Psychotherapy*, 5(1): 11–35.

Hoffman, S. and Gazit, M. (1996) To Touch and be Touched in Psychotherapy? *Changes*, 14(2): 115–16.

Holloway, E. L. (1995) *Clinical Supervision: A Systems Approach*. Thousand Oaks, CA: Sage.

Holub, E. A. and Lee, S. S. (1990) Therapists' Use of Nonerotic Physical Contact: Ethical Concerns, *Professional Psychology: Research and Practice*, 21(2): 115–17.

Horton, J. A., Clance, P. R., Sterk-Elifson, C. and Emshoff, J. (1995) Touch in Psychotherapy: A Survey of Patients' Experiences, *Psychotherapy*, 32(3): 443–57.

Hughes, J. (1990) *The Philosophy of Social Research*, (2nd edn). London: Longman.

Hunter, M. and Struve, J. (1998) *The Ethical Use of Touch in Psychotherapy*. Thousand Oaks, CA: Sage.

Hutchins, R. M. (ed.) (1952) *Great Books of the Western World 7: Plato*. Chicago: William Benton.

Hycner, R. H. (1993) *Between Person and Person*. New York: The Gestalt Journal Press.

Hycner, R. H. and Jacobs, L. (1995) *The Healing Relationship in Gestalt Therapy: a Dialogic/Self Psychology Approach*. New York: The Gestalt Journal Press.

Imes, S. (1998) Long-term Clients' Experience of Touch in Gestalt Therapy, in E. W. L. Smith, P. R. Clance and S. Imes (eds) *Touch in Psychotherapy: Theory, Research and Practice*. New York: The Guilford Press.

Jacobs, T. (1995) Discussion of Jay Greenberg's Paper, *Contemporary Psychoanalysis*, 31(2): 237–45.

Jehu, D. (1994) *Patients as Victims: Sexual Abuse in Psychotherapy and Counselling*. Chichester: Wiley.

Jennings, S. E. (1998) *Introduction to Dramatherapy: Theatre and Healing, Ariadne's Ball of Thread*. London: Jessica Kingsley.

Johnson, S. M. (1987) *Humanizing the Narcissistic Style*. New York: W. W. Norton.

Kaye, J. D. (1996) Towards a Discursive Psychotherapy, *Changes*, 14(3): 232–7.

Kelly, A. E. and McKillop, K. J. (1996) Consequences of Revealing Personal Secrets, *Psychological Bulletin*, 120 (3): 450–65.

Kepner, J. I. (1993) *Body Process: Working with the Body in Psychotherapy*. San Francisco: Jossey-Bass.

Kertay, L. and Reviere, S. L. (1993) The Use of Touch in Psychotherapy, *Psychotherapy*, 30(1): 32–40.

Kupfermann, K. and Smaldino, C. (1987) The Vitalizing and the Revitalizing Experience of Reliability: The Place of Touch in Psychotherapy, *Clinical Social Work Journal*, 15(3): 223–35.

Leder, D. (1984) Medicine and Paradigms of Embodiment, *The Journal of Medicine and Philosophy*, 9: 29–43.

Leder, D. (1984/5) Toward a Phenomenology of Pain, *Review of Existential Psychology and Psychiatry*, 19(2–3): 255–66.

Leder, D. (1990) *The Absent Body*. Chicago: The University Of Chicago Press.

Liedloff, J. (1986) *The Continuum Concept*. London: Penguin.

Lipowski, Z. J. (1988) Somatisation: the Concept and its Clinical Application, *The American Journal Of Psychiatry*, 145(11): 1358–68.

Liria, A. F. (2000) From Interpretation to Commentary: Truth and Meaning in Psychotherapy, *Journal of Psychotherapy Integration*, 10(3): 325–34.

Lowen, A. (1976) *Biogenergetics*. New York: Penguin.

Lundeen, E. J. and Schuldt, W. J. (1992) Models of Self-Disclosure in Psychotherapy, *Psychology: A Journal of Human Behaviour*, 29(2): 8–13.

McCann, I. L. and Pearlman, L. A. (1990) Vicarious Traumatization: A Framework for Understanding the Psychological Effects of Working with Victims, *Journal of Traumatic Stress*, 3(1): 131–49.

McDougall, J. (1974) The Psychosoma and the Psychoanalytic Process, *International Review of Psychoanalysis*, 1: 437–59.

McDougall, J. (1989) *Theatres of the Body*, London: Free Association Books.

McDougall, J. (1993) Countertransference and Primitive Communication, In A. Alexandris and G. Vaslamatzis (eds) *Counter-Transference: Theory, Technique, Teaching*. London: Karnac.

McIlwraith, B. (1993) An Analysis of the Driving Position in the Modern Motor Car, *The British Osteopathic Journal*, XI: 27–34.

McLeod, J. (1994) *Doing Counselling Research*. London: Sage.

McLeod, J. (1996) The Emerging Narrative Approach to Counselling and Psychotherapy, *British Journal of Guidance and Counselling*, 24(2): 173–84.

McLeod, J. (1997) *Narrative and Psychotherapy*. London: Sage.

McLeod, J. (2000) Narrative Processes in Experiential Therapy: Stories as Openings. Paper presented at the *BAC Counselling Research Conference*, The University of Manchester, 20 May.

McLeod, J. and Balamoutsou, S. (1996) Representing Narrative Process in Therapy: Qualitative Analysis of a Single Case, *Counselling Psychology Quarterly*, 9(1): 61–76.

McNamee, S. and Gergen, K. J. (1992) *Therapy as Social Construction*. London: Sage.

McNeely, D. A. (1987) *Touching: Body Therapy and Depth Psychotherapy*. Toronto: Inner City Books.

Martin, E. (1987) *The Woman in the Body*. Milton Keynes: Open University Press.

Martin, E. A. (1990) *The Concise Medical Dictionary*, 3rd edn. Oxford: Oxford University Press.

Mason, J. (1996) *Qualitative Researching*. London: Sage.

Masson, J. (1990) *Against Therapy*. London: Fontana.

Mathers, N. and Rowland, S. (1997) General Practice: A Post-modern Speciality? *British Journal of General Practice*, 47: 177–9.

Mathew, M. (1998) The Body as Instrument, *Journal of the British Association of Psychotherapists*, 35: 17–36.

Mechanic, D. (1972) Social Psychologic Factors Affecting the Presentation of Bodily Complaints, *New England Journal Of Medicine*, 286(21): 1132–9.

Merleau-Ponty, M. (1962) *The Phenomenology of Perception*. London: Routledge & Kegan Paul.

Merleau-Ponty, M. (1968) *The Visible and the Invisible*. Evanston, IL: Northwestern University Press.

Morrison, A. L. (1997) Ten Years of Doing Psychotherapy While Living with a Life-Threatening Illness: Self-Disclosure and Other Ramifications, *Psychoanalytic Dialogues*, 7(2): 242–56.

Norcross, J. C. and Goldfried, M. R. (eds) (1992) *Handbook of Psychotherapy Integration*. New York: Basic Books.

Norfolk, D. (1993) Bedding Design: A Professional Appraisal, *The British Osteopathic Journal*, XII: 13–16.

O'Dowd, T. C. (1988) Five Years of Heartsink Patients in General Practice, *British Medical Journal*, 297: 20–7.

Orbach, S. (1994). Working with the False Body, in A. Erskine, and D. Judd (eds) *The Imaginative Body*. London: Whurr.

Ots, T. (1990) The Angry Liver, the Anxious Heart and the Melancholy Spleen, *Culture, Medicine And Psychiatry*, 14(1): 21–58.

Parker, I. (1996) Networks Festival (letter to the editor), *Changes*, 14(3): 249.

Parker, I. (1998) Constructing and Deconstructing Psychotherapeutic Discourse, *The European Journal of Psychotherapy, Counselling & Health*, 1 (1): 65–78.

Parker, I. (ed.) (1999) *Deconstructing Psychotherapy*. London: Sage.

Parlee, M. B. (1998) Situated Knowledges of Personal Embodiment, In H. J. Stam (ed.) *The Body and Psychology*. London: Sage.

Parlett, M. and Page, F. (1990) Gestalt Therapy, in W. Dryden (ed.) *Individual Therapy: a Handbook*. Buckingham: Open University Press.

Perls, F. S., Hefferline, R. F. and Goodman, P. (1951) *Gestalt Therapy: Excitement and Growth in the Human Personality*. New York: Julian Press.

Pilgrim, D. (1992) Psychotherapy and Political Evasions, in W. Dryden and C. Feltham (eds) *Psychotherapy and its Discontents*. Buckingham: Open University Press.

Prochaska, J. O. and Norcross, J. C. (1994) *Systems of Psychotherapy: A Transtheoretical Analysis*, 3rd edn. Pacific Grove, CA: Brooks/Cole.

Radley, A. (1998) Displays and Fragments: Embodiment and the Configuration of Social Worlds, in H. J. Stam, (ed.) *The Body and Psychology*. London: Sage.

Ramachandran, V. S. (1998) *Phantoms in the Brain*. London: Fourth Estate.

Randell, P. (1989) A Contribution Towards a Psychodynamic Theory in Osteopathy, *European Journal Of Osteopathy*, 1: 3.

Randell, P. (1992) The Crisis of Clinical Theory Supporting Osteopathic Practice: A Critique and New Proposal, *The British Osteopathic Journal*, ix: 5–7.

Reich, W. (1983) *The Function of the Orgasm*. London: Souvenir Press.

Reich, W. (1990) *Character Analysis*, 3rd edn. New York: Noonday.

Richards, G. (1996) *Putting Psychology in its Place*. London: Routledge.

Richert, A. J. (1999) Some Practical Implications of Integrating Narrative and

Humanistic/Existential Approaches to Psychotherapy, *Journal of Psychotherapy Integration*, 9(3): 257–78.

Riikonen, E. and Smith, G. M. (1997) *Re-Imagining Therapy: Living Conversations and Relational Knowing*. London: Sage.

Roberts, A. (1999) The Field Talks Back: An Essay on Constructivism and Experience, *British Gestalt Journal*, 8(1): 35–46.

Rock, I. and Palmer, S. (1990) The Legacy of Gestalt Psychology, *Scientific American*, 263(6): 48–61.

Rodin, G. M. (1991) Somatization: a Perspective from Self Psychology, *Journal of the American Academy of Psychoanalysis*, 19(3): 367–84.

Rowan, J. (1998) Linking: Its Place in Therapy, *International Journal of Psychotherapy*, 3(3): 245–54.

Rubenfeld, I. (2000) *The Listening Hand: How to Combine Bodywork and Psychotherapy to Heal Emotional Pain*. London: Piatkus.

Sampson, E. E. (1998) Establishing Embodiment in Psychology, in H. J. Stam (ed.) *The Body and Psychology*. London: Sage.

Samuels, A. (1985) Countertransference, the '*Mundus Imaginalis*' and a Research Project, *Journal of Analytical Psychology*, 30: 47–71.

Samuels, A. (1993) *The Political Psyche*. London: Routledge.

Sandler, J. (1988) *Projection, Identification, Projective Identification*. London: Karnac Books.

Sarafino, E. P. (1994) *Health Psychology: Biopsychosocial Interactions*. New York: John Wiley.

Sayers, D. L. (1949) *The Comedy of Dante Alighieri: Cantica 1*, trans. D. L. Sayers. London: Penguin.

Sayers, J. (1996) On Kissing, Touching and Shaking Hands, *Changes*, 14(2): 117–20.

Schwandt, T. A. (1997) *Qualitative Inquiry*. Thousand Oaks, CA: Sage.

Schwartz-Salant, N. (1982) *Narcissism and Character Transformation*. Toronto: Inner City Books.

Schwartz-Salant, N. (1986) On the Subtle-Body Concept in Clinical Practice, in N. Schwartz-Salant and M. Stein (eds) *The Body in Analysis*. Wilmette, IL: Chiron Publications.

Schwartz-Salant, N. and Stein, M. (eds) (1986) *The Body in Analysis*. Wilmette, IL: Chiron Publications.

Seligman, C. (1995) The Therapist as Patient in Interminable Treatment: A Parallel Process, in M. B. Sussman (ed.) *A Perilous Calling: the Hazards of Psychotherapy Practice*. New York: John Wiley.

Seltzer, M. (1992) *Bodies and Machines*. New York: Routledge.

Servanschreiber, D., Tabas, G. and Kolb, N. R. (2000) Somatizing Patients: Part II, Practical Management, *American Family Physician*, 61(5): 1423–8.

Shaw, J. and Creed, F. (1991) The Cost of Somatization, *Journal of Psychosomatic Research*, 35(2/3): 307–12.

Shaw, R. (1994a) An Exploration into the Relationship between Visualisation, Somatised Pain and the Unconscious, *Changes*, 12(1): 18–23.

Shaw, R. (1994b) Literature Review of Somatisation, *British Osteopathic Journal*, XIII: 28–31.

Shaw, R. (1995) Mind-Body Dualism: An Historical Perspective and its Prevalence Within Contemporary Medical Discourse, *British Osteopathic Journal*, XVII: 35–8.

Shaw, R. (1996a) Towards an Understanding of the Psychodynamic Processes of the Body, *Psychodynamic Counselling*, 2(2): 230–46.

Shaw, R. (1996b) Towards Integrating the Body into Psychotherapy, *Changes*, 14(2): 108–14.

Shaw, R. (1997a) Somatisation and Importance of Integrating the Body into Psychotherapy, *Mind Your Body Seminar Series*, Merseyside Psychotherapy Institute, Liverpool, January.

Shaw, R. (1997b) The Unknown Body: An Exploration into Somatic Processes. Paper presented at *The Association of Student Counsellors Annual Conference*, York University, March.

Shaw, R. (1997c) Towards a Sociology of Lived-Body Experience, *The Journal of Contemporary Health*, 6: 61–4.

Shaw, R. (1998) Shame: An Integrated Approach to the Preverbal Becoming Verbal, *Changes*, 16(4): 294–308.

Shaw, R. (1999) An Exploration of the Embodied Experience of Psychotherapists in the Therapeutic Encounter. Paper presented at the *Second World Congress for Psychotherapy*, Vienna, Austria, 6 July.

Shaw, R. (2000a) The Embodied Psychotherapist: An Exploration of the Therapist's Somatic Phenomena Within the Therapeutic Encounter. Ph.D. Thesis, University of Derby.

Shaw, R. (2000b) Shame: An Integrated Approach to the Preverbal Becoming Verbal: One-day workshop at *Supportcentre Against Incest,* Oslo, Norway, 15 March.

Shilling, C. (1993) *The Body and Social Theory*. London: Sage.

Skultans, V. (2000) Narrative Illness and the Body, *Anthropology and Medicine*, 7(1): 5–13.

Smith, E. W. L., Clance, P. R. and Imes, S. (1998) *Touch in Psychotherapy: Theory, Research and Practice*. New York: The Guilford Press.

Speedy, J. (2000) The 'Storied' Helper: Narrative Ideas and Practices in Counselling and Psychotherapy, *European Journal of Psychotherapy and Health*, 3(3): 361–74.

Spinelli, E. (1994) *Demystifying Therapy*. London: Constable.

Spinelli, E. and Marshall, S. (eds) (2001) *Embodied Theories*. London: Continuum.

SPTI (1999/2000) *Handbook for Gestalt Psychotherapy*. Nottingham: The Sherwood Psychotherapy Training Institute.

Stake, J. E. and Oliver, J. (1991) Sexual Contact and Touching Between Therapist and Client: A Survey of Psychologists' Attitudes and Behavior, *Professional Psychology: Research and Practice*, 22(4): 297–307.

Stam, H. J. (ed.) (1998) *The Body and Psychology*. London: Sage.

Stern, D. N. (1985) *The Interpersonal World of the Infant*. New York: Basic Books.

Straus, E. W. (1966) *Phenomenological Psychology*. London: Tavistock.

Stryer, L. (1981) *Biochemistry*, 2nd edn. New York: Freeman.

Sussman, M. B. (ed.) (1995) *A Perilous Calling: the Hazards of Psychotherapy Practice*. New York: John Wiley.

Synnott, A. (1993) *The Body Social*. London: Routledge.

Szasz, T. (1987) *Insanity: The Idea and its Consequences*. New York: Wiley.

Talbot, A. (1998) Listening with the Body, *Australian Journal of Psychotherapy*, 17(1–2): 34–56.

Thompson, E. (2001) Empathy and Consciousness, *Journal of Consciousness Studies*, 8 (5–7): 1–32.

Thorn, B. E., Shealy, C. and Briggs, S. D. (1993) Sexual Misconduct in Psychotherapy:

Reactions to a Consumer-Oriented Brochure, *Professional Psychology: Research and Practice*, 24(1): 75–82.

Toombs, S. K. (2001) The Role of Empathy in Clinical Practice, *Journal of Consciousness Studies*, 8(5–7): 247–58.

Tune, D. (2001) Is Touch a Valid Therapeutic Intervention? *Counselling and Psychotherapy Research*, 1(3): 167–71.

Turner, B. S. (1995) *Medical Power and Social Knowledge*, 2nd edn. London: Sage.

Turner, B. S. (1996) *The Body and Society*, 2nd edn. London: Sage.

Turp, M. (1999) Working with Body Storylines, *Psychodynamic Counselling*, 5(3): 301–17.

Waitzkin, H. and Britt, T. (1989) Changing the Structure of Medical Discourse: Implications of Cross-National Comparisons, *Journal of Health and Social Behaviour*, 30(4): 436–49.

West, W. (1994) Post-Reichian Therapy, in D. Jones (ed.) *Innovative Therapy*. Buckingham: Open University Press.

Westen, D. (2002) Assessing Personality Disorders and Personality Change in Psychotherapy. Paper presented at the *Society for Psychotherapy Research (UK) Annual Conference*, Ravenscar, North Yorkshire, 24–7 March.

Wilkinson, H. (1997) *Notes on the Supportive Therapeutic Use of Touch in Counselling*. Scarborough: Psychotherapy Training Institute.

Wilson, J. M. (1982) The Value of Touch in Psychotherapy, *American Journal Of Orthopsychiatry*, 52(1): 65–72.

Winnicott, D. W. (1971) *Playing and Reality*. London: Tavistock.

Woodmansey, A. C. (1988) Are Psychotherapists out of Touch? *British Journal Of Psychotherapy*, 5(1): 57–65.

Wosket, V. (1999) *The Therapeutic Use of Self: Counselling Practice, Research and Supervision*. London: Routledge.

Wright, K. (1991) *Vision and Separation*. London: Free Association Books.

Yoshida, K. A. (1993) Reshaping of Self: A Pendular Reconstruction of Self and Identity Among Adults with Traumatic Spinal Cord Injury, *Sociology of Health and Illness*, 15(2): 217–45.

Zahavi, D. (2001) Beyond Empathy: Phenomenological Approaches to Intersubjectivity, *Journal of Consciousness Studies*, 8 (5–7): 151–67.

Index